THE POLITICS
OF THE ESSAY

THE POLITICS
OF THE ESSAY

FEMINIST PERSPECTIVES

—

edited by
Ruth-Ellen Boetcher Joeres
and Elizabeth Mittman

Indiana
University
Press

BLOOMINGTON AND INDIANAPOLIS

The paper used in this publication meets the minimum requirements of American
National Standard for Information Sciences—Permanence of Paper for Printed
Library Materials, ANSI Z39.48-1984.

Manufactured in the United States of America

Library of Congress Cataloging-in-Publication Data

The Politics of the essay : feminist perspectives / edited by Ruth-Ellen
Boetcher Joeres and Elizabeth Mittman.
    p.   cm.
  Includes bibliographical references and index.
  ISBN 0-253-33109-9. — ISBN 0-253-20788-6 (pbk.)
  1. Essay.   2. Feminist literary criticism.   3. Literature—Women
authors—History and criticism.   I. Joeres, Ruth-Ellen B., date.
II. Mittman, Elizabeth, date.
PN4500.P65   1993
809.4'0082—dc20   92-25121

1 2 3 4 5   97 96 95 94 93

Contents

WOMEN'S ESSAYS AS POLITICAL INTERVENTION

Acknowledgments

First and foremost, we would like to thank our contributors, whose creative and differing approaches to the essay made our work on this volume a process filled with new discoveries. The perspectives they brought to this project from a wide variety of national, cultural, and historical contexts have given the book a particular richness. Like any such endeavor, this one has, of course, involved not just the two of us and our contributors but many others who have helped us in a variety of ways. We would like to express appreciation to the University of Minnesota Graduate School, especially to its graduate research funding committee, which has underwritten the work on our volume on several occasions. The University of Minnesota German Department deserves our grateful acknowledgment as well for its generous support, ranging from assistance with various costs to general encouragement. Particular friends and colleagues — especially Nancy Armstrong, Marilyn Frye, Renate Hof, and Lisa Roetzel — supported and advised us in many helpful ways. We also very much appreciate Susan Griffin's special contribution to our volume, without which our book would be incomplete. And finally, the students in seminars on women and essays at the Universities of Minnesota and Munich gave us many marvelous ideas and encouragement. Their enthusiasm and interest spurred us on.

RUTH-ELLEN B. JOERES AND ELIZABETH MITTMAN

THE POLITICS
OF THE ESSAY

Red Shoes

SUSAN GRIFFIN

The imprisonment which was at one and the same time understood as the imprisonment of the female mind has a larger boundary, and that is the shape of thought itself within Western civilization.

It is an early memory. Red shoes. Leather straps criss-crossing. The kind any child covets. That color I wanted with the hot desire of a child.

On one level, one thinks simply of the conditions of imprisonment which affected, for instance, the intellectual life of George Sand. How it was necessary for her to dress like a man in order to attend the theatre with her friends. She wanted to be in the section just beneath the stage, and women were not allowed in that section. This transgression was a necessary one if she was going to, as she did, enter the realm of public discourse within her mind.

When was it I first heard the title of the film, "The Red Shoes"? My older sister had seen it. Did she speak of it with my mother? I must have overheard it. I was often excluded from such conversations. I was too young. And my mother preferred my sister.

The female world, bounded as it is, contains, as does any world, rich layers of meaning. It is not simply that a woman must stay within this world, but that signification itself is kept away from it. Whatever lies within the confines of the feminine province is defined *sui generis* as either trivial or obscene (as in housework, or lovemaking) and as such not fit for public discourse.

I was I suppose shopping with my grandmother in the department store with the X-ray machine that made a green picture of the bones in my feet. I have the vague feeling my grandmother finds red impractical.

In this light it is no wonder that the novel became a literary form so widely practiced by women, a genre in some of its popular manifestations, and in some phases of its development, dominated by women. The novel is allowed to describe what we think of as the private sphere of life, which is also the sphere of life given over to women. And is it any wonder that so many "classic" novels written by men have a heroine at the center of the story? *Anna Karenina. Madame Bovary.*

In my mind, as I remember my grandmother, I can feel the shape of her larger body next to mine. Her elbows are wrinkled in a way that fascinates me. The flesh on her forearms hangs in beautiful white lobes, not so different than the lobes of her breasts.

Why is it the novel can enter the private sphere in a way, for instance, that the essay cannot? One answer presents itself immediately. The novel is fiction. It is not true. It exists in an epistemological category unto itself. Yes, it is lifelike, it evokes or even, as is said metaphorically, creates realities; still the reality of fiction is not to be confused with *reality.*

I cannot remember whether or not my grandmother let me have those shoes. Despite her somberness in my presence, a mouth habitually turned down, and her air of dutiful weariness at having to raise a child at her advanced age, she has another side. I am twenty-one years old when she pulls a black silk robe out of a closet where she has kept it for years, and gives it to me.

In the public imagination the feminine world has the same flavor as a fictional world. It is present but not entirely real. Men enter the home in the evening, as darkness descends. They may eat there, play with the children, make love, confess certain feelings, hidden during the day, to their wives, sleep, dream, but all that fades away into near obscurity with the dawn when they must emerge again into the world of work.

Perhaps she did buy me those red shoes. I can see them now in my closet which was also her second closet, the closet of the black silk robe, the place where she kept her rarer treasures, her two fur coats, worn only on the more special occasions . . . and, am I embellishing here, her sweater with the rhinestones on it, or were they pearls? Whenever I wore those red shoes, which was as often as I could, they gave me secret sustenance, the liberatory feeling of a rebellion conspired between my grandmother and me.

Secrets within the private life are like obscurities within an obscurity. Private life is *private*, walled off, unseen, unscrutinized. To write a history of the private life is a recent departure, an ingenuous idea, and has an erotic edge, not only because of the sexuality which is part of private life, but because in doing so one penetrates a contained world. The secret alcoholism or indiscretion or sexual abuse within a family history is, being an obscurity inside an essentially obscure world, seemingly less real than the rest of private life, and has even more the flavor of fiction. At the same time, the novel, being fiction, is congruous with this world. It is formed to the contours of the way we hold the private life in our minds.

When I put the red shoes on it was not only on special occasions. I wore them even on ordinary days. They followed me into a child's world, one that no adult ever saw. If I took them off to play in the sand or the mud, they witnessed me from the sidelines, and kept my secrets.

In fiction the whole life of the body, of sensuality is opened to view. The form of the novel or the short story and even more of the poem allows the reader to enter imagined experience as if within a body. Pain, pleasure, color, taste, sound, smells are evoked. The literary devices of fiction are meant to admit this material world.

I wore them walking the twelve blocks I regularly walked to school. The shoes became so much a part of me that I forgot I was wearing them. I let my mind wander. I looked into the windows of the houses along the way and imagined the lives of the inhabitants.

In depicting the sensuality of the world and our bodily experience of it, fiction is also portraying the mind itself which always thinks in a sensual context. Without the body, it is impossible to conceive of thought existing. Yet the central trope of our intellectual heritage is of a transcendent, disembodied mind. As the essay moved further away from meditation and reflection, further from what we call "confessions" and closer to science, with its claim of objectivity, it began to resemble more and more this celestially detached brain. At a fairly recent point in the history of the essay it became a radical act to use the pronoun "I."

Perhaps she did not buy me the red shoes. But even if that were true, the fact is she might have.

The idea of the entirely autonomous mind has a subtext, and that is the desire for unlimited freedom from natural limitations.

In the lay and ken of her soul, this was a possibility. As I imagine that she gave me the shoes, which perhaps she did, I am bringing part of her soul into being.

And yet limitations are a necessary predisposition for any existence, including the existence of something we suppose to be abstract and cerebral, like the essay. And when the essay is built on the purposeful "forgetting" of the body, these limitations paradoxically grow greater. The form of the essay circumscribes imagination. At its edges many other imagined possibilities are hovering.

Was this the reason for her attachment to the peach-colored bedspreads. They covered the single beds where she and my grandfather slept. They had a luxuriant feel, suggesting an erotic dimension that otherwise was absent in her house.

To speak of housework, or childbirth, or sexuality, or rape in the form of the essay represents, in each instance, a crumbling of the fortifications erected by a masculine world against the feminine world. But still, in each instance, the sensual reality of these phenomena is stripped away so that they may enter public discourse. And when these subjects are made into sciences, they gain a certain legitimacy. Though it is often marginal, as in Home Economics.

Or perhaps not entirely absent, but never more open, never so frank, as in those bedspreads. They were luminously sexual, the sort of bedcover Mae West might have had. Of course we never spoke of this quality. It could never be spoken, only suggested.

One might think that because fiction brings one into a fully sensual world, the subject matter would be more rigidly policed. But this is not the case. The idea that fiction is untrue allows it a greater radius. I am thinking of Virginia Woolf's *Orlando*. At the time of its publication, it was her most popular novel. What she suggested about the malleability of gender was far more palatable in this form than in her essays which treated the subject, by comparison, more conservatively.

The bedspreads were symbolic of many aspirations. She cosseted a desire to be socially elevated. In her mind we were finer than all our neighbors, though I, with the working class language of my father, and my childish ignorance of manners, constantly endangered our superiority.

Just as the reader is protected by the supposition that fiction is not true, so too, the author of fiction is shielded by this idea. Stories can be told that otherwise could not. But what is even more interesting is that because fiction evokes particular social and natural worlds in their entirety, many possible stories exist inside the narrative world implicitly, without being explicitly described. They exist as possibilities or even likelihoods. A door to a barn is described. The narrator does not open that door. But it exists. And therefore the reader can imagine what is behind the door. The shape of circumstances in both *Jane Eyre* and *Wuthering Heights* suggests sexual abuse. One knows a racist political history has preceded *Their Eyes Were Watching God*. Neither writer nor reader need have admitted these events fully into consciousness. The experience is part of the reality that is conjured.

I was fascinated by my grandparents' bedroom. The family story was that they slept in a double bed until one day my grandmother woke to find my grandfather's hands around her neck. He was having a dream. I am certain the significance of the dream was never discussed. Only thereafter they slept in single beds. I can't remember when I heard that story. Now it is as if I've always known it.

But unless one knows the history of racism or the configurations of sexual abuse, one does not see them in the narrative. They are felt perhaps, sensed, but not delineated, unnamed.

In this bedroom, they lived as if in separate worlds. I liked to watch my grandmother at her dressing table, trying on her earrings, her perfumes; I felt privileged to catch a glimpse of her fleshy body, her long pendulous breasts emerging from her corset. I preferred to look at my grandfather's desk when he was absent. What I loved best was his collection of fountain pens.

Reading a book about the documentation of torture in Brazil I come across this distinction made by Thomas Nagel: "the difference between knowledge and acknowledgement." He defines "acknowledgement" as "what happens to knowledge . . . when it becomes officially sanctioned, when it is made part of the public cognitive scene." The essay is a forum for the "public cognitive scene."

One evening when my grandparents went out and I was alone in the house I was pulled as if by a magnet to my grandfather's desk. I wanted to write with his fountain pen, which he never let me use in his presence. But the ink was heavy in it. Many times I had seen him shake it down to the nib, and so I did this, but not with the same experienced gesture. The ink sailed across the room in a sure trajectory toward my grandmother's satin bedspreads. Both covers were evenly spattered.

The integration of knowledge into public consciousness is more than a simple act of education. Perception itself in human consciousness is a social act. It is not only that knowledge and language are socially derived, but the moment of perception itself is prismatic. A single viewer will react differently when part of an audience. Certain responses are amplified. A small gesture made on the stage, whose meaning otherwise might be ignored or even forgotten, brings the whole theatre to laughter. In the assembly of others, perception becomes a demarcated event. And, as it is said in the same book about torture in Brazil, the process of transforming knowledge into public acknowledgement is also "sacramental."

I tried to wash the spots out but only made them worse. I can feel the terror of discovery now. It is hot under my skin. I would have preferred the scene to be private, between my grandmother and me. I was rarely physically punished. But she beat me this once, with a belt. My father and grandfather were in the next room, and I was angry at them, not because they failed to intervene, but because they were witnesses at all.

Sitting in the public gardens that are close to my house, I hear a white-haired woman exclaim to her friend, "The color is so intense!" Their bent bodies are as if curled together around a rose bush. The gardens are tiered and shaped like an amphitheatre and so her voice travels easily. It is an extraordinary moment. All at once I am pulled into her passion and the brightness of the roses, and I begin to think how closely twinned in human consciousness are experience and the expression of experience. Something happens, indefinable yet palpable, as all of us in the garden are pulled simultaneously toward the sound of this old woman's voice, and the color of the rose.

What was it I did not want them to know? That I had committed a crime and been found out? Or that I had become abject, shamed by the pain itself of my punishment. I had been in such abject states before, when, through the neglect of my mother, I was cold, frightened, perhaps hungry. Afterwards I would feel a profound embarrassment. Writing of his experience of torture, Jean Améry recalls that "one never ceases to be amazed that all those things one may . . . call his soul, or his mind, or his consciousness, or his identity are destroyed when there is that cracking and splintering in the shoulder joints." It is this that is humiliating, and as Améry writes, "The shame of destruction cannot be erased."

After a time, I leave my bench and walk up the tiers of the amphitheatre. I hope to catch a glimpse of these two women. In my imagination I have already given the speaker a rich mystical life. But they are gone.

Such a memory is perhaps more easily recalled when it is only an abstraction of itself. One says, "I was tortured," or, "I had a difficult childhood," without entering the experience in any concrete way, and thus also without reliving the feeling of destruction. But sensuality and abstraction are mutually dependent. In the mind, the capacities are inseparable.

I had wanted to see the old woman's face. There was something in the tone of her voice which lead me to believe she had crossed that barrier which we so often erect against what is seen. Did she fall into the color of the rose?

Fiction, as opposed to the essay, is often viewed as an escape from reality. The storyteller can make up a world, and has no moral reason to stay loyal to this one. Shame and suffering can be left at the boundaries of this imagined world.

I imagined the color of the rose to be red. As I entered the garden I saw a rose whose deep burgundy color drew me. This red is replete with associations. Some of them wonderful. Some terrible.

But any really good story includes both pain and pleasure, sorrow and joy, in infinite complexities. And any imagined world, if it is to be believed, will soon be replete with its own requirements, consequences, and limitations, just like this world.

Falling into that color, was she not also falling into herself, as I fall into myself now, my own memories of red, and my own redness. For me this is still a color heavy with menses and childbirth, with violence and loss. But in her voice I hear something different. All that yes, but an added dimension, a kind of lightness, an aspect of this color that comes to one perhaps only in old age.

The freedom that fiction affords is not a freedom from concrete limitations but from the limitations on the mind imposed by ideas. This is a secret liberation, the same liberation given by direct experience. For the limits of physical reality are not the same, nor as distinct in experience as the limitations described in abstraction. As John Berger writes in his long work on the peasants of Alpine France, those who live on the land, "never suppose that the advance of knowledge reduces the extent of the unknown."

It is easy for me to imagine beginning to perceive another dimension of color in old age. Imagining this I am pulled toward a future I have never until now predicted.

The extent of the unknown borders all language. One's relationship with it is erotic. One has a passion to know. But one can never entirely know what is other. Telling a story, no matter how much you know, you are very soon pulled into unexplored territory. Even the familiar is filled with unexpected blank spaces. The usual Sunday drive is all of a sudden a wild ride into terra incognita. You are glad to be going, but there is a vague feeling of discomfort. Where are you?

This is not a dimension of color acknowledged in our culture. Still, it exists within the culture. It has been painted. I am thinking of the work of Helen Frankenthaler. Color as she paints it takes a different place in the mind. Or rather one might say the mind takes place in the color. One is infused with it, the same way one is taken in by water, swallowed.

I am thinking of a Sunday drive with my grandparents. We went to the country place of friends. They had an orchard filled with peach trees. I have remembered it all of my life. The vividness of the peaches I pulled from the trees. The sharply sweet taste in my mouth, nothing like store-bought fruit.

Is this experience of color had by some in old age, and others who are artists, a return to an earlier state of mind, the beginner's mind of infancy? To a perception untutored, not yet muted by the mediating presence of language?

Now as I remember that peach, it is a taste indistinguishable from the shapes of trees, the tall grass surrounding them, the summer heat, the breeze blowing, the sight of my grandmother in a white blouse standing on the ladder. And was there a kitten, or am I confusing the memory of my great-grandmother's garden, and her kitten, with this one?

There are of course two experiences of the red color of that rose. One is acknowledged. It is the social red, the historical red, the red, as Merleau-Ponty writes, "that is a punctuation in the field of red things." The other red is unacknowledged, it exists in an exiled region of consciousness. But can they be separated, these two reds? And what of the tension one feels between experience and the forms experience assumes in the imagination. One feels it while writing. The words are not quite right. They betray. Lie a little. Fail to make a perfect fit. Take off in another direction entirely on their own.

Of course I am embellishing. I doubt that my grandmother wore white. It is the color one is supposed to wear if one is a woman in a pastoral setting.

In recent critical discourse, the awareness that in the mind experience is replaced with a construction of experience has led to a despair of the possibility of describing reality. But in the sway of this despair, how do you point out a lie? How do you answer the contention that torture in Brazil never took place?

That day in the country I breathed in a certain state of mind. One that I did not have before with such force. Later, when I encountered the same mood in certain paintings, certain myths, I not only mixed my memory, but also my hope, with these images.

I love that moment in writing when I know that language falls short. There is something more there. A larger body. Even by the failure of words I begin to detect its dimensions. As I work the prose, shift the verbs, look for new adjectives, a different rhythm, syntax, something new begins to come to the surface.

Looking back, I see a maze of associations I must have had with the color red. I know my mother also loved the color red. That she would have bought me those shoes unhesitatingly. That she wore bright red lipstick. That she used red henna on her dark brown hair. But I cannot remember if I thought of her that day I chose red shoes.

The manner of telling lies in public life is seldom direct any longer. Far more pervasive is the habit of ignoring an event of great significance. No official need argue that torture never existed. The torture is just never mentioned. No one goes to trial. No torturer is ever named. A general, vague reference is made to troubling events of the past which must be changed. The actuality of the torture begins to fade from public consciousness.

She had faded away from my life. I could not remember her at all as my mother, but only as a woman I would visit, and whom I liked. Liked her in a way unaccountable even to myself.

Among those who were tortured or those who lost a loved one to torture there are two reactions. Some wish to evade the memory at all costs. Even though the memory is always there in some form, the pain of recall is too excruciating. Others live to tell the truth, or hear it told, and never tire of the telling. Of course, this is also too simple. For most of us, who have not been tortured, but experienced lesser pains and fears, the two impulses, to remember and tell, or to deny and forget, are side by side, and mixed together.

She was not easy to remember. It was not only neglect, but abuse I suffered from her, a nastiness when she would drink, that came from her, as if from a demon, and which she herself would forget the next day.

I underline this passage in a recent issue of the *Paris Review*, in which Nathalie Sarraute is being interviewed. " . . . it seemed impossible to me," she said, "to write in the traditional forms. They seemed to have no access to what we experienced."

It seems possible to me then that even as a child I would be drawn to the color red, and yet also welcome my grandmother's interdiction. It is certainly not a practical color. It won't get you anywhere.

Form can be transgressed for transgression's sake, but it can also be transgressed in an attempt to lean in a certain direction. It is a tropism toward the light and heat of another knowledge. And is this knowledge a memory?

Even so I cannot forget my desire to wear red. Even if my grandmother failed to buy me those shoes, years later as an adult woman I make up another story. I investigate the possibility that she did buy them. This is not an escape from desire. It is instead an instigator of grief. I learn more fully what it is I have lost.

What we would wish to remember and what we might wish to forget are so intricately woven. Would we perhaps like to forget the life of the body, of the inner self, the private world, the world of children and childhood, of sucking and orgasm and death? This world which is a privacy within a privacy, protected by the double walls of house and skin, the conventional forms of expression and silence.

It is not the inner place of red I am seeking but the right to wear it outwardly. To wear it brazenly. Like a sequined dress. Or a scarlet letter.

There is then a hypnotic movement of the mind. We are used to it. We move back and forth from fiction to essay. From private to public. The arc of the pendulum has put us to sleep. But when the two poles meet, and the swaying stops, someone in us awakens.

It is one thing to love the color red and quite another to wear it openly. For my mother, wearing red was an act of defiance, a flag of another kind. Despite everything, she has won some territory for me, her daughter. I am like the daughter of Madame Bovary. The daughter of the fallen woman.

Bringing the public world of the essay and the inner world of fiction together, is something sacrificed? The high ground. Perspective? Distance? Or is it instead a posture of detachment that is renounced, a position of superiority. The position of one who is not immersed, who is unaffected, untouched. (This is, of course, the ultimate "fiction.")

And she, my mother, was the daughter of a respectable woman. But that is not the whole story. My grandmother had her own rebellion. She was a club woman. In the organization that was defined as auxiliary to my grandfather's club, she was made president. The proceedings of the club were secret. It was a secret realm of power, a fictional world, closed off from that other world, described as real life.

But there is always the other side of the coin. Behind the "superior" stance of the essay a quality of fragility is concealed. Theory pales when faced with the complex world of experience. Almost as soon as any idea reaches the page, another argument comes to mind.

And while it is true that in the realm of ideas one can diminish the reality of everything outside these ideas, this is at best a temporary diminishment and one that always rebounds upon the self. For ultimately this diminishment requires a lessening of one's own knowledge, one's perceptual experience, and even, existence.

It was to these clubs that my grandmother wore her best finery. Treasures sequestered from her closet, the closet of the fur coats and the black silk robe, which was also my closet.

On the other hand, the realm of experience longs for more than knowledge. What goes on in the private body, in the inner quarters of the mind, cannot fully be redeemed, nor even understood, without public acknowledgement. I am thinking of the tears of the victim who has finally heard her assailant convicted. In this case paradoxically it is not an imprisonment which takes place so much as a liberation from the imprisonment of an enforced privacy.

On the nights when the family could attend dinners or occasions given by my grandmother's club we were given little party favors and corsages. These had been made by the women in their secret sessions together. They contained bits of plastic fruit, sprays of pine, sparkles, all tied together with a bit of ribbon, most often red.

Is it possible to write in a form that is both immersed and distant, far-seeing and swallowed? I am thinking now that this is what women have been attempting in the last decades. Not simply to enter the world of masculine discourse, but to transform it with another kind of knowledge.

My grandmother has been dead for nearly two decades, and now my mother, who is old herself, has become respectable. Yet it is an astonishing moment for me now, to recall these two women, and myself as a child, my red shoes, my mother's rebellion, my grandmother's secret wardrobe, the inner meanings of these, and the threads of meaning that reach out like tendrils in the larger landscape of mind.

If I rise from my desk, leave my pen and paper behind, walk to the door, the play of life before me and inside is suddenly dazzling in its intensity. Is it because I am thinking about consciousness that suddenly my experience sharpens? And when I return to write, will I be able to reshape the form so that more of this world falls on the page? One can spend a whole life writing, I think to myself, and still hardly begin.

An Introductory Essay

RUTH-ELLEN BOETCHER JOERES AND ELIZABETH MITTMAN

> Only recently have I begun to concatenate
> my experiences into patterns distinct from
> the narrative ground in which they are
> embedded: This process I call essay-writ-
> ing.
>
> Nancy Mairs, *Plain text*

As a literary form, the essay has always caused problems for those who would define it, whose futile efforts to pin it down range from the poetic to the utterly stolid. But it is also a problem for its practitioners, whose own often more vague attempts to specify what they are doing are mere approximations, even to them. (For example, in the introduction to his own collected essays, Aldous Huxley calls the essay "a literary device for saying almost everything about anything. . . .") Everybody—but most especially the Central Europeans (Lukács and Adorno are the best known, but they by no means exhaust the list)—seems to get into the business of defining. And nobody is particularly successful at it. For some, the result is a persistent uneasiness about where the essay "belongs" in the standard division of genres. Others would elevate it to the status of "anti-genre," a site for critical reflection, for subversive—precisely because it is non-systematic, unscientific—thought. In any case, it is generally consigned to a netherworld of something different, borderland, extra-ordinary, becoming the subject of academic conference sessions with titles like "Boundary Genres" or "Marginal Literature." Analogies are also often drawn to other genres, the letter, for example, or the journal or diary—in fact, all of those genres that are connected with what we now often call personal narratives. The essay's precarious position between the non-fictional and the fictional also causes discomfort. Literary critics want to know where it "fits" and are disturbed by the fact that it seems to stretch the fabric of definition at the seams.

At the same time, the essay is in a sense utterly traditional. It emerges from a patriarchal European/white origin. As the creation of Michel de Montaigne, it came into its own in the aristocratic world of French manners in the sixteenth century, and even if Montaigne was viewed at the time as an innovator and a radical—even if we acknowledge that now—there is also no denying that the genre originated in wealth and privilege, that it was the product of a nobleman whose experiences, translated in his essays into observations on life in general, were hardly common or usual even in sixteenth-century France. Thus the label "elite" has been attached to the form: the elitism not only of a social class, but certainly also of a particular gender, although neither of these is marked, but rather taken for granted as the norm. Montaigne belonged to the gentry; he was a gentleman, someone who most often would be placed, and would place himself, in a class separate from and superior to other classes. It is probably not a coincidence that the critical discussion of the essay in this century emerged in full force during the era of New Criticism, especially in the 1950s and 1960s, when the purity of distance and the paramount importance of "objectivity" were stressed. In such a discussion, the characteristics most usually attached to the essay are formal ones. The essay is seen as having a purifying function, as that which extrapolates meaning and form from something far messier, the chaos of experiences—what Nancy Mairs in the epigraph above calls her "narrative ground." Form thus becomes a controlling, clarifying element.

GENDER AND GENRE

A feminist who reads an essay by Montaigne today can indeed admire the structure, the use of words, the turn of phrase. She will have greater difficulty with the content, which is not only dated and often remote, but also in many ways alien to us as women and, if it is to be understood, in need of "translation" into an idiom that we can relate to ourselves. Not an unusual practice for most women as we have always had to translate apparently universal assumptions into a language that we can see as relevant to us. Essays might well have been written for the edification of women (Montaigne did such, for example), but women were then the objects of attention, hardly active agents in the process: they were described or addressed; they did not do the describing or the addressing. Though its inclusion of the personal/autobiographical would seem to be consonant with the subjective trimmings long considered acceptable for women writers, the essay as such is relatively new for women, whose use of the genre has not always been as self-evident as it now is. Women, who were in any case only rarely represented in the world of letters at the time of Montaigne and Francis Bacon, could not be expected to employ a genre that exuded experience, wisdom, and contemplation, none of which fell within the province of their expected behavior. As a matter of fact, it is really only in the past century that women in greater numbers have begun to claim the essay as a form of their own.

Approaching the extensive critical literature that has been written on the essay can be daunting. Focusing on the specificities of gender greatly simplifies the process, however, since virtually nothing has been written on the subject of women and essays from a feminist perspective. This volume intends to redress that lack. Our collection of articles and essays is a first attempt to examine what it is that women undertake when they choose the essay for their own purposes, when they appropriate the form for themselves and do with it as they wish. It perhaps will come as no surprise that the women whose essays are discussed here are often activists, political progressives, no matter what their national origin, no matter what their chronological location: whether they are the nineteenth-century French radical feminist reformer Flora Tristan or the contemporary African-American essayists Audre Lorde and June Jordan or the German terrorist Ulrike Meinhof. It takes a certain degree of radical thinking to appropriate a literary form unintended for you and to make it conform to your own wishes, and at least among the essayists discussed here, the label "radical" frequently fits.

Which is not to say that all women essayists can be labeled radicals. The one woman essayist most often mentioned in the standard critical discussion on the genre is, of course, Virginia Woolf, whose elegant and decisive essays form a major part of her oeuvre. But even among the recent critical writings on the essay, Woolf has not been analyzed specifically as a woman essayist; she may be used to illustrate the theories and ideas of whoever is writing about her as an example of what that particular critic thinks an essay is, but gender is rarely a factor in the discussion of her essays *as essays*. Woolf, in other words, is included in the standard literature because she is a "good" essayist. In that context, she simply becomes another man. But however she is viewed and despite her compelling importance for women and particularly for feminists, she cannot be put into the radical camp. Her own essay on the essay (to which Pamela Mittlefehldt and Tuzyline Allan make reference) perhaps best describes her far-from-radical perspective: for her, the essay clearly served the function it did for Montaigne and so many others, namely a space for contemplation, measured thinking, respite from the frenetic world. Hardly a battleground for rebellion, despite the energizing effect her words have since had on their readers.

So, faced with virtually no critical literature on the subject, we have forged ahead on our own. In the process, we have become aware of a number of challenges to such an investigation, some inherent in the very nature of the project of studying a genre, others relatively specific to the idea of the relationship of women writers to a particular literary form. The very elusiveness of a stable entity we can call "genre," for example, creates roadblocks as we try to enter into a critical discussion of women's essays. Do the attempts to describe the essay as an open form, a non-linear, reflective, playful medium, provide an opening on the basis of the notion of *écriture féminine*? Margret Brügmann ponders such an approach (and its shortcomings) in her analysis of Hélène Cixous' "The Laugh of the Medusa." Or can we describe and enter a space of difference through the gendered content of women's essays? The essay as such of course demands a response on the level of content. In some ways, the substance contained within the form can be regarded as everything; one distinguishing feature of the form itself is its transparency; it is busy being no-thing, framing the message invisibly. This predominance of content over form helps to determine Lourdes Rojas' and Nancy Saporta Sternbach's focus on the political content of Latin-American women's essays, and Pamela Mittlefehldt's insistence on content as absolutely dominant over form in the essays of African-American women writers.

For a feminist undertaking such as ours, an important addition to the specific challenges of formal study of a genre is, as we have already implied, to ask questions of its history. It is to ask whether the use of the label "essay" has been a deliberate choice for the authors or is simply part of the leveling process that calls any short, generally non-fictional prose piece an essay. (Or, for that matter, most scholarly articles — look at the subtitles of virtually any academic anthology published today and you will find the designator "essay.") It is to ask why a certain form might have been chosen; how the genre affects the content, the presentation of the content; whether the use of that genre is understood to be for all writers, or whether cultural assumptions have led to its selection (or exclusion) by a certain gender or class or nationality. It is to ask whether the function of the genre is unchanging or has shifted within the course of the genre's history. It is to ask what has happened as it has begun to be used by nontraditional proponents of the form, namely those who are not white middle- or upper-class men. It is also to ask literary/aesthetic questions: about the role of the speaking/narrating subject, the importance of the voice, and other issues of structure. It is to concentrate particularly on the cultural implications of the essay as genre, and how these have affected and continue to affect its production and its use.

DIFFERENCES/DIVERSITY

By diversifying the project even more, by moving beyond our own national boundaries and bringing in studies of essays by women of different nationalities and cultures, as we have done in this volume, the topic becomes even more intriguing. We have learned that the approaches to the essay as genre may well be affected by the national origin of the essayists. Despite the multiple and diverse cultures of Latin America, for example, there is, as Lourdes Rojas and Nancy Sternbach point out, a widespread perception among Latin Americans of essays as political instruments, and not just when they are in the hands of women or feminists. An echo of this in the United States is certainly the radical-feminist essay, which is by definition political, overt, not at all a part of the contemplative world. The most extreme manifestation of the essay as overtly political in this anthology is certainly the case of Ulrike Meinhof, the focus of Arlene Teraoka's article. In any case, all of these digress from the traditional perception of the essay as removed, distant, or introspective.

The picture is further complicated when we consider not just nationality, but also specific historical location. The studies in this volume span the last two centuries, from Flora Tristan, Florence Nightingale, and a host of nineteenth-century Latin-American essayists, to Christa Wolf, Carmen Martín Gaite, and

Audre Lorde. A particular historical context plays, as always, an important role in how the essay is perceived, how it is written, what it contains, or, indeed, who writes it. The farther back we go, the less likely we are to find a woman essayist. The essay, as we have indicated, was not to all intents and purposes within the woman writer's domain for the first three hundred years of its existence as a genre, and those women who chose the form in the last century did so within a decidedly patriarchal context.

Although this volume concentrates on women essayists, the presence of Montaigne and Bacon, the fathers of the form, cannot be wished away. Nor should it be; they offer an important contrast to their female successors. Nevertheless, we are fully aware of the dangers of any sort of generalization of gender as a category: when it comes to seeing "female" and "male" characteristics in the essay, these observations are suspended on a line between acculturated assumptions (social constructs) and what seems actually to characterize women's essays in general, but they are not easily pinpointed nor proved. We have observed traits that may characterize a certain type of essay by women (the radical-feminist essay, for example, or the borderland nature of essays by *mestizas* like Gabriela Mistral and Victoria Ocampo), but broadening those assumptions to include all women, all nationalities, all times and places, is foolish. This volume represents instead an effort to approximate, to approach (like the original meaning of essay (*essai*) itself): to approach and explore and "attempt" the genre as it is employed by women, and see where such an effort leads us.

The very indefinability of the essay opens up interesting spaces for a variety of discussions and approximations, for a certain intriguing freedom. What these articles and essays represent is a discussion about what the essay appears to be in a variety of contexts. The slippery nature of the form can be observed on many different levels: we direct your attention particularly to the section on genre-crossings, to Amy Kaminsky's discussion of borderlands, to the inclusion by both Elizabeth Mittman and Ruth-Ellen Joeres of letters that they also define as essays. Not all essays are what are called philosophical essays, carefully crafted arguments on this or that point. Think of the range of essays discussed in this one volume alone: everything from the careful precision of Virginia Woolf to the introspective and often lengthy ruminations of Christa Wolf, from the academic style of Carmen Martín Gaite to the polemical pieces of Audre Lorde and most of the Latin-American women essayists. We would be hard put to find much that is a basis for commonality in such a great variety of textual practices.

In fact, the very act of attempting to define the essay is itself marked by the difficulty that these conflicting characteristics present. If there is anything that can be said to hold true for all essays, it would have more to do with structure than with specific content. We may "essay" the following definition: the essay has at its core an argument that welds its various parts together. Essays make a case for something; they not only present evidence, they also interpret that evidence. From experience, they glean observation. Logic is a vital rhetorical strategy essays use to construct their arguments. Yet the content itself exceeds that logic, at least on occasion—think of the essay's power and/or desire to persuade, which certainly exceeds the simple presentation of logical facts or orderly observations. And here we already begin to encounter diversity. Certainly, essays are also frequently marked by a tendency to wander around a subject, to investigate various paths toward a point, to enjoy the possibility of digression, of playfulness. Not all essays are philosophically constructed as neat and solid arguments; they often partake of the elliptical, the elusive, the indirect.

Still, we should not conclude that the essay is not recognizable as a genre: Katherine Snyder's careful comparison of Florence Nightingale's novel fragment "Cassandra" with the essay that it became in its later version highlights some of the fascinating differences between the two genres, thereby more clearly defining each, at least as Nightingale conceived them in her particular context. Similarly, Eileen Sivert's explication of Flora Tristan's essays—no matter what their overt form—makes clear that the essay itself can take on any number of identifiable guises. Constance Sullivan's investigation of the ways in which Carmen Martín Gaite introduced elements of the personal essay into her academic writing gives us yet another contrastive lens through which we can view the essay.

It is perhaps not merely paradoxical but in fact appropriate to the consideration of such a "non-genre" that by raising the question of women and essays we have found ourselves in the middle, not of a sterile discussion of genre and form, but of issues of class, race, subjectivity, gender-based constructions and perceptions of women, differences, the role of radical politics in writing, the effect of culturally prescriptive messages on those who are excluded. This is certainly a result of the nature of feminist inquiry, an always contextually grounded undertaking: we do not study a text in pristine isolation, à la New Criticism; we inquire about its roots, its surroundings, its consequences. We heed the power of words and the ways in which those words are presented. The essay is a form that emerged from the genteel male world of French aristocracy, yet it ultimately made its way into the hands of women writers, many of them ardent and committed feminists who represent many contexts of their own, none (or few) of which resemble Montaigne's exclusive world, or Bacon's patriarchal framework, or even E.B. White's gentle, ironic New England in the first half of this century. How did the essay get here? What happened to it along the way? What effect does its use by women have on them? Are they even aware of its patriarchal history? What makes them select the form?

And how do they make it their own?

POLITICS

The reasons behind our choice of title *The Politics of the Essay* are by now perhaps becoming clear. While the articulation of the bourgeois individual may have been radical within Montaigne's own historical context, it has, in the centuries since, become a conservative standard by and with which modern society helps to anchor itself. Literary criticism as an institution has tended to de-emphasize the politics of the essay. But politics is in fact the central issue in this book: politics as power, how it is exercised, where it is embedded. The politics/power of the word as well as the form: who holds it? who wrests it away? and how does that work? We mean not just the traditional sense of political content that is observable in some essays (those by the radical feminists, the Latin Americans, Flora Tristan, Ulrike Meinhof, for example), nor the less obvious political overtones in the essays by Gabriela Mistral, Victoria Ocampo, Florence Nightingale, Christa Wolf, or Carmen Martín Gaite, but the politics of certain constructions of self and of that self's expression that may (or may not) inhere within the formal parameters of the essay. In this broader sense, then, all of the contributions in this book deal with politics, not just the final section. In light of the essay's history, subjectivity, for example, becomes a political issue if we view the expressed presence of a subject—most often an explicitly present narrative "I"—in terms of the problem of author/authority. Whatever else may be claimed about the essay as a democratic form, as a rebellious response to the rigidity of the dogmatic tracts that preceded it and to which it responded, it is also true that Montaigne left the public world in which he had been prominent to write his essays and based them on the authority of his experience in that world. Experience is indeed the/an authorizing force in the essay.

And what sorts of experiences do women call upon? Are they different from the usual experiences called upon in the essay? Is the author (still) authoritative? How do women essayists mark their specifically gendered voice within the generically masculine form? The East German writer Christa Wolf's frequently quoted phrase about "the difficulty of saying 'I' " is often applied by feminist critics to women as a cryptic summation of the problematic relationship between women and subjecthood. And when we come down to talking about essays, it is important that we pay attention to that aspect of the essay, namely the (constructed) presence of the author, the sole source of authority. In the case of Wolf, as Elizabeth Mittman points out, the appropriation of the essayist's specific kind of authority can lead to some apparent contradictions.

But it is not only the author who is of interest and importance here. Another entire set of questions can and should be raised in this context about audience. What happens when we add the reader as a factor in the process of essay production and think about the essay as dialogue, as initiating discussion, as inviting reaction, response? In this instance, it is important to realize that many essays originated—particularly in the case of women essayists—as talks or speeches. Nancy Sternbach and Lourdes Rojas investigate the relationship between speech/talk and essay in their article on Latin-American women essayists, as do Ruth-Ellen Joeres and Pamela Mittlefehldt; Barbara Sichtermann's essay was indeed a speech before it became the essay we have translated for this volume. How does the transition between speech and essay take place? What elements of the speech persist? Is an audience specified? How do relationships play a role in connecting the essayist and her readers? Are those readers also addressed in part or in some fashion as listeners?

WHERE DO WE GO FROM HERE?

Of course there is also the nagging question of why: why study anything as apparently removed from reality as genre? Isn't such a preoccupation with genre, with the kind of definition that so often turns normative and prescriptive, precisely what we as feminists would normally spend our time denouncing? What does this add to our knowledge? More importantly, how does such knowledge help us to live, function, act? If we spend too much time on the removed and isolated niceties of form, won't we be neglecting the content that really makes up our lives?

In response to such questions, we would like to suggest one way in which a study of the essay, and, by extension, the practice of the essay, might be of value to us as feminists, particularly as academic feminists. To this end, we have deliberately begun our volume with a "real" essay written especially for us by Susan Griffin, whose "Red Shoes" provides a sort of paradigm of what we mean when we claim that a study of women and essays is not only appropriate, but illustrative, useful, and enjoyable. Susan Griffin is both an academic and an activist writer/essayist, and we can take a page from her book and the book of other radical feminists like Audre Lorde, Charlotte Bunch, or Gloria Anzaldúa, who already are clearly aware of what we now present as a suggestion: namely, that the essay is in many ways the ideal form for the presentation of feminist ideas. Activists have long known this: with their paramount goal of communication, they have always realized the need for a written form that resembles the speech — that invites dialogue and connection, that is straightforward, comprehensible, yet impassioned; that allows and indeed assumes a personal presence — that has such flexibility that it can take a variety of forms, whatever is most appropriate for the purpose at hand. In its status as a borderline genre, the essay already seems to connect with women, whose sense of marginality and not-belonging is still so present. Even in the standard (non-"political") descriptions of the essay, we find resonances with what we think of when we examine the social construct that is woman, or what we consider to be the project(s) of feminism: the unsystematized nature of the essay, its spontaneous and almost accidental quality, its assumed opposition to doctrinaire, disciplinary thinking, its focus on personal experience, its cultivation of diversity, its stress on particularity, its "happy inheritance of meaninglessness" (as Barbara Sichtermann puts it), its concern with knowledge that is intimately connected with the author, its emphasis on objects and the importance of things. In fact, as Ruth-Ellen Joeres suggests in her article on radical feminist essays, when one reads the critical literature on essays, one quickly gains the sense that whereas essayists, the actors and agents, are almost always defined very clearly as "masculine," the essay itself is placed over and over again into a space that is uncannily feminine, at least as the qualities adhering to the "feminine" have been defined since the eighteenth century. Essays are called a mixture of anecdote, description, and opinion. Essays are said to focus on a little world, on details.

Essays seem, according to Theodor Adorno, to form patterns of relationships "rather than a straight line of necessary consequences. . . ." Essays stress process rather than product. Or as Graham Good says, "The essay is an act of personal witness. The essay is at once the *in*scription of a self and *de*scription of an object."

If all of this is so, then the essay seems perfectly designed for feminist projects. It is certainly much more appropriate than the dry, imitative, and often muddy scholastic treatises that academic articles generally are. To choose deliberately the form of the essay is to step away from a path of obedient submission to the academic world in which feminism, the formerly activist movement, is now firmly ensconced. It is to say that we value the form in which we present our thoughts as much as we do their content. It is to say that we do not choose to imitate everything the male university has taught us and has told us is correct. It is to assert ourselves. It is to acknowledge that we are above all determined to connect with each other, with an audience, and to communicate with that audience.

And on a practical level, it is to select a form that brings us closer to fulfilling the feminist aim of reaching and connecting with a widely-based audience. The essay can help us do that, particularly if we have adapted it to our own ends, if we have taken away its aura of elitism by making the subject matter our own. If we view the use of the essay as an announcement to others (not to mention ourselves) that our choice of it means the renunciation of jargon and the acknowledgement that our experiences and our ideas can best be expressed in a form that does not reek of the rigidity and stultification of most academic prose.

It is not that feminist scholars haven't already been using essays, or varieties thereof. Think, for example, of the writings of Marilyn Frye, Patricia Williams, Adrienne Rich, or Bernice Johnson Reagon. But they tend to be the exception rather than the rule. Although activist feminists have long since recognized the virtue of the essay form, academic feminists in contrast seem bent upon separating themselves from activism and tying themselves ever more firmly to academe, especially in the way in which they record their ideas. As a result, there is an ever present and expanding gap between the feminist language of the academy and that of the nonacademic world. And that seems very much to go against the grain of our being, the very purposes of our diverse but related projects. If the essay—with its openness, its accessibility, its sense of initiated dialogue, its emphasis on the particular and the concrete, its stress on dynamic process—could become an alternative form for feminist critical writing, we suspect that our writing as academic feminists would be enormously enriched.

We hope that our volume will be viewed as a first stage in a discussion of the particular benefits of the essay for us as feminist scholars, writers, readers, and activists, American and nonAmerican alike. Our investigation of what women from various cultures and times have done with the genre is merely a part of the larger project of developing our own visions and versions of the essay.

Women's Essays

Genre-Crossings

CHAPTER ONE

From Novel to Essay

Gender and Revision in Florence Nightingale's "Cassandra"

KATHERINE V. SNYDER

"About Cassandra I see that I was mistaken. I did not exactly take Cassandra for yourself, but I thought that it represented more of your own feeling about the world than could have been the case."[1] Thus wrote Benjamin Jowett, Regius Professor of Greek at Oxford, in a letter to Florence Nightingale sometime between May and July of 1861. Their correspondence had begun the previous summer when Arthur Hugh Clough, Nightingale's secretary and an undergraduate contemporary of Jowett's, asked Jowett to comment on a three-volume work by Nightingale which included her essay, "Cassandra." Although the letters immediately preceding Jowett's polite retraction no longer survive, we can deduce that in them Jowett mistook Nightingale for the subject of her essay and Nightingale rebuked him for this misapprehension. In assigning the identity of Cassandra to Nightingale herself, Jowett may have been responding to the fact that there *is* no Cassandra, after the title, in the essay that he read.[2] However, in an earlier, novelistic version of the manuscript, there *was* a Cassandra or at least a character who rhetorically renames herself after the cursed prophetess of ancient myth:

> "Oh! Call me no more Nofriani, call me Cassandra. For I have preached & prophesied in vain. I have gone about crying all these many years, Wo to the People! And no one has listened or believed. And now I cry, Wo to myself! For upon me the destruction has come." [Add. MS 45839, f. 269][3]

Cassandra and Nofriani are absent from the essay as it was eventually published; Nightingale's dismissal of both figures occurred in the course of revising the manuscript several years after its composition. Her editorial decisions, more process than strategy, resulted in a significantly altered text. The first phase of the novel's development had featured a heroine who told her own tragic life-story; a later but still novelistic recension made its world available through the agency of a masculine narrator; the final transformation of "Cassandra" is an authoritative, anonymously narrated, essayistic account of the

tragic situation of all women in society. The temporary intervention of a masculine "interpreter" distanced the narrative voice from the feminine subjectivity at issue in Nightingale's social critique. This transitional regendering of the
narrative persona marked what was ultimately a generic transformation of the
text: from autobiographical novel to non-fictional essay.

The shift from feminine to masculine subjectivity does not reflect an essential gendering of these prose genres but rather the literary and social history
behind them. Nightingale wrote first in, and then against, a novelistic tradition
whose linkage to the needs and resources of middle-class women was apparent
as early as the mid-nineteenth century.[4] Despite the publication of such influential Victorian women essayists as Harriet Martineau and Mary Russell Mit-
ford, the essay was understood almost exclusively in terms of its masculine lineage. Indeed, the nineteenth century's endorsement of what Joel Haefner has
termed the "dual father theory" of the essay's origins was heartfelt. Alexander
Smith's popular 1863 essay, "On the Writing of Essays," for example, focuses
almost exclusively on the dual heritage of Montaigne's familiar essay and Bacon's rational essay; some forty years earlier, William Hazlitt "extended the
mythos of two generic giants by pinpointing Addison and Steele as literary
'sons' of the father, Montaigne" [Haefner, 261]. The location of the essay's
"proper" origins—determining where and to whom it "belongs"—in this po-
larized yet complementary patrilineage effectively eliminates the need for a
challenging myth of an essayistic mother. Because it subsumes the usual role of
the personal/familiar/feminine other within its own self-division, the two-fa-
ther system displaces the feminine altogether, contributing to the historical neglect of women's essays and the devaluing of "feminine" style in essayistic
practice.

Taxonomical distinctions between personal and rational notwithstanding,
nineteenth-century readers of both of these essayistic kinds took the immediate
presence of the author and his consciousness as a preeminent and uniting generic feature. From this perspective, the essay is nonfictional and mimetic—it is
an expression of the writer's actual experience and essential self. However, the
terms "fiction" and "non-fiction" do not map precisely onto "novel" and "essay." Just as the label "autobiographical novel" already breaks down any pure
or exclusionary opposition between fiction and non-fiction, the essay occupies
an indeterminate discursive space between fiction and non-fiction. That is to
say, the essay, whether familiar or formal, constructs a writerly self who resembles the author's historical self but whose verisimilitude in this area as in
others—Montaigne's inaccurate quoting from sources is the recurrent
example—is not beyond question.[5] Late twentieth-century language-based theories, citing "the Death of the Author" [Barthes], encourage us to read essays
as purely linguistic constructions, whose free-playing signifiers construct an
"author" who does not otherwise already exist in the "world." Celeste
Schenck articulates the political bind that this theoretical bias presents to the
burgeoning field of women's autobiography, but its relevance for theorizing the
essay should be readily apparent: "A feminist reading of women's writing

would argue . . . that women, never having achieved the self-possession of post-Cartesian subjects, do not have the luxury of 'flirting with the escape from identity,' which the deconstructed subject may enjoy" [288]. If we focus exclusively on language and "absence" in our attention to essayistic subjectivity, we risk sacrificing the experience of historical women authors and we risk losing gender as a category of significance.

Importantly, the status of the author and her own experience concerned Nightingale's audience and Nightingale in her revisions. For the writer and for her readers, the appropriateness of the genre of "Cassandra" was intimately connected to the gender of its writer. By denovelizing "Cassandra," Nightingale was attempting to distance herself from her heroine's story and problems, but her revisions generated an uneasy proximity of a different kind. Without the mediation of the novel's characters, the essay's unveiled account of women's confinement within the bounds of proper society seemed to her contemporary male readers like indecent exposure. Nightingale's revisions may have been a bid for authority or even a sign that she had attained it, but the essay that they yielded found no welcoming reception from Nightingale's contemporaries.

"Cassandra" comes at the end of the second volume (subheaded "Practical Deductions") of Nightingale's *Suggestions for Thought to Searchers after Religious Truth*. Nightingale wrote this theological tome in 1850 and 1851, a period during which she was profoundly, even suicidally, depressed; her despair was largely a response to her family's seemingly insurmountable resistance to her desire for active public work.[6] However, in 1853 Nightingale received from her father an independence of £500 per year, and several months later she accepted a post as the Superintendent of an Institution for the Care of Sick Gentlewomen in Distressed Circumstances at 1 Upper Harley Street in London. In 1854 she left for the Crimean War and the nursing work that was to make her an international legend.

When Nightingale returned from the Crimea, she set about revising the manuscript of *Suggestions*, including the section called "Cassandra." She went on, in late 1859 and 1860, to have the extensively revised manuscript privately printed up in a three-volume review edition, with wide margins for annotations. The six copies in this edition were sent to her father, her uncle Samuel Smith, Richard Monckton Milnes, Sir John McNeill, John Stuart Mill, and Benjamin Jowett.[7] Nightingale undertook no further revisions of "The Stuff," as she customarily called it. An unknown number of copies, probably very few, were printed in 1860; these books were identical to the review copies but without the wide margins.[8] *Suggestions for Thought* never became publicly available, but "Cassandra" was reprinted in 1928 as the appendix to Ray Strachey's *The Cause* and reprinted again as a monograph by the Feminist Press in 1979. "Cassandra" has reached readers only in its heavily revised form.

In its early incarnation as a fictionalized autobiographical novel, "Cassandra" begins (following an epigraph retained in the revised version) this way:

The night was mild & dark & cloudy. Nofriani was walking to & fro before the beautiful facade of a Palladian palace. All was still. Not one light shining through the window betrayed the existence of any life stirring within. "I, I alone am wandering in the bitterness of life without," she said. She went down where on the glassy dark pond the long shadows of the girdle of pines the tops of which seemed to touch heaven, were lying. The swans were sleeping on their little island. Even the Muscovy ducks were not yet awake. But she had suffered so much that she had outlived even the desire to die. [Add. MS 45839, f. 237].[9]

Reentering the palace and throwing herself down on her balcony, Nofriani "start[s] up, like the dying lioness who fronts her hunters," then bemoans the way society stifles women's moral and intellectual energy and the way women respond by withdrawing into a fantasy world. She puts it bluntly: "In the conventional society, which men have made for women, & women have accepted, women must have no passions, they must act the farce of hypocrisy, the lie that they are without Passion" [MS 239]. But then, in a more fanciful vein, she calls upon the "young maidens of the 'higher toned classes' " to speak, thereby causing phantasms to appear,

the phantasms, the larvae of the most beautiful race of the world, the maidens of the ranks, whose white hands have never been made hard by toil. Graceful & lovely, pure & etherial they floated by & their thoughts and fancies took shape & form at the word of the Magician [Nofriani]. With each maiden there was a Phantom one! There were two, three, twenties, hundreds, ever varying, ever changing, but *never* was she *alone*. With the Phantom companion of her fancy, she talked, not love, she was too innocent, too pure, too full of genius and imagination & high toned feeling for that, but she talked, in fancy of that which interested her most . . . or if not that, if not absorbed in endless conversations, she saw herself engaged with him in stirring events, circumstances which called out the interest wanting to her. [Add. MS 45839, f. 239-40].[10]

The chapter concludes with an atmospheric, spiritual, and artistic crescendo in which the narrator likens the effect of "fleecy clouds" veiling the moon's "flood of radiance" to "the wings of the Almighty overshadowing suddenly the world, as in that inspired representation of Him in Michael Angelo's Sistine Chapel" [MS 244].

In the next chapter, Nofriani pursues her theme of the mental and emotional deprivation of women by society, but here she reclines beside a fountain on a fiercely hot day with her brother, Fariseo, as her audience. This discussion, a kind of dramatic dialogue, continues through the next five chapters, apparently over some time since chapter three takes place during a snowstorm. It encompasses a critique of the family and marriage, a contrast between ideal and actual life, and the possibility of the coming of a female Christ. The piece ends with Nofriani on her deathbed at the age of thirty, with Fariseo among the mourners recounting her last requests and her final words: "Free, free, oh! divine Freedom, art thou come at last? Welcome, beautiful Death!" [Add. MS 45839, f. 287].

These final words are virtually the only ones retained as indirect discourse in the essayistic version; in that later version, however, they are attributed to some unspecified "dying woman to her mourners." Elsewhere in the essay, Nightingale removed Nofriani's speeches from their quotation marks and changed "I" of her first-person singular narration to the first-person plural—women as "we"—or to the more generalized third-person plural—women as "they." With these changes in the personal pronoun comes a shift in tense—the historical past of one woman's life is transposed to the present condition of women in general. One paragraph, for example, originally read:

> Thus I lived for over seven years dreaming always, never accomplishing—too much ashamed of my dreams, which I thought were "romantic," to tell them where I knew that they would be laughed at, if not considered wrong. So I lived, till my heart was broken. I am now an old woman at thirty . . .

Nightingale then revised it to read:

> Dreaming always, never accomplishing, thus women live—too much ashamed of their dreams, which they think "romantic," to tell them to be laughed at, if not considered wrong. [Add. MS 45839, f. 263][11]

In this example, the shift in person and tense coincides with certain other alterations. These alterations, which characterize the revision of the manuscript as a whole, can be grouped into two categories. First, she cut or disguised autobiographical details, such as "at thirty," Cassandra's age at death and Nightingale's age when she first wrote "Cassandra." At the same time, she excised stylistic details that may have seemed overly fanciful, or "romantic," such as "till my heart was broken." In fact, the two categories of revised or excised material tend to overlap because Nightingale fictionalized many details of her life by framing them in fanciful (or sometimes highly spiritualized) language and settings.

Nightingale's revisions resemble the self-censorship described in the passage from "Cassandra"; that is, women's concealment of their "romantic" dreams suggests a paradigm for Nightingale's own censorship of "romantic" or "dreamy" passages in her manuscript. This censorship eliminated the exotic settings and atmospheric effects of the original version, including those that open and close the first chapter; it even foreshortened accounts of women's compensatory fantasy life that were themselves particularly fanciful, like the description of Nofriani conjuring up the phantasmic maidens. By eliminating the descriptions themselves, the essay actually enacts the censorship that the novel describes.

In an earlier, pre-Crimean journal entry, Nightingale articulated the threat of fantasy and the necessity for regulating it through concealment: "Every different kind of suffering is ranged under the one comprehensive word: Fancy, & disposed of with the one comprehensive remedy: Concealment or Self-Command which is the same thing" [Add. MS 43402, f. 35].[12] But despite Nightingale's indictment of fantasy as the source of all suffering, we may infer that such "fancies" were important to her early imagining of "Cassandra" as a novel written for her eyes only. They were a way for her to acknowledge the problem of these consuming daydreams for women while indulging in them at the same time. In other words, the fancies involved in the writing of "Cassandra" as an autobiographical novel were both a symptom of and a form of therapy for what ailed Nightingale.

However, in reimagining "Cassandra" as a public text for a male audience, Nightingale distanced the subjectivity of her authorial voice from the problematics of feminine subjectivity that it treats. By toning down the fancifulness of her text, she made the authorial consciousness of her essay seem immune to the very fantasies that the piece exposes. The genre of the essay thereby resolves the seeming paradox of Nightingale's equation of "self-command" with "concealment"; the generic transformation that reallocated her own experience to other women not only reflects Nightingale's assumed or achieved distance from fantasy but may have actually been a way for her to attain this emotional distance.

Both the novel and the essay versions of "Cassandra" involve what I have been calling distancing, although by different means and with different implications.[13] Cecil Woodham-Smith's biography of Nightingale, for example, gives this account, unfortunately without attribution, of an episode from Nightingale's own life that reappears in the novelistic and essayistic incarnations of "Cassandra":

> In the spring of 1851 she unexpectedly met Richard Monckton Milnes at a party given in London by Lady Parthenope [Nightingale's sister]. She had not seen him since the day she refused him, and she was shaken. He came across to her and said lightly: "The noise of this room is like a cotton mill." She was deeply wounded— how could he speak as if she were an ordinary acquaintance?[14]

In "Cassandra" the novel, Nofriani finishes her discussion with Fariseo about marriage thus:

> "Oh! How cruel are the revulsions which women suffer! I remember, on the ruins of Palmyra, amid the wrecks of worlds & palaces & temples, thinking of one I had loved, in connection with great deeds, noble thoughts, devoted feelings. I saw him again. It was at one of those crowded parties of Civilization which we call Society. His words were, 'the buzz tonight is like a manufactory.' Yet that man loved me still.
>   And now, I have soon done with this world. The life of it has departed from me."
> [Add. MS 45839, f. 278]

The essay "Cassandra" renders the anecdote this way:

> How cruel are the revulsions which high-minded women suffer! There was one who loved, in connection with great deeds, noble thoughts, devoted feelings. They met after an interval. It was at one of those crowded parties of Civilization which we call Society. His only careless passing remark was, "the buzz tonight is like a manufactory." Yet he loved her. [Add. MS 45839, f. 278]

Nightingale's earlier, novelized version of the encounter is marked by several features. For one, Nofriani's sorrowful apostrophe, "Oh!", and her "end is nigh" refrain (repeated with variations throughout the chapter) signify the relevance of the anecdote to the suffering of the first-person speaker. Another important feature of the novelized version is the defamiliarized geographical and historical setting. The exoticism and belatedness of "the ruins of Palmyra, amid the wrecks of worlds & palaces & temples" set up a disjunction with the mundane contemporaneity of "Society" and the "manufactory." This disjunction characterizes the novelistic version as a whole, with its Italianate and aristocratic characters in their timeless Romance world discussing specifically mid-nineteenth century, English, and upper middle-class pursuits like "the Opera, the Exhibitions, the debate in the House of Commons & the caricature in Punch" [MS 243]. The romantic characters and scenery disguise the "real" writing subject and her Victorian milieu, but the artificial literariness and the jarring inconsistency of the romantic trappings constantly give themselves away. They are finally less a disguise than the self-conscious construction of a different world and a different self.

When Nightingale excised the components that contributed to the novelistic world of "Cassandra," she established an essayistic world that appeared more realistic and objective: more realistic because of the familiar frame of reference within bourgeois Victorian society, and more objective because the narrator is not the subject of the narrated anecdote. The essayistic anecdote, with its disinterested, rational teller and its recognizable, plausible context, would tend to appear authoritative to an upper-class male Victorian reader. In short, the essayistic anecdote makes a truth claim of a kind that the novelistic anecdote does not. However, the process of transformation in the above sequence underlines the point that both autobiographical novel and essay are mediated forms that depend on generic expectations for their effect. Both the novelistic and the essayistic versions use the anecdotal device and the figure of the representative individual to epitomize the problems of women as a whole. The "other woman" of the essay bears an unmistakable resemblance to the "other woman" in the novelistic version who is Nofriani. Moreover, both Nofriani and the "one" who meets her former lover are distinct from the author; both figures are part of the narrative strategies by which Nightingale distanced her own experience.

One crucial difference is that the novel has Nofriani narrating her own life story while the essay imagines some "one" other than its writing self as the object of its speculation.[15] While retaining the romantic theme of the clash between transcendent love and conventional society, the rational voice of the essay poses the anecdote of thwarted love as somebody else's problem. The essayistic anecdote is no longer part of the sequence of a self-told life history but a block of evidence used to build the case against conventional society. Yet the essay condemns conventional society in a voice that allies itself (at least in part) with just that social convention which excludes "great deeds, noble thoughts, devoted feelings" from everyday life and contains them in fiction. I qualify my assertion about the alliance of Nightingale's essayistic voice with social (male) authority because of her sympathy, however distanced, for the female victims whose cause she promotes. It is conceivable that the essayistic voice betrays a kind of hybridization of the emotional investment of the Nofriani narrator and the cool disinterest of the anonymous third-person narrator, but to me this dialogism betokens not a heteroglossic vitality (my vocabulary here is, of course, Bakhtinian) but a conflicted self-division. Rather than having it both ways, Nightingale experiences a double bind: masculine privilege is both the object of her social critique and the ultimate source from which she seeks discursive authority.

The denovelization of "Cassandra" was facilitated by a transitional defeminization of its narrative voice and identity. Nightingale began "Cassandra" as a novel using a third-person omniscient narrator, but one whose voice is largely subordinate to the speaking "I" who is Nofriani. By the final stage of the essay's revision, there is still an omniscient narrator but no Nofriani; her subjectivity is repressed by this authoritative, writing persona.

There was, however, an intermediate stage somewhere between novel and essay that featured a masculine first-person narrator. As soon as Nofriani has an audience, the male audience of her brother, some ambivalence over the relations between audience and speaker surfaces. This ambivalence expresses itself in the form of pronoun trouble. When her brother first appears in chapter two, his comments are marked with "said Fariseo" or "he said." But several pages into the chapter, a question he puts to Nofriani is marked with "I said," which is crossed out and replaced by "said Fariseo." For his next speech, the text sticks with "said I" with an explanatory "I am Fariseo" in parentheses. The oscillation between "he said" and "I said" continues, but in the following chapters the use of the first-person voice for Fariseo's speech stabilizes. And in the last chapter, the voice telling the story announces its identity:

> Before I go on, I had better tell who "I" am. My name is Fariseo. I am one of those, who are called the Cynics of the age, who openly confess their own selfishness, admit the wants of the times, & preach that we should bear with them, making this confession not with sorrow of heart, nor well-trained resignation, but without shame & without difficulty, as, on the whole, the best state of mind. I am the brother of poor Nofriani, & I tell her story as she told it me, one day when I blamed her for not finding her happiness in life as I & her contemporaries have done, & she answered that I did not know whether her life had been such that she could either find happiness in it or alter it. I made some few notes of our conversation, for it occurred a short time only before her death. My poor sister! She died at 30 wearied of life, in which she could do nothing & having ceased to live the intellectual life long before she was deserted by the physical life. I saw her on her death-bed, & giving way to the tears and exclamations natural on such occasions, was answered by her. [Add. MS 45839, f. 286]

None of the intermediary oscillation between first and third person is apparent in the final printed version since both characters were ultimately excised, leaving only the words of Nofriani, initially transmitted through a third-person narrator and then reported by Fariseo, finally in the form of direct, written descriptions of the general plight of women.

The regendering of the narrative persona can be read as part of Nightingale's bid for the approval of her selected audience of male readers.[16] However, an unspoken but nevertheless stringent critique of Fariseo's masculine point of view complicated her design. The unspoken critique is palpable, for example, in the longest passage that was cut from the manuscript, a passage that occurs in the same chapter as the pronominal oscillation that ultimately alters Fariseo's status. Nofriani has been trying to answer Fariseo's uncomprehending questions about her despair by using a variety of anecdotes and arguments. Finally, she turns her attention to the fountain, with its "beautiful solitary spire of water," beside which they are sitting:

> "See, it struggles up towards heaven again. And this time it will succeed. Behold, it scales Infinity. It is rising higher and higher. That mighty heart will climb to heaven. Now it has conquered Earth. It is out of the sphere of its attraction. Oh! it is rising now! It has ascended up on high. It is leading Gravitation captive. The earth cannot reach it to pull it down again. Shoot up, brave spirit, brave spirit, soar higher! Thou hast mastered matter. Be of good cheer, thou hast over come the world. . . .
>
> Alas! where is it now? Its impulse is exhausted; its strength is at an end; its life is blasted; its struggles done; its hope destroyed. And it falls lifeless on the grass— it, which had so lately been striving to heaven. For it is dead. . . .
>
> The ungrateful ground had been fertilized by it. It struggled to the skies—& it watered a weed. It thought to scale Infinity—& it made verdant a blade of grass."
> [Add. MS 45839, f. 253–55]

In response, Fariseo tries to "improvise a 'Ballata' for her benefit, to shew [sic] her that her sick fancies were not those of all the world":

> "See, how the infant founts spring & gambol & dance in the sun-beams! There is one! He is shooting with his tiny arrow at the sun. He stands, the mimic Apollo, erect & fearless & laughing sends the missile at the mark. And when the harmless arrow falls playful at his foot, he runs, with joyous laughter, back, & hides his merry face in his mother-fountain, while he tells her how the sun held out his noble hand to catch the infant spear, & could not. . . .
>
> There, pouring his joyous soul in song, he waves his little lance on high. Glad morning vision of *light* and merry *life* as brothers! Not long does he remain there, but eager to rejoin his Mother Earth, down he springs—& his sister fount welcomes him back with her glad eyes. In loving triumph, she holds up her watery mirror, while he, the daring little soarer, successful Icarus, admires his scatheless wings. [Add. MS 45839, f. 255–57]

The chapter ends with Fariseo's words; no commentary is necessary (or possible, since he has become the narrator) to criticize his version of the *paysage moralisé*. Nofriani's eloquent silence censures his sketch, a family drama that uncritically contrasts the unrestrained, phallic activity of the water-baby brothers with the passive mirroring of the "mother-fountain," "Mother Earth," and "sister fount." He doesn't get it, but we get it and so, implicitly, does Nofriani. His translation of Nofriani's interpretation unwittingly reveals the limitations of his masculine perspective and vindicates Nofriani's complaint.

In this intermediate phase between novel and essay, the text reveals a man's failure to understand a woman's suffering through the uncomprehending words of a man himself, hardly a flattering reflection on male editors, real or within the text. The irresolvable dilemma of a masculine perspective that is authoritative yet obtuse dramatizes the conflicted nature of Nightingale's transformation of "Cassandra" into an essay. She revised her writing to impress male figures of authority in her personal life and in the intellectual community, but these readers were affiliated with the conventional social authority that she criticizes in "Cassandra." Her relation to her readers thus motivated but also constricted Nightingale's revisions. The gaps that remain in her essay, evident in the manuscript's palimpsestic traces of the novel, bear witness to Nightingale's sense of the irreconcilable demands posed by her male audience.

Nightingale's revisions transformed *Suggestions* from private writing—her concealed response to the emotional and intellectual privations of enforced domesticity—to public writing intended for an audience wider than one. But while the revisions prepared her writing for publication, what publication meant for Nightingale is not entirely clear. It may well have been unclear, or at least conflicted, for Nightingale herself. In a letter to Sir John McNeill, Nightingale claimed that she wrote the first volume, entitled *Suggestions for Thought to Searchers after Religious Truth among the Artisans of England*, with the artisans in mind:

> Eight years ago I had a large and very curious acquaintance among the Operatives of the North of England, and among those of what are called Holyoake's party in London. The most thinking and conscientious of our enormous artisan population appeared to me to have no religion at all.
>
> I then wrote the first part of what I have ventured to send you, without the least idea of publishing it. And it was read in MS by some of them. . . .
>
> Till this last spring I never thought for a moment of printing it. But just now I have had six copies done of which I send you one. No one knows of it. And, till after my death, I would never have it published, certainly not with my name.
>
> My reason for sending it you is to ask you, should the subject interest you enough, to be so good as to say *at your leisure* whether you think it would be after my death at all useful among the "Atheist" Operatives, as they are called. [Add. MS 45768, f. 112][17]

The complexities within this single letter confound any simple bifurcation between private and public writing. Nightingale could write for a particular audience and purpose, and even show the manuscript to that audience, without having "the least idea of publishing." Moreover, she claimed that any publishing would have to be both posthumous and pseudonymous. But in the letter that accompanied the copy of *Suggestions* she sent to John Stuart Mill, Nightingale wrote that "I never intended to print it *as it was*. But my health broke down. I shall never now write out the original plan. I have therefore printed the ill S.S. [Suggestions to Searchers?] as they were, mainly in order to invite your criticism, if you can be induced to give it" [Add. MS 45787, f. 1].[18] To McNeill she disavowed any premeditated aim to publish, but to Mill she only denied that she premeditated printing it in its present state.

The inconsistencies in Nightingale's different accounts of her intentions suggest her ambivalence toward further revising and publishing *Suggestions*.[19] The problem of self-publicity was standard for Victorian women autobiographers. It was scandalous for a Victorian woman to publish her memoirs during her lifetime; a respectable woman let her family, usually her children, publish her memoirs posthumously, typically in a small, privately-printed edition for distribution to family members only.[20] Our understanding of Nightingale's ambivalence over publishing is further informed by a frequent theme in her private journals and correspondence during the post-Crimean years: the annoyance and dangers of publicity. Soon after returning from the Crimea, she condemned the popular attention her work had received:

[T]he publicity & talk there have been about this work have injured it more than anything else—and in no way, I am determined, will I contribute to making a show of myself. On this ground I have determined to sit for no one as a public character unless the Queen desire it. I desire privacy for the reason that I consider publicity to have injured what is nearest to my heart. [Add. MS 43402, f. 162]

In a private note from the same period, Nightingale connected the exploitative superficiality of publicity to her troubled relation with her family:

What have mothers & sisters ever done for me? They like my glory—they like my pretty things. Is there anything else they like in me? I was the same person who went to Harley St and who went to the Crimea. There was nothing different except my popularity. Yet the one who went to Harley St [illegible: "that"?] person was to be cursed, & the other to be blessed. The popularity does not signify much one way or other. It has hurt me less in the Crimea and vantaged me less at home than I expected. Good Public! It knew nothing what I was really doing in the Crimea. Good Public! It had known nothing of what I wanted to do, & have done, since I came home. . . . Yet, this adventitious, this false popularity based on ignorance has made all the difference in the feeling of my "family" towards me. [Add. MS 43402, f. 179]

Nancy Boyd makes the point that while Nightingale may have protested against publicity, she nevertheless used her public image as the saintly and maternal "lady with the lamp" to promote her work [188].[21] And, in fact, during this period Nightingale published *Notes on Nursing*, which fed the Nightingale legend and thereby facilitated her work on army sanitary reform. Nightingale's preoccupation with other projects following her return from the Crimea also helps to explain her decision not to continue work on *Suggestions*.

The feedback from Nightingale's selected readers did not influence her accomplished revisions since their responses came only *after* the printing of the review copies. However, their commentary may have dissuaded her from continuing to revise. The quantity as well as the nature of their suggested revisions were daunting—only Mill suggested minor changes, whereas both Jowett and McNeill advised substantive changes that would actually undo the revisions she had already made. Jowett explicitly advocated back-tracking—"[S]uppose you were to publish the novel & imaginary conversations as they stood originally" [Quinn and Prest, 8]—as well as numerous other changes. A reversion to novelistic form was implicit in McNeill's critique as well:

> [I]t is through the imagination rather than through the reason that the masses are influenced especially in matters of religion and . . . without appeals to the imagination and a certain romance of mystery it would at this time be impossible to produce any considerable impression. [Add. MS 45768, f. 122]

McNeill's remarks link genre to class. The workers, implicitly childlike or even childish in their dependence on fiction, might be induced to accept the bitter pill of religious truth if it were sugar-coated with "a certain romance of mystery." His evaluation of the capacities of the working classes "at this time" indicates the paternalism, however benevolent or visionary, underlying his class bias; if fiction controls the masses, McNeill seems to reason, then it can be used to exert control over them. McNeill's advice combines a species of social Darwinism—a theory of "human kinds" that locates the working classes low on the evolutionary ladder—with an evolutionary theory of literary kinds in which primitive genres like fiction forerun more advanced forms of rational discourse.[22]

One connection between these parallel theories of human kinds and of literary kinds—class and genre—is the category of gender. If the way to a worker's intellect is through his imagination, then the ideal explorer of these uncharted territories would be the upper middle-class woman. As a woman, she would be sympathetically childlike yet instinctively maternal. She would share the workers' primitive tendency towards fiction, and she would be suited to "raise" the intellectual young of society. Moreover, as upper middle-class she would be morally obliged to share the imperialist burden of spiritual and social instruction. Nightingale envisioned herself in this multi-faceted role in a letter to Jowett from this period: "If I were what I was 8 years ago, I would have a Working Men's Children's School . . . to teach them all the laws of Nature (known) upon this principle, that it is a religious act to clean out a gutter and to prevent cholera" [Quinn and Prest, 17–18]. Her association of working men with their children and her sense of herself as a maternal, spiritual teacher cum head nurse support the view of class and gender relations suggested by McNeill's comments on literary form.[23]

Both McNeill and Jowett emphasized the issue of audience (possibly to deflect their criticisms from the writer onto her readers and thereby to soften the blow), but their responses as readers are not, as my comments above indicate, separable from their feelings about Nightingale as a woman. Jowett's initial response to *Suggestions*, directed to Clough since he had not yet been introduced to Nightingale, took the writer's situation into account:

> In a few places there appeared to me a trace of passion (shall I say?) which weakened the form of what was said. Feeling there should be, for feeling is the only language which everyone understands. But I thought that here and there I traced some

degree of irritation in the tone. I hardly like to notice it, for it is probably only the unavoidable weakness of illness which always impairs the power of expression much more than [the] power of mind and thought. [Add. MS 45795, f. 19]

He interpreted the "weakened . . . form" as a product of the "weakness of illness," linking physical and literary weakness to uncontrolled "passion." In a later letter to Nightingale that comments explicitly on "Cassandra," Jowett's concern with "weakness" resurfaced:

> But I think it would add to the effect of what is said . . . if the difficulties of the subject were more considered e.g., the extremely small number of women (or indeed of men) who are capable of fulfilling an ideal or carrying out an original walk of life; — the weakness which is often found precisely in the character most likely to form a sentimental idea; — the dangers which women must incur unless they could be supposed to be quite impassible. [Quinn and Prest, 4]

While he included men in a conciliatory parenthetical gesture, for him weakness was an attribute of illness and of passion, and therefore especially of women, those who are most susceptible to a "sentimental idea."

Despite his agreement with Nightingale that the "value" of her papers depends on "their being a record of your own experience" [Quinn and Prest, 8], Jowett repeatedly objected to just this feature of her writing:

> it would add to the effect of what is said . . . if the reflection on the family took less the form of individual experience; this appears to me to lessen the weight of what is said & may, perhaps, lead to painful remarks. [Quinn and Prest, 4]

> The difficulty I should find would be to separate the part which expresses your own feelings & thoughts from those which belong to other characters. [Quinn and Prest, 9]

Even in its revised essayistic form, "Cassandra" was still too emotional and too personal for Jowett's sense of decorum. Apparently, it seemed even more personal and emotional than a fully novelized version might have because no characters interpose between writer and reader; as nonfiction, it displays undisguised the feelings and experience of the author. To Jowett, the non-fiction essay left the woman writer indecently exposed, whereas fictionalized, novelistic trappings would provide fittingly modest attire for "Cassandra" and for Nightingale's life.

Whereas Nightingale's male readers saw the essayistic version of "Cassandra" as too revealing, I see it as a cover-up. Having witnessed the fragmentation and cancellations of the manuscript, I regard Nightingale's essay as inhibited and concealing, a form of protective self-censorship rather than liberated self-empowerment. While I grant that Nightingale's revisions reflect a new control over her fantasy life and may even have helped her to gain that control, it is a control that comes at a heavy price. Aligning herself with the masculine authority that was the subject of her critique may have enabled Nightingale to accomplish the social reforms that were her goals, but it played havoc with the voice of "Cassandra." The gaps and other structural and tonal peculiarities

that characterize the essay testify to Nightingale's gendered and generic predic-
ament, yet at least one recent critic has seen in them a subversive feminist poetics.[24]

The combination of defeat and resistance, of co-optation and subversion, in
Nightingale's "Cassandra" resonates in the response of an early reader and
feminist essayist in her own right. Virginia Woolf's landmark essay, "A Room
of One's Own," published in the year following the belated public appearance
of "Cassandra" in *The Cause* (1928), alludes several times to Nightingale's essay. Distinguishing her own essayistic style from that of "Cassandra" in which
"Florence Nightingale shrieked aloud in agony," Woolf nevertheless partly derives her feminist poetics from the practice of Nightingale as an essayistic foremother. Thus, Woolf's prediction of the second coming of Judith Shakespeare
echoes yet modifies the prophesy in "Cassandra" of a female savior. The belated reception that Nightingale's essay found in Woolf does not indicate that
"Cassandra" was ahead of its time, but rather that Nightingale was entrenched
in her historical moment.

NOTES

An earlier version of this article was presented at a 1989 MLA special session, "Illu-
minating the Lady with the Lamp: Writings by and about Florence Nightingale." I
would like to thank the participants in that session, Linda Peterson, Nancy Armstrong,
and the editors of this volume for helping to guide this essay along its way.

1. Jowett-Nightingale correspondence, Balliol College Library, Oxford University.
An abridged version of this letter is reproduced in Quinn and Prest, 8.

2. Although Nightingale may have reproved Jowett's identification of her as Cassandra, she refers to herself as "poor Cassandra" in a letter to a cousin; see Cook, 1913,
1:116. Furthermore, many years after his retraction, in the established intimacy of their
correspondence, Jowett could playfully address Nightingale: "My dear Cassandra, Are
you really 'Cassandra,' as I suspect when I see the title of Mr. Grant Duff's article in the
'Contemporary Review'? I thought that Cassandra prophesied what was true but that
nobody believed her. I am afraid that he may give you the labour of preparing an answer." According to Quinn and Prest, 264, "Rocks ahead; or the Warnings of Cassandra," by W. R. Greg appeared in the *Contemporary Review* in 1874.

3. "Cassandra," Add. MS 45839, f. 269, Nightingale Papers, British Library.

4. Christ documents the link in nineteenth-century literary criticism (as well as in
nineteenth-century literary production) between heroic masculinity and non-fiction
prose, exploring the sexual politics implicit in the gendered and generic Victorian ste-
reotyping of "lady novelists," "feminine poets," and "men of letters."

5. The dialogue between fiction and nonfiction and the patching-together of quotations are two features of the essay which have encouraged its recent reconceptualization
along the lines of Bakhtinian novel theory. But despite the "intergeneric" [Haefner],
a-generic, or anti-generic [Bensmaïa] heteroglossia of both the novel and essay genres,
the historical importance to Nightingale and her contemporary readers of an organic/
evolutionary model, positing the family relation as well as the taxonomic distinction
between novel and essay, warrants our attention here.

6. For accounts of Nightingale's emotional and intellectual outlook during this period and after her return from the Crimea, see the standard biographies by Cook and Woodham-Smith. See also Showalter, 1981.

7. This list of recipients is from Quinn and Prest, xii. Neither Woodham-Smith nor Showalter mentions Nightingale's father or uncle, although Showalter [1981, 407] includes historian J. A. Froude among Nightingale's selected readers of *Suggestions*.

8. Copies of the narrow-margin book are in the British Library and in the Florence Nightingale Museum.

9. To preserve Nightingale's voice, I have left her distinctive orthography—her ampersands and her underlinings—intact.

10. These phantoms resemble the ones in an 1847 letter Nightingale wrote to her friend, Mary Clarke Mohl ("Clarkey") soon after her marriage:

> We must all take Sappho's leap, one way or other, before we attain to her repose—though some take it to death and some to marriage and some again to a new life even in this world. Which of them is the better part, God only knows. Popular prejudice gives it in favor of marriage. . . . In single life, the Stage of the Present and the Outward world is so filled with Phantoms, the phantoms, not unreal tho' intangible, of Vague Remorse, tears, dwelling on the threshold of everything we undertake alone, Dissatisfaction with what is, and Restless Yearnings for what is not . . . love laying to sleep those phantoms (by assuring us of a love so great that we may lay aside all care for our own happiness . . . because it is of so much consequence to another. [Woodham-Smith, 45]

11. The printed edition varies slightly from the revised manuscript here—"to tell them where they will be laughed at, even if not considered wrong" [Stark, 39]—and elsewhere in "Cassandra." These differences indicate that Nightingale made further revisions in proofs which are no longer extant. Most of these late revisions are minor. Several changes, however, are more substantive, including two discursive footnotes added in the proof stage which can be read in Stark, 50 and 53. Another substantive revision in proof tones down a scathing analogy comparing marriage to prostitution. The passage originally read:

> And now they are married. . . . The woman is as often a prostitute as a wife. She prostitutes herself, if she has sold her person for an establishment, as much as if she had sold it in the streets. She prostitutes herself, if, knowing so little of her husband as she does, she begins immediately, without further acquaintance, to allow him the rights of a husband over her person. She prostitutes herself, later, if, against her own desire, she allows herself to be made the blind instrument of producing involuntary children. It will be said, & truly, that, when she marries, her husband understands all these privileges as granted, & that she would drive him mad & deceive his understood expectation, if she did not grant them. But how is she to ascertain her husband's opinion on these points before marriage? [Add. MS 45839, f. 277]

Only the sentence about allowing "the rights of a husband over her person" was excised from the manuscript initially, but the entire passage was further abbreviated in proof to read: "And now they are married. . . . The woman who has sold herself for an establishment, in what is she superior to those we may not name?" [Stark, 48].

12. Many critics have commented upon Nightingale's pre-Crimean struggles against day-dreaming, a habit which she compares to "gin-drinking" [Add. MS 43402, f. 54]; see especially Stark's introduction to "Cassandra," 8. Like the strategic invalidism of her later years, Nightingale's early brushes with madness can be interpreted as a response to social and domestic demands which were both overwhelming and confining; see Pickering, 1976, 165–177 and also Showalter, 1985, especially 62–66.

13. "Distancing" is a useful paradigm for describing the activity of Nightingale's different generic discourses, but it is nevertheless problematic, not because it implies that there is a "real" historical experience to which the narrative refers, but because the es-

sayistic and novelistic representations achieve proximity and connection with her experience as much as distance and separation. The important point here is that neither essay nor novel is intrinsically "closer" to Nightingale's actual experience but that each achieves its relative distance (or closeness) through a different generic code.

14. Woodham-Smith, 70. It is worth reiterating here that Monckton Milnes was one of the recipients of the limited editions of *Suggestions* which included the fictionalized sketch of their encounter cited here as well as Nightingale's comments on the sketchiness of modern poets which mention Monckton Milnes along with Tennyson, one of his intimates, and Mrs. Browning. While we cannot know precisely what Nightingale meant to achieve by communicating her views of their thwarted love and his poetic skill in this manner, it certainly complicates our understanding of Nightingale's preparation of "Cassandra" for her male audience.

15. Sidonie Smith holds that "[t]he doubling of the 'self' into a narrating 'I' and a narrated 'I' and, further, the fracturing of the narrated 'I' into multiple speaking postures mark the autobiographical process as rhetorical artifact and the authorial signature as mythography" [47]. My reading of Nightingale's imagining of Nofriani as the speaking self in her fictionalized autobiography implicitly accepts this position, although here I explicitly emphasize the alterity of the "one" who is the nonspeaking object of the essayistic discourse.

16. It is possible that what I have identified here as a stage of revision between novel and essay (in which Fariseo serves as the first-person narrator) may actually have occurred as part of Nightingale's pre-Crimean writing of the novel. If the shift did occur in the course of her early "private" writing (for her eyes only), its significance would have more to do with her writing as an early symptom and therapy than as a later bid for authority.

17. This letter is marked "30, Old Burlington Street, London W. May 17/60." Nightingale sent McNeill the portion containing "Cassandra" about three months later (in a letter marked "August 29/60"): "I send you the Parts Second and Third of the religious 'stuff' (confidential) of which I sent you the first part some time ago" [Add. MS 45768, f. 118].

18. The letter is on lined paper in a school-girl hand: either a copied letter or Nightingale assuming the ingénue. Nightingale writes of sending the second and third parts to Mill on Sept 28, 1860 [Add. MS 45787, f. 23].

19. In his iconoclastic and essentially hostile study, F. B. Smith uses the discrepancies between the letters to her different readers to argue that Nightingale was self-aggrandizing and manipulative. He also casts doubt on Nightingale's relation to the artisans, citing the lack of evidence for Nightingale's relation to the working-class secularist G. J. Holyoake or to the Northern artisans. However, Smith weakens his argument when he suggests that Jowett humored Nightingale but "dodged her repeated requests to edit the work," and that "[o]nly good, grave John Stuart Mill . . . directly annotated Miss Nightingale's text" [185–86]. The voluminous Jowett-Nightingale correspondence which spans over 33 years evinces, to the contrary of Smith's animadversions, deep mutual respect. Moreover, Cook's biography reports that Jowett annotated *Suggestions* in detail: "The proof copy of 'The Stuff,' with Mr. Jowett's annotations, was one of Miss Nightingale's most cherished possessions" [1:472]. Unfortunately, Cook does not cite the location of this artifact, and I have been unable to discover it.

20. I am grateful to Linda Peterson for this information about autobiographical publishing practice and for her insight into its parallels with Nightingale's declared intentions and ultimate distribution of *Suggestions* to her coterie of male readers. For more on permissible genres for Victorian women's autobiographies, see Peterson's chapter, "Martineau's *Autobiography*: The Feminine Debate over Self-Interpretation."

21. Mary Poovey also argues that Nightingale participated in her own popular misrepresentation as a "saving angel" in her chapter, "A Housewifely Woman: The Social Construction of Florence Nightingale."

22. The idea that fiction gratifies a primitive urge is shared by post-Darwinian genre critics well into the twentieth century, including the classic formulation in E. M. Forster's *Aspects of the Novel*: "For the more we look at the story (the story that is a story, mind), the more we disentangle it from the finer growths that it supports, the less shall we find to admire. It runs like a backbone—or may I say a tapeworm, for its beginning and end are arbitrary. It is immensely old—goes back to neolithic times, perhaps to paleolithic. Neanderthal man listened to stories, if one may judge by the shape of his skull" [26].

23. My analysis of class and gender interactions is influenced by Mary Poovey's discussion of Nightingale's participation in British imperialism at home and abroad; she illuminates the gendered and classed implications of Nightingale's post-Crimean "campaign for nursing": "as an imperialistic program, we can see that it had two related fronts. The first was the 'domestic' front within medicine . . . her object was to carve out an autonomous—and ultimately superior—realm for female nursing. The second front was the 'foreign' front of class . . . her object here was to bring the poor and their environment under the salutory sway of their middle-class betters" [188].

24. In a 1989 MLA paper, Elaine Showalter suggested that the structural peculiarities of Nightingale's "Cassandra," like those of Margaret Fuller's "Woman in the Nineteenth Century," present a political challenge to conventional masculine rhetoric.

WORKS CITED

Bakhtin, Mikhail M. *The Dialogic Imagination: Four Essays*. Edited by Michael Holquist; translated by Caryl Emerson and Michael Holquist. Austin: University of Texas Press, 1981.

Barthes, Roland. "The Death of the Author." In *Image, Music, Text/Roland Barthes; essays selected and translated by Stephen Heath*. New York: Hill and Wang, 1977.

Bensmaïa, Réda. *The Barthes Effect: The Essay as Reflective Text*. Translated by Pat Fedkiew. Minneapolis: University of Minnesota Press, 1987.

Boyd, Nancy. *Josephine Butler, Octavia Hill, Florence Nightingale: Three Victorian Women Who Changed Their World*. London: Macmillan, 1982.

Christ, Carol. " 'The Hero as Man of Letters': Masculinity and Victorian Nonfiction Prose." *Victorian Sages and Cultural Discourse: Renegotiating Gender and Power*. Edited by Thaïs E. Morgan. New Brunswick: Rutgers University Press, 1990.

Cook, Edward T. *The Life of Florence Nightingale*. 2 vols. London: Macmillan, 1913.

Forster, E. M. *Aspects of the Novel*. San Diego: Harcourt Brace Jovanovich, 1927.

Haefner, Joel. "Unfathering the Essay: Resistance and Intergenreality in the Essay Genre." *Prose Studies: History, Theory, Criticism* 12 (3) 1989: 258–73.

Jowett, Benjamin. Jowett-Nightingale Correspondence. Balliol College Library. Oxford University.

———. Letter to Clough. Additional Manuscript 45795. Nightingale Papers. British Library.

Nightingale, Florence. *Cassandra: An Essay*. Edited by Myra Stark. Old Westbury, N.Y.: Feminist Press, 1979.

———. *Notes on Nursing; What It Is, and What It Is Not*. Boston: W. Carter, 1860.

———. *Suggestions for Thought to Searchers after Religious Truth*. 3 vols. Privately printed. London: Eyre & Spottiswoode, 1860.

———. Private papers. Additional Manuscript 43402. Nightingale Papers. British Library.

_____. Letter to McNeill. Additional Manuscript 45768. Nightingale Papers. British Museum.

_____. Letter to Mill. Additional Manuscript 45787. Nightingale Papers. British Museum.

_____. "Cassandra." Additional Manuscript 45839. Nightingale Papers. British Museum.

Peterson, Linda. *Victorian Autobiography: The Tradition of Self-Interpretation.* New Haven: Yale University Press, 1986.

Pickering, George. *Creative Malady.* New York: Dell, 1976.

Poovey, Mary. *Uneven Developments: The Ideological Work of Gender in Mid-Victorian England.* Chicago: University of Chicago Press, 1988.

Quinn, Vincent, and John Prest, eds. *Dear Miss Nightingale: A Selection of Benjamin Jowett's Letters to Florence Nightingale, 1860–1893.* Oxford: Clarendon, 1987.

Schenck, Celeste. "All of a Piece: Women's Poetry and Autobiography." In *Life/Lines: Theorizing Women's Autobiography.* Edited by Bella Brodski and Schenck. Ithaca: Cornell University Press, 1988.

Showalter, Elaine. *The Female Malady: Women, Madness and English Culture, 1830–1980.* New York: Pantheon, 1985.

_____. "Florence Nightingale's Feminist Complaint: Women, Religion, and *Suggestions for Thought.*" *Signs* 6 (1981): 395–412.

Smith, Alexander. *Dreamthorp; A Book of Essays Written in the Country.* London: Stratham, 1863.

Smith, F. B. *Florence Nightingale: Reputation and Power.* London: Croom Helm, 1982.

Smith, Sidonie. *A Poetics of Women's Autobiography; Marginality and the Fictions of Self-Representation.* Bloomington and Indianapolis: Indiana University Press, 1987.

Strachey, Ray. *The Cause: A Short History of the Women's Movement in Great Britain.* London: Virago, 1978.

Woodham-Smith, Cecil. *Florence Nightingale 1820–1910.* New York: McGraw-Hill, 1951.

Woolf, Virginia. *A Room of One's Own.* New York: Harcourt Brace Jovanovich, 1929.

CHAPTER TWO

The Boundary-Crossing Essays of Carmen Martín Gaite

CONSTANCE A. SULLIVAN

A prize-winning author of novels and short stories from the beginning of her literary career, Carmen Martín Gaite (born in Salamanca in 1925) had achieved by 1980 a solid reputation as one of Spain's foremost writers of fiction.[1] She is also a prolific writer of various kinds of essays. However, literary critics in Spain and elsewhere who share the Western predilection for genres such as theater, novel, and poetry over the essay have studied Martín Gaite's essays primarily as they elucidate or have relevance to her fiction. This explains why her volume of narration and memory, *El cuento de nunca acabar* [*The never-ending tale*, 1983], is the only one of her volumes of essays that has been the theme of academic literary criticism; it might also explain why none of her book-length essays has been translated into English.[2] But Martín Gaite is also an academic historian with a doctorate from the University of Madrid. She has published both historical essays and essays of literary criticism. It is the uneasy juncture of the historian and literary critic with the writer of personal essays that is the focus of my discussion.

The boundaries I mention in my title are the traditional generic distinctions between the subjective personal essay and the erstwhile objective academic prose of historical narration and analysis or of literary criticism. I am not unaware that some theorists of the essay define very closely what may be deemed to fall within the realm of "the essay" as genre, and that academic essays and book-length essays are beyond that pale.[3] However, my point here is not to redefine or re-theorize the essay but to describe the process by which Martín Gaite ever more confidently blends her subjectivity into academic essays in defiance of that kind of sub-generic definitional taxonomy. My perception is that Carmen Martín Gaite's way of writing academic essays gradually evolved into highly subjective non-fictional prose studies, in other words, very "personal" essays where she no longer hid the female subjectivity that always lay behind her thematic interest in the specific topics of her historical and literary re-

search. To me, the blurring of the distinctions between the academic or scholarly essay and the personal essay that Martín Gaite effects has been the cause
of widespread mislabelling by Hispanists of her latest book of nonfiction, *Usos
amorosos de la postguerra española* [*Love and courtship customs in post-civil
war Spain*, 1987]. The subjective involvement of the writer with her material
and her inclusion of her own memories in it as data have led literary Hispanists
to label this book "memoirs."[4] That label strikes me as an inaccurate characterization of the informality of the dialogue that the author seeks to establish
with her readers, the lack of chronological sequence in the distinct topics reflected upon in each chapter, and the purposeful inclusion of quotations from
archival texts that amplify and generalize her individual memory of the period
to include an entire generation of Spaniards. In similar fashion, Martín Gaite's
book of critical essays on Spanish women writers, *Desde la ventana: Enfoque
femenino de la literatura española* [*From the window: Feminine focus in Spanish literature*, 1987], is a personalized reading. In this case too, and unlike her
earlier essays, the writer's critical voice is self-consciously female and her sensitivity to the contexts in which women wrote is obviously feminist, although
she explicitly denies that these readings are feminist.

My purpose here is to focus on the essays that Carmen Martín Gaite has
published in book form in order to raise some questions about how this Spanish woman writer uses the essay as an expressive vehicle.[5] At the center of my
inquiry is the issue of how much or how little Martín Gaite distinguishes between academic essays of historico-cultural analysis or literary criticism, and
what is called the personal essay, in terms of the distance—the "objectivity" or
"subjectivity"—of her narrating and interpreting voice from the material.
Some related questions are the degree to which the author genders her essayistic voice as female and the dynamics of the social and literary context that
might explain the increasingly clear feminism of her essays, while she continues
to reject the label of "feminist" to describe them.

I perceive a gradual, if not always consistent, change of voice in Martín
Gaite's academic essays. That is, her initial posture remains fully within the traditional assumption that the essayist who writes narrative/interpretive history
is both objective and generically male. That posture subsequently evolves into
the confident self-presentation of the Teller of the Narratives of History and
Literature as female, a specifically situated female with a profound subjective
involvement with the facts and interpretations contained in her text. I am proposing that, for a number of reasons that have to do with her novelistic career,
her credentialization as a historical scholar, and the permutations of Spain's
social and cultural history of the last twenty years (including the feminist
movement and Martín Gaite's varied responses to it), she blurs the line between
the erstwhile "objective" historical or literary critical essay and the traditionally acceptable subjectivity of the personal essay. Isabel M. Roger characterizes
Martín Gaite's fiction as describing over time a gradual "trajectory toward the
lyrical novel," that is, as developing from the narrative voice's distance from
the story to highly subjective or self-involved narrators. Others have called this

a blurring of distinctions between fiction, autobiography, and history. I see a similar trajectory in Martín Gaite's academic historical and literary essays. In my view, her growing confidence in this subjective blending of boldly stated personal views with the objectivity of the documented fact so dear to the academic essayistic endeavor eventually extends to her assertions of what kinds of "facts" count as documentation. She includes the dailiness of women's lives, even of her own life, as documentary evidence in her interpretive historical essays. In her book of literary criticism, that dailiness is a perspective that the critic shares with women writers in her national tradition.

Carmen Martín Gaite interrupted her fictional creation to spend six years (1963–1969) assembling the research materials for, and writing, her biography of Melchor Rafael de Macanaz. This eighteenth-century politician's tenacious efforts to firm the Bourbon monarchy's control over Spanish society in the face of traditionally entrenched Church power were betrayed by three successive kings, and he became a victim of the Inquisition. Full of the scholarly accoutrements of multiple footnote citations and ample bibliography, this biography is presented, or narrated, by a distant if sympathetic voice that hides any indication of its subjectivity, including its gender. Only in the author's introduction is there a sense of the person who accomplished the research and writing, and of that person's motivations.[6] That brief introductory comment about the serendipitous way the topic occurred to her is as personal as Martín Gaite gets in her first historical study, in this case a carefully documented biography. The academic coolness of the Macanaz volume as a whole stands out clearly when contrasted with the elaborate, dramatically personalized explanation of why and how she came to write it. That 1971 essay was first published in the *Revista de Occidente*, a rather scholarly journal, and Martín Gaite later included it in 1973 in her first collection of essays, *La búsqueda de interlocutor y otras búsquedas* [*The Search for a conversational partner and other searches*, 1973]. In 1970 she was clearly aware of, and adhering to, the constraints of a required objectivity and the ostensible "ungenderedness" of the traditional masculine generic voice in academic historical essays. The greater subjectivity of the personal essay, however, permitted her to dramatize her encounter with the written remnants of Macanaz's life, quite as if she and her object of study were characters in a novel:

My first trip to the Simancas Archives, in the spring of 1966, was a decisive event in firming up the relationship between Macanaz and me that, coinciding as it did with my own personal discouragements and fatigues, was threatening a total break. . . . In Simancas I finally met face to face this prisoner about whom I already knew so much, I got to know him in his exile, in his old age. . . . I felt him grow old, . . . his stubbornness moved me. [1973:50–51]

At that moment I swore to be faithful "to my dead man" with the same seriousness with which I could have sworn it to him at an altar, I knew that he only had me, and that I absolutely would never fail him. . . . Since that day, holding Macanaz's hand, I entered into his old age, I dropped my doubts and my impatience,

> I decided to let myself follow the branches of that story without thinking whether it would have an ending or not. . . . [54]
>
> We were good for each other. His company drew me out of my constant hurry, and many melancholies and personal upsets. . . . [55]

Here the subjective involvement of the personal essayist in the task of finding information on a historical figure is narrated as a passionate and mutual commitment to another individual. The book, on the other hand, reveals nothing of the sort. There, the reporting or narrating "I" is de-personalized, ungendered, and objective in stance and language as it recounts the documented facts of Macanaz's life and long trial.[7]

All eleven personal essays and the short story included in *La búsqueda de interlocutor y otras búsquedas* elaborate on one theme: that one's knowledge of self comes from being reflected in the mirror of an accepting interlocutor who follows and interacts with our tale of identity (our "stories" of who we are). These essays, written from 1960 to 1972, can be relatively abstract, they can read like memoirs, or, in the case of the final three essays and the short story, they can speak to society's construction of concepts of gender and how it restricts women in tragic ways.[8] With the exception of Martín Gaite's self-dramatizing presentation as historical researcher in the essay on Macanaz that I mentioned above, the essays in this volume contain a speaking voice that uses what tradition and custom have taught us is the generic masculine: the essayist refers to Man and Mankind, all persons are the masculine impersonal "one" (*uno*), and the femaleness of the memoirist in the notice of her friend Aldecoa's death is veiled—here Martín Gaite could be any one of Aldecoa's Salamanca and Madrid male companions, as far as the language, the content, and the perspective reveal [27–39]. In all fairness, Martín Gaite uses that traditional patriarchal model of "grammatical correctness" because it was the only one available in the 1960s. But she also withholds anything very personal from these early personal essays. The lament/memoir on Aldecoa's presence in her life, for example, ends with the submergence of the remembering female self into a writing generation of which they were both members. However, the three essays on women and the short story about the ennui and frustration of an unhappily married woman have as their common theme the deeply negative effects on women of societally imposed images of what should make them happy, yet does not. Martín Gaite's grammatical usage stays the same, but her sympathetic understanding of the self-alienating effects on women of externally imposed images of the feminine ideal is not typical of the Spanish intellectual mentality of the 1960s. That theme is the explicit focus of Martín Gaite's essay on the effects of advertising on women. Nevertheless, in the essay "Las mujeres liberadas" ["Liberated Women," 95–101], she attacks the stridency of the emerging feminist movement in the Western world and the absurdity—as she sees it—of women leaving or refusing to enter the institution of marriage, while they recreate similar heterosexual relationships without the commitment of a marriage ceremony. She concludes that feminists are afraid of commitment to another human being on an intimate basis and that they are flailing about uselessly in a solitude imposed on them by a false ideology.

That essay's round condemnation of feminists—early, flamboyant, loud feminists who held marches, waved placards, expressed anger openly, protested their exclusion from male clubs and restaurants and government offices—seems to reflect chagrined embarrassment at what she perceives to be the vulgar behavior of these women. It also reflects Martín Gaite's need to hold on to her ideals of heterosexual institutions like marriage and her own ideas concerning what women should aspire to in life. It is followed by an essay on Flaubert's Madame Bovary and Hollywood's Marilyn Monroe, whose suicides Martín Gaite finds to be only one of the similarities between these two well known public representations of women. To her mind, both of them failed to deal with their inner reality, their authentic selves, in attempts to conform to the gender prescriptions for women that their society provided in romantic literature or the celluloid world of Hollywood. Beyond the fact of her decision to include them, the juxtaposition of these three female-centered essays and the short story of blocked communication and ennui that closes the volume highlights the contradictions and the pain that Martín Gaite saw inhabiting female lives when something outside themselves determines what they should be and what they should desire of their existence. But there we see as well the dilemma of a writer whose own life held deep contradictions: she did not want to be a *Señora*—a submissive and subservient married woman whose only interest was husband, children, and home—but she had been brought up to believe deep inside her that both God and society meant that to be her natural destiny. Effectively employing gender analysis before feminist theory had come to make distinctions between sex, sexuality, and gender and to prioritize the latter as a category of analysis, the essays on the effects of advertising on women's self-image and on Bovary and Monroe clarify the essayist's deprecations of early feminist protest. She had been taught that decent women of good breeding simply do not make such noise, they do not participate in loud and public protests about patriarchy. Thus, this collection contains the first outright refusal by Martín Gaite to consider political feminism as a viable posture, as well as the internal contradictions between her feminist sensibilities and that rejection of feminism, a constant tension in this author's subsequent essays, both historical and literary.

As a by-product of her long archival research on Macanaz, Martín Gaite "found" the topic of eighteenth-century Spanish women's lives and loves. The book that resulted, *Usos amorosos del dieciocho en España* [*Love customs in eighteenth-century Spain*, 1972], now considered a classic study of eighteenth-century Spain, focuses on women's lack of education, their forced leisure, the creation of a new class of rich women—the future bourgeoisie—who imitated the fashions and customs of the nobility, including the practice of having a *cortejo* (a male companion who substituted for a husband in the social realm of parties and promenades and theater- and opera-going, whose main task was to accompany and serve these idle, bored women; the custom was considered

highly scandalous in its time and later). Her sources included music, dance, opera, fashion statements, sermons, satires in the press, literary and artistic representations of eighteenth-century women in Spain. Martín Gaite carefully
cites all these disparate sources, and each chapter consists of the author's dialogue with excerpts from those varied sources. The tone of her prose here is
much more personal than it was in the study of the life and trials of Macanaz.
Her narrative "I" in the Macanaz biography was unobtrusive, that of a com-
piler of facts, but in this study she makes little attempt to hide her negative view
of society's refusal to educate women or allow them any meaningful role in the
institutions of enlightened reform as she reflects, chapter by chapter, on different aspects of what that meant for women's lives and spirits.[9] This study asserts
that eighteenth-century women, out of their extreme boredom, invented for
themselves a set of customs and behavioral patterns that at least occupied their
time, if not their minds. The author seems filled with a sense of outrage at the
waste of those lives and at the concurrent and subsequent condemnations of
their invented pastimes by male authors of both the Old Regime and the bourgeois nineteenth century, and by the Spanish Church.

Considered as a whole, the book contains a good deal of internal redun-
dancy, for in each chapter or essay Martín Gaite discusses whatever factors she
believes relate to the topic at hand. That informality of treatment leads her to
talk about the birth of a consumer society in her reflections on fashion and
luxury but also of men's avoidance of marriage and political interests of the
Old Regime in stable families. An etymological study of the term cortejo, for
example, wanders from Spanish to Italian and French society, to antiforeign
sentiment in eighteenth-century Spain, and female boredom. An essay on conversational style includes descriptions of styles of dress and body language, and
considerations of social class differentiations. Any one of these chapters can be
read independently; the book is not structured chronologically as a narrative of
a century.

It is in this collection of scholarly historical essays around a large and complex topic that the author begins to blur the lines between historical
scholarship—objective, based on archival research on traditionally accepted
sources—and the interpretive personal essay. Love Customs in Eighteenth-
Century Spain is a passionate book expressing both understanding of the circumstances of women and irritation at the lives they led. It offers a sharply
critical analysis that is grounded in the author's sense of female solidarity with
Spanish women of ostensibly privileged classes of the past whose lives were circumscribed both by lack of any access to formal education and by role prescriptions that insisted that women of privilege do nothing at all.

The process of developing her own voice into an unembarrassed, confident
woman's voice is one of fits and starts with Martín Gaite. It is an incomplete
process because of the continuing contradictions in her writing and the tensions in the cultural and literary context in which she wrote. However, a major
change in her essayistic voice occurred with El cuento de nunca acabar [The
never-ending tale, 1983]. This collection of short personal essays around the

theme of the origins and nature of narration reasserted the writer's primary interest in telling stories, be they historical biographies, lived anecdotes of public or private history, things remembered and things dreamed. It is at the same time a work of literary theory and a challenge to the tone, content, and form used in academic theoretical discourse.[10] It is aggressively disjointed, a compilation and distillation of notes and scattered comments written over years in a series of notebooks. Without a visible order, circling over itself, biting its own tail, it is indeed a never-ending story about what it is to tell stories.

In this collection of essays on narration, Martín Gaite states outright that she has never been able to respect the division between kinds of writing—what she resisted in grade and high school as the difference between writing as reportage/summary (*redacción*) and writing as invention. Within these essays she combines anecdotal stories both autobiographical and taken from others' experience with analysis of how the human urge to narrate stems from the child's interest in listening, then the discovery of the need to be the protagonist of a story or of the telling of a story, and the excitement of learning the code of writing where the child can invent a listener/reader, a reader who is in the first instance the child who writes the narrative. There are many themes in this collection of essays—including loneliness, rejection, a desire to create a self-image that will command respect and attention without allowing anyone (even one's self) to apply a stereotyped label onto that self and make it rigidly unchangeable, relationships between children and the adults around them, the insights to be learned from watching children play, and narrating/writing as play, as dialogue, and as self-creation. She uses with insistent frequency the daily contact of a parent (a mother) with children and their perceptions and frustrations as a starting point for reflections on the origins of the urge to narrate. She recalls her own childhood experiences with toys, books, and people, tying these and her adult insights to reiterative explorations of narrative as a process. The reader never is allowed to forget that these are a woman's reflections.

Thematically and in the form she adopts here, the writer rejects quite firmly the jargon and the artificial stiffness, purported linear clarity, and magisterial authority of academic literary theorizations. She insists that a narrator/writer must first find or imagine a listener/reader, for the text depends on the appropriate listener/reader who intervenes—and is invited by the good (effective and interesting) narrator to intervene in the creation of the text—with questions and requests for authentication of the narrator's knowledge of the story told. Martín Gaite here elaborates on one of the constant themes in her essays and fiction: that without a listener/reader who takes the time to receive a story narrated calmly and in all its details and digressions, there is no effective storytelling. And, if story-telling is asserted as a way to know the self, there are no effective narrations of the self without dialogue with that other.

The spontaneity and spiraling structural complexity of the essays in *El cuento de nunca acabar,* and their anecdotal and experiential content gendered as female, make this book an axis of change in the essays of Carmen Martín Gaite. Here she lets fly with her own views, her own preferences as to how to

write, and what matters as content in the tales one tells—biography, cultural
history, novel, or short story. At one point she mentions that a young male professor gave her a lengthy bibliography of texts on literary theory that she read
until she decided that what she wanted to do with her thinking on narration
was not like what those academic essays did. She stopped reading literary theory, and she hides her erudition on the subject by belittling that reading and
omitting all scholarly accessories in this book. In fact, Martín Gaite begins the
collection by playing with the idea of scholarly organization of her materials:
she elaborates a description of how difficult it was for her to begin to make
sense of the years of notebook annotations to herself on the topic of narration,
and of her attempt to organize the notes, to record then the moment when she
throws aside the cards and their delineated and separate categories—not in defeat but in defiance—and proceeds to write her circular essays on the general
topic, weaving subtopic into subtopic as she elaborates on her thoughts essay
by essay.

   Love Customs in Eighteenth-Century Spain is a precursor and parallel text
to *Usos amorosos de la postguerra española* [*Love and courtship customs in
post-civil war Spain*], her historical study of gender reconstructions in post-
Civil War Spain, and also envisions her future analyses in *Desde la ventana*
[*From the window*] of how the circumstances of women writers in Spain affected their writing. In the introduction to *Love Customs in Eighteenth-Century Spain* she indicates the thematic interest that would tie them to each other:

> It had already been giving me much food for thought—almost since I myself had
> begun to suffer from it—that the majority of women, be they of flesh and bone or
> fictional (who are frequently modelled after those of flesh and bone) need with
> such a peculiar vehemence to adjust their behavior to patterns underwritten by pre-
> vailing opinion, whether that opinion is of a majority or a minority. From which I
> deduced that if one wants to know something about women and their significance
> in a specific epoch, it is the models that that epoch has proposed to them, and why
> it has proposed them, that one needs to analyze and understand. [xvii-xviii]

She goes on to claim that there are specific connections between the eighteenth-
century customs she studies, present-day Spain, and her personal history:

> And if I myself, to speak of a specific case, were to stop a moment to analyze my
> own way of thinking, choosing, and acting (which, although it doesn't interest me
> here, probably influences surreptitiously, unfailingly, everything I say and write), I
> could not, however uncomfortable it might be for me, omit consideration, along
> with the handful of preferences we are always pleased to exhibit, of a series of read-
> ing materials that worked on the sensibilities of those of us who were girls of nine
> to fifteen during the Civil War, a task that would make me contemplate a study of
> the romance novel (*novela rosa*) . . . and that would take me back to the nineteenth
> century and Romanticism. . . . [xix]

Those are exactly the topics that Martín Gaite would eventually study—gender
construction, and the romance novel (among other texts)—in her two 1987 essays.

Martín Gaite's 1987 *Usos amorosos de la postguerra española* [*Love and courtship customs in post-civil war Spain*] is a profoundly revealing study of Spanish culture under the Franco dictatorship, a book of interrelated essays that analyze causes and effects of the restrictive gender education forced on the generation of Spaniards who were adolescents when the Civil War ended in 1939. Its organizing theme is that those circumstances and the interpersonal relationships they inspired precluded authentic communication and understanding between men and women of Carmen Martín Gaite's generation, just as the differences in socio-economic and cultural circumstances between the immediate postwar period and the post-Franco democratic Spain inhibit intergenerational understanding.

It is this book of essays that disconcerts Martín Gaite's critics because it incorporates her own memories of the lives of young people in the 1940s and 1950s. Academic critics and reviewers are reluctant to accept Martín Gaite's major innovation both here and in her eponymous 1972 book of encounters with the realities of eighteenth-century women's lives. That innovation is to constitute the facts of the daily lives and concerns of women and girls as historical data. She had already fictionalized many of her personal memories in her novels, most especially and recently in *El cuarto de atrás* [*The Back Room*, 1978]. But her introduction to the 1987 historical essay on postwar Spain reiterates its connection with her earlier *Love customs*, in case the parallel titles failed to make her point. In this book she was combining her memories not with fiction, as in her novel, but with other relevant documents:

> Some friends of mine commented that they had read [my earlier monograph] "like a novel," and I started to reflect on the relation between history and stories and to think that, if I had managed to give a novelistic treatment to those materials drawn from archives, I might also try an experiment in the reverse: I could try to apply a criterion of the historical monograph to the materials that, because they proceeded from the archive of my own memory, on other occasions I had elaborated into the form of novels. [11–12]

Thus she considered archival materials an essential complement to her own remembrances in this new effort at historical analysis in this case of her own time, a history she and her generation had lived.

Carmen Martín Gaite's analysis of the construction of gender ideas and concepts in the early years of the fascist regime of Francisco Franco won a best-essay prize offered yearly by Anagrama, its publisher, and was an immediate best-seller that went into multiple editions in its first year. Part of the public's enthusiasm for this essay's analysis of how a combination of intentional and circumstantial factors can shape the self-perception of an entire generation of men and women stemmed from the fact that the middle-class reading public in the "new Spain" of the 1980s had become noticeably female. Women had discretionary money to spend on books, the education to appreciate them, the time and the desire to read, and those female book-buyers were eager to read works by and about women. The unshackling of the feminist movement from its Franco-era illegality and consequent underground status was important in shaping Spanish women's renewed interest in their own history. But the response to Martín Gaite's 1987 essay was also a by-product of the new freedom from censorship assured by the democratic constitutional government and the Socialist party in power. In the decade following the death of General Franco in 1975, there was an urgency in Spain to undo the ideological framing of that right-wing dictatorship, to look at the country's history with more objectivity and more intellectual rigor. There were numerous memoirs and biographies of people important or forgotten in the Franco era, new histories of every moment of Spain's near and distant past, studies of how the ideological intentionality of the State and its allies, the army and the Church, shaped minds and people's sense of individual identity.

The power of Martín Gaite's text resides in its foregrounding of interpersonal relationships that depended on self-concepts as well as a concept of the essence and role of the other — in this case, the heterosexual other — and of how the Franco regime from the end of the Civil War until about 1953 strove to remold gender concepts in the minds of all Spaniards. Carmen Martín Gaite's generation, those young people who came to adulthood in the 1940s, were the ones on whom the full power of the State and its allied institutions worked to instill a fiercely retraditionalized idea of the natural correctness of the strongly patriarchal family. Women were to aspire only to marriage and to accept with good grace their dependence on and subordination to the will and the whims of the husband-father, and later of the sons. The book looks at various types of information from the era, from confidential government planning and implementational documents newly accessible to scholars, to the advice columns in women's magazines and other print media, to the sermonizing of the Catholic Church and the forced passage of all young adults through mind-control educational agencies like the *Sección Femenina* of the Spanish Falange for women and compulsory military reserve training and service for men. Neither sex could marry without having completed this "national service" to the State's satisfaction.

Martín Gaite uses a tone of high irony that often is sarcasm in this book; her narrative and analytical voice is harsh and definitely female. She includes as valid historical data the experience of young women like herself and her sister; she includes anecdotal materials told in a historically-situated first person that amplify the many citations from documentary sources that support her argument. And she has the temerity in this book to examine not just her own and her female generation's formative years and what it did to their lives and self-image but also what happened to Spanish men.

The overall point of *Usos amorosos de la postguerra española* is that the rigidly traditional patriarchal concepts of gender that were instilled in women and men of her generation of the immediate postwar period led to a permanent and damaging barrier to honest communication, real conversation and understanding, between women and men of that generation. She concludes that their formative experiences had obviated even the possibility of heterosexual mutual comprehension and coexistence in marriage or friendship. Her dedication of the book to women of her generation and their children explains that she wants the younger generation—that of the "new Spain" of democratic freedoms and more liberal ideas—to understand what had made their parents the people they are: conservative, afraid of change, rigid in their ideas of what is right and what is wrong in moral and social terms.

The essays in this historical analysis are relatively independent of each other and the book has no narrative chronology. Rather, each reflects along a certain informal line of thought on a subtopic of the phenomenon Martín Gaite addresses in the book as a whole: ideological remythification of Spanish cultural traditionalism; limitations of women's life goals to heterosexual marriage and economic dependency; postwar Spanish social fabric; rebellious women; scarcity, hunger, and long courtships (in one chapter); the forced hypocrisy of courtships and the cult of female virginity; the shortcomings of the educational system and censorship. In each essay the author includes quotations from women's magazines, popular songs, films, radio programs, government documents, and newspapers. Mixed with these voices is the frequent voice of the writer: "I remember . . . ," "all the children of my generation . . . ," "my sister and I used to . . . ," "every Spanish boy and girl. . . . " This voice is speaking mainly to those of her generation who shared the same experiences and remembered many of the same things from the first twelve to fifteen years of the postwar period.

The informality of Martín Gaite's dialogue with her memory, her audience, and the voices from popular and official sources that she quotes is complemented, not contradicted, by the footnotes and bibliography she adduces to these essays. The multiplicity of voices in dialogue here precludes the book from being the memoir of only one woman's youthful life; they transform it into an evocation and analysis of the social history of a shared existence in the not-too-distant past. The book asserts a woman's perspective on that past, a woman who recognizes that her generation's formation of ideas about gender took place in the painful period she evokes. Peering at that process from one angle and another, she attempts to comprehend the impossibility of mutual comprehension between men and women of her generation, of authentic intimacy, of marriage. With and in this text, which I consider one of the richest cultural texts of the last fifteen years of Spain's self-examination, Carmen Martín Gaite achieved a confident female voice, a voice unmistakably her own, in an essay of historical and cultural analysis that was feminist in its sensitivity.[11]

At the core of *Desde la ventana: Enfoque femenino de la literatura española* [*From the Window: Feminine Focus in Spanish Literature*], also from 1987, are four interpretive essays of literary criticism of texts by Spanish women of various periods. These essays explicitly attempt to understand the femaleness, the Spanish femaleness, of those texts. The organizing metaphor, or concept, of these critical essays is that Spanish women writers have always had to look out on the world from interiors, through windows, and not by being out in the world. According to Martín Gaite, enclosure colored these women's texts; it inheres in their perspective on the world, a perspective that permitted them to see without being seen. The collection is framed by two very personal essays that recall the author's mother and her encouragement of her daughter's writing, as well as the private angle of vision—from the window—that her mother had on the outside world of Spanish society.

Desde la ventana's first critical essay exemplifies the author's skittish relationship with academic theoretical essays (like, but not as extreme as, the relationship in El cuento de nunca acabar), with feminism, feminists, and feminist literary criticism. She situates herself as a perceiving subject who again only half-reveals what she has read about women as writers and readers:

> During the last few years, by means of the questions put to me by interviewers, writers of doctoral theses, and audiences at colloquia in which I have participated, I have become aware that the polemic about feminine writing inspires passionate interest; and in my spare time I have informed myself a little bit about it. More than anything, it has been a number of female professors at North American universities, to which I have been invited rather regularly, who have earnestly recommended to me some books of feminist criticism that, according to them, were necessary reading. But the tone of the works that have come into my hands, almost always written by English-speaking female authors, I found boring and professorial, quite removed from the humor and narrative approach with which Virginia Woolf [in A Room of One's Own] declared herself to be excluded from the patriarchal methodology of learned men.
>   The term "feminist criticism" that, while it fails to convince me very much, is the one everyone uses, tries to work toward its own definition . . . and establish its parameters in opposition to those elaborated by men. [13]

She seems to agree with Elaine Showalter's concept [in "Feminist Criticism in the Wilderness"] that women write within models and language established by men, and thus end up writing a double-voiced discourse. But Martín Gaite then goes on to make a gesture that distances her both from feminist awareness of dominant-group influence on women's minds and discursive strategies, and from any sense in the readers of her essay that she herself, as a well-educated middle-class Spanish woman who writes, ever had difficulties with finding her own voice within a strongly masculinist institution like Spanish literature:

> Personally, I have never deemed it a stigma to be a woman or to have received the greater part of my instruction from the spoken or written discourses of men. But I realize that, particularly in other historical periods, the desire to make the influence of patriarchal criteria accord with the desire to make one's own voice heard may have presented a huge conflict for the woman writer. [16]

The evidence of her own previous work would seem to contradict Martín Gaite's assertion that her writing career, and her achievement of a unique voice in her work, did not entail the struggle she agrees other women might have had. Why does she believe it necessary here to distance herself from such problems, especially when her readings of Spanish women writers' texts in this volume of essays emphasize her cultural and gender-based understanding of the difficulties they faced? Why does she simultaneously present feminist critical concepts and the suggestion that they are pedantic, overly dependent on male paradigms, and lifeless?

One powerful incentive to such assertions is the almost total resistance to feminism shown by the Spanish academic community and the news media of the 1970s and 1980s. Feminists continue to be portrayed in both of these cultural institutions as aggressive man-haters, wildwomen on the margins of society. Carmen Martín Gaite's reluctance to be associated with that image, even through the totally appropriate application of the adjective "feminist" to her work, is shared by many other younger women writers in Spain today, who want, as she does, to achieve validation in and from the mainstream culture and the men who control its movement. Like the nineteenth-century women in Spain who broke with gender prescriptions in their writing careers but who reinforced in public the gender system's ideal for women as domestic angels, many of today's Spanish women writers sidestep any application of the word "feminist" to their often deeply feminist writing.[12] Still in the thrall of the traditional gender concepts that were so forcefully re-instilled by the Franco regime, Spanish cultural institutions represent feminists as deviant, "unfeminine" women.

Carmen Martín Gaite's increasingly subjective, self-involved fiction and essays clearly imply her youthful self-perception as a misfit and outsider, someone the prevailing system's rules and standards did not permit, a *chica rara* ("strange girl") who went against the current because of her desire to go beyond the limiting gender boundaries presented to her historical moment. While she could not comfortably bring herself to an outright challenge to her culture's gender prescriptions, she has broken through the prevailing boundaries between the genres of objective history/story of time and the permissibly more subjective personal essay, just as she increasingly blended her self into her fiction. More confident in the late 1980s because she is a successful novelist, credentialled as a historian, and newly surrounded by women writers and feminists, Carmen Martín Gaite seems to have overcome any timidity at the idea of challenging academic and cultural institutions with her own views, not only of what the novel can be but of what an academic essay can be: she has gradually come to place her subjectivity as a Spanish female at the center of both these forms of writing.

NOTES

1. Joan Lipman Brown's *Secrets from the Back Room: The Fiction of Carmen Martín Gaite* provides not only a fine discussion of this author's works but a bibliography of her publications to 1980 and Martín Gaite's lengthy autobiographical sketch in both the original Spanish [193–206] and in English translation [20–34]. Linda

Chown's interpretive biographical section on Martín Gaite in *Narrative Authority and Homeostasis in the Novels of Doris Lessing and Carmen Martín Gaite* [23–43] translates into English small portions of interviews in Spanish with the author published by others elsewhere. See also Roger and Butler de Foley.

Critics have seen strong autobiographical elements in Martín Gaite's fiction; the articles in Servodidio and Welles's *From Fiction to Metafiction: Essays in Honor of Carmen Martín Gaite* (1983) address that tendency, as do the studies listed in Isabel Roger's 1988 bibliography of this author's writings and critical essays about her work.

2. One of Martín Gaite's previously unpublished essays has been translated by Marcia Welles: "The Virtues of Reading," *PMLA* 104, 3 (May 1989): 348–53. After my study was completed, María G. Tomsich's translation of Martín Gaite's 1972 book on eighteenth-century Spanish women was published with the title *Love Customs in Eighteenth-Century Spain* (University of California, 1991). The translator notes in her Preface [xiv] that she condensed or removed certain passages of the original text for this translation. Among these omissions are the book's final chapter on eighteenth-century language and significant aspects of the author's erudition in footnotes and in the text.

3. See, for example, Graham Good, "The Essay as Genre," *The Observing Self: Rediscovering the Essay* (1988): 1–25; and ix–xii.

4. Two recent examples of this phenomenon are Steve Summerhill's "Dialogue and Memory: The Essays of Carmen Martín Gaite," which suggests that the book's nature as memoir is diminished by its scholarly accoutrements of quotations and bibliography, and David K. Herzberger's equation of this apparent reworking of materials the author had already fictionalized in 1978 with the memoirs of politicians and other public figures of the Franco era who did, following the latter's death in 1975, write their personal stories [44]. How memoirs here are distinct from autobiography is a question still to be asked.

5. I will not address here the numerous newspaper and magazine articles that the author has not seen fit to publish in book-length collections.

6. The introduction begins by recalling an afternoon's casual reading in the autumn of 1962 of Ferrer del Río's history of Charles III's reign, where Martín Gaite was reminded of the story of Macanaz's life and written Spanish history's denigration of his initiatives:

> From that moment on, my curiosity to fill in such a confused and marginalized *historia* [in Spanish, the word means both story and history] grew so fiercely that the desire to dig into the inexplicable trial that brought Macanaz to fame, exile, jail, and death finally took the place in me of any other intellectual project.
>
> Some people, who knew of my former dedication to literature, were surprised at this unexpected turn of my attention and there were even some who became seriously indignant at how absorbing and stubborn was my new zeal to follow the tracks of a dead man, because, according to them, he was vocating in the way of my true vocation. This, aside from the fact that it's very debatable, might lead us to think about the relationship that false stories can have with true stories, and to many other irrelevant questions, such as, for example, the question of whether one does have to stick implacably to a fixed line of work. [xvii]

All English translations here are my own unless otherwise indicated; I have intentionally retained Martín Gaite's syntax and punctuation although it may read awkwardly in English. All page references are to the Spanish editions.

7. Were it not for the delicate but absolutely thorough disassociation of the author's personal voice and interpretive perspective from the subject matter in *El Conde de Guadalhorce, su época y su labor* [*The Count of Guadalhorce*, 1977], Martín Gaite's biography of Macanaz might get the nod as her least personal writing. She had been concerned to make Macanaz come alive by creating a narrative thread between the documents she cited. With the Guadalhorce biography, however, she reconstructed the man's life almost solely by quoting at length from his personal papers and official gov-

ernment statements praising his works as an engineer. The fact that she adds nothing to it is obscured by her tactic of omitting footnotes. Even her prefatory note to the reader in the Guadalhorce biography is dismissive:

> Given the anti-academic nature of this biography, which simply aspires to situate the figure of Guadalhorce in the framework of an era whose political events have been thoroughly studied elsewhere, I have not found it opportune to burden the reader with footnotes identifying sources for the quotations with which I have embellished it. All the references can be gleaned from the bibliography. [11]

This was a commissioned hagiography, and Martín Gaite is almost totally absent from this book as an overt perceiving self, just as she keeps that book on Guadalhorce absent from her autobiographical reflections on her literary activities. See Brown, 20–34.

8. A second edition of this book of essays in 1983 omits the short story that closed the original edition and adds six more essays that do not seem as closely related to the connecting theme; my discussion, therefore, refers to the 1973 edition.

9. Good narrators, as she says in *El cuento de nunca acabar*, always reveal their situationality to their readers or listeners—how did you see/know this? why are you telling this story?—are questions a narrator must answer. In her academic essays, the author places her answers to such necessary questions in introductions or prefaces, until her two 1987 books break that pattern.

10. A sensitive and eloquent discussion of *El cuento de nunca acabar* is found in El Saffar (1984); Pope, Bush, El Saffar, and Kaminsky (1988), experiment together with the themes and forms of literary criticism that are suggested by Martín Gaite's book on narration, in a fascinating critical conversation *à quatre*.

11. A masculine view of a similar topic, but handled much differently in the sense that women's experiences are presented "from the outside" and that the main point is not gender constructions, is Rafael Abella, *La vida cotidiana en España bajo el régimen de Franco* [*Daily life in Spain under the Franco regime*, 1985].

12. Answering a question about this phenomenon that I had put before the conference in a paper I gave the day before, the Spanish novelist and journalist Rosa Montero stated that "To label you a feminist is the same thing as labelling you a [social and cultural outsider]." Panel on Spanish Women, International Symposium on "Spain Toward the Twenty-First Century," Ohio State University, April 1990.

WORKS CITED

Abella, Rafael. *La vida cotidiana en España bajo el régimen de Franco*. Barcelona: Editorial Argos Vergara, 1985.

Brown, Joan Lipman. *Secrets from the Back Room: The Fiction of Carmen Martín Gaite*. University, Mississippi: Romance Monographs, 1987.

Butler de Foley, Isabel. "Hacia un estudio del tiempo en la obra narrativa de Carmen Martín Gaite." *Insula* 39 (July–August 1984): 18.

Chown, Linda. *Narrative Authority and Homeostasis in the Novels of Doris Lessing and Carmen Martín Gaite*. New York and London: Garland, 1990.

Del Villar, Arturo. "Carmen Martín Gaite." *La estafeta literaria* (October 1–15, 1978): 8–11.

El Saffar, Ruth. "Shaping the Chaos: Carmen Martín Gaite and the Never-Ending Tale." *International Fiction Review* 11, 1 (Winter 1984): 125–30.

Good, Graham. *The Observing Self: Rediscovering the Essay*. London and New York: Routledge, 1988.

Herzberger, David K. "Narrating the Past: History and the Novel of Memory in Postwar Spain." *PMLA* 106 (January 1991): 34–45.

Martín Gaite, Carmen. *La búsqueda de interlocutor y otras búsquedas*. Madrid: Nostromo, 1973. Second edition, Destino, 1982.

_____. *El Conde de Guadalhorce, su época y su labor*. Madrid: Colegio de Ingenieros de Caminos, Canales y Puertos, 1977.

_____. *El cuarto de atrás*. Barcelona: Destino, 1978. *The Back Room*. Translated by Helen Lane. New York: Columbia University Press, 1983.

_____. *El cuento de nunca acabar*. Madrid: Trieste, 1983.

_____. *Desde la ventana: Enfoque femenino de la literatura española*. Madrid: Espasa-Calpe, 1987.

_____. *El proceso de Macanaz. Historia de un empapelamiento*. Madrid: Moneda y Crédito, 1970. Second edition, *Macanaz como otro paciente de la Inquisición*. Madrid: Taurus, 1975.

_____. *Usos amorosos del dieciocho en España*. Madrid: Siglo XXI, 1972. Translated by María G. Tomsich, as *Love Customs in Eighteenth-Century Spain*. Berkeley, Los Angeles, and Oxford: University of California Press, 1991.

_____. *Usos amorosos de la postguerra española*. Barcelona: Anagrama, 1987.

_____. "The Virtues of Reading." Translated by Marcia Welles. *PMLA* 104 (May 1989):348–53.

Medina, Héctor. "Conversación con Carmen Martín Gaite." *Anales de la literatura española contemporánea* 8 (1983): 183–94.

Olba, Mary Sol. "Carmen Martín Gaite: La lúdica aventura de escribir." *Insula* 39 (July–August 1984): 19.

Pope, Randolph D., Amy Kaminsky, Andrew Bush, and Ruth El Saffar. "*El cuento de nunca acabar*: A Critical Dialogue." *Revista de estudios hispánicos* 22 (1988): 107–34.

Roger, Isabel M. "Carmen Martín Gaite: Una trayectoria novelística y su bibliografía." *Anales de la literatura española contemporánea* 13 (1988): 293–317.

Servodidio, Mirella, and Marcia L. Welles, editors. *From Fiction to Metafiction: Essays in Honor of Carmen Martín Gaite*. Lincoln, NB: Society of Spanish and Spanish-American Studies, 1983.

Summerhill, Stephen J. "Dialogue and Memory: The Essays of Carmen Martín Gaite." Paper presented to the Kentucky Foreign Language Conference, Lexington, April 1989.

CHAPTER THREE

Flora Tristan

The Joining of Essay, Journal, Autobiography

EILEEN BOYD SIVERT

The essay has traditionally been seen as an open-ended form, one that follows few rules and is difficult to define. In sixteenth-century France, when Montaigne was writing, the word *essai* "had come to mean an exercise, test, a trial or food sample" [Fraser, 20]. For Montaigne, the essay was a means of testing his reading, his observations, and, most important, his own mental faculties and judgment. Because testing presupposes a number of possible outcomes or points of view, it allows for uncertainty and for the possibility of changing one's mind. Such openness might well be at odds with another conventional trait of the essay, particularly common to those of Montaigne: the notion that, as the study of an individual's personal views and judgments, the essay can serve as commentary on, or even as a model for, the behavior of humanity in general. The possibility of different interpretations, and the variable form of the genre, would seem to open the essay to everyone, but the model offered fit only half of humanity. It is no accident that Theodore Fraser accepts the following as a sufficiently precise and yet broad enough definition of the essay: "first the work must bear the stamp of the author's particular temperament; second, it should clearly reflect *his* fundamental thought patterns; and third, it should reveal *his* most personal feelings or convictions on any topic with which it deals" [Fraser, 6, emphasis mine].

Early authors and readers of essays were presumed to be educated males, and the behavior of upper-class men was the essay's subject. Yet men's writing is usually seen as linear, chronological, and logically ordered, and that of women fragmented, subjective, and personal. The essay appears to invite female authors by its very form or lack of one. Why, then, have women been underrepresented or underacknowledged in the genre? Is it because the writing subject of the essay (traditionally male) is the essay's subject?[1]

But what of the female subject? In what way does the female-authored essay constitute a subjectivity that differs from that of her male counterparts?

One way to get at the problem is to look at essays through the related genre of autobiography. If essays are commonly seen as a testing of the writer's judgment and thought processes based on her or his own life and observations, autobiography tends to be more an account of the writer's life. Yet my own critical essay will show these distinctions to be arbitrary. Female subjectivity does not fit into neat categories. My view of what constitutes an essay—an open-ended personal observation of, and comments on, the writer's life and surroundings, leading to observations on the human condition, and written in a way that is unencumbered by rigid rules of form—can serve as well to describe female autobiography and journal writing. In the same way, Domna Stanton's writing on "autogynography," autobiographical writing by women, sheds light on female subjectivity and the essay. Stanton claims that "[b]ecause of woman's different status in the symbolic order, autogynography . . . dramatize[s] the fundamental alterity and non-presence of the subject, even as it asserts itself discursively and strives toward an always impossible self-possession" [Stanton, 16]. While female-authored essays, similar to those of Montaigne, are best seen as process rather than finished product, I would suggest that the process itself is different. In the essay, as in autobiography, the female "I," as opposed to the male, is "not simply a texture woven of various selves; its threads, its life-lines [come] from and extend . . . to others. By that token, this 'I' represent[s] a denial of a notion essential to the phallogocentric order: the totalized self-contained subject present to itself" [Stanton, 16].

My project is a study of that same interconnectedness among genres as well as individuals. I propose to concentrate on three books by Flora Tristan (1803-1844), whose genres are not as clearly distinguished as conventional categorization would have it: *The Workers' Union* [*L'Union ouvrière*, 1843], a book of polemical essays written in an attempt to bring about universal unionization and the constitution of a working class; *Le Tour de France* [1843-44], an intimate journal kept by Tristan as she traveled around France publicizing *The Workers' Union* and its ideas; and *The Peregrinations of a Pariah* [*Les Pérégrinations d'une paria*, 1838], an autobiography depicting Tristan's search for her own place in society. But the names of genres by which these works are commonly designated are deceiving, and they might better be called essay-like books or prose reflections: autobiographical experience informs the thought behind what is called a book of essays; the autobiography itself moves beyond Tristan's life to observe and reflect upon universal human problems; and Tristan's journal wanders from very personal, self-directed thoughts to details of everyday life and the more general commentary these details elicit.

If the essay as a literary form has sometimes been seen as marginal, so too have the writings and even the life of Flora Tristan, who lived on the edges of society in a number of ways. Born to an upper-class Peruvian father and a middle-class French mother, she was raised in the slums of Paris. Because her parents' religious wedding in Spain was never registered with the civil authorities, Tristan was considered illegitimate. She was a self-educated woman and fled the so-called legal protection, which was in fact abuse, of her husband, who later shot her on a Paris street and was sent to prison for attempted murder. The blurring of distinctions one can read in Tristan's personal life, as she moved among the Peruvian aristocracy, the French bourgeoisie, and the French and English working classes, can be seen in her writing as well. A reading together of the separate but related forms reveals that the boundaries thought to exist between essay and autobiography, or essay and journal, are fragile indeed.

Yet the conventional limits transgressed by Tristan go beyond genre and class. Let us not forget that the traditional essay was written as a means of sharing experience, personal opinion, and judgment with one's readers. One of the questions for female authors in a patriarchal society is that of the authority of the speaking subject. How does one to whom history has denied not just authority, but also full emancipation, assume that authority and offer her own experience and judgment as a guide to the reader, and what are the consequences? How, indeed, does she find her readers?

I will begin with a discussion of *The Workers' Union*, bringing in the more personal *Tour de France* and *Peregrinations of a Pariah* later, because I find it fruitful to read Tristan's experience in publishing *The Workers' Union* as a metaphor for woman's struggle to make her voice heard. Flora Tristan had already put her opinion in print before publishing *The Workers' Union*. She had little trouble publishing pamphlets on women's issues, her autobiography, or *Promenades dans Londres*, a description of the misery of the English working class. *The Workers' Union*, however, unlike the earlier published works, was not a depiction of Tristan's or of women's personal experience, and it was French, not English, working-class misery that was detailed in its pages. Suddenly the means of publication were closed off. *The Workers' Union*, advocating universal unionization and the right to work, as well as equal pay for equal work, was too dangerous to the property-owning class, including the owners of the presses. The book was a challenge not only to the bourgeoisie but also to followers of the social utopians Saint-Simon and Fourier, and to those workers or artisans-turned-owners who claimed to speak for the workers (male workers, that is). Consequently, Tristan's voice was silenced. When even those editors known for publishing working-class literature (Pagnerre and Gosset, for example) refused what she called her "little book," it was clear that she would have to find a means outside the usual system of publishing to convey her message to working-class men and women. The only means available to her was to go door-to-door collecting subscriptions to finance publication of her work. The enumeration of subscribers at the end of her several prefaces makes it clear that Tristan is outside the normal power structure, beholden to no editor, speaking to and for the "little people," mostly workers. Her voice then, is her own.

An even more striking consequence of the circumstances of the publication of this "little book" is the way in which it dissolves the hazy line (a haziness already characteristic of the essay form) between inside and outside, between literature and its referent. The essay can be seen figuratively as a dialogue between author and reader (writers of essays commonly use conversational style and address the reader explicitly within the text). The reader's own lived experience plays a part in a productive reading of the text. In the case of *The Work-ers' Union*, the essay becomes not a figurative but a true dialogue in which the response of the workers to whom it is addressed is to give small contributions in order to extend that dialogue to increasing numbers of readers. In this way, the most important aim of these essays, the constitution of a working class and the joining of disparate workers in a universal union, moves beyond the covers of the book and is achieved on a small scale by the very act of a publicly fi-nanced publication. Indeed, the door-to-door collection of subscriptions for *The Workers' Union* brought Tristan face-to-face with the readers whom she had to persuade of the book's validity before it could be published. The second edition, made possible by additional subscribers, came out in the same fashion, while publication costs of the third edition were borne entirely by the workers of Lyon after Tristan's lengthy stay in their city.

Flora Tristan's travels around France following the book's publication con-stitute an expansion of the dialogue that had already gone beyond the limits of her pages. Her tour is based on the tradition among artisans of traveling the country (the "tour de France") after their apprenticeship in order to refine their skills by working with different "compagnons." "There is nothing more to be said, nothing more to be written, for your wretched position is well-known by all," Tristan writes in the beginning of *The Workers' Union*. "Only one thing remains to be done: to act by virtue of the rights inscribed in the Charter" [*WU*, 37]. She thus combines her desire for action with her realization of the difficulty, even impossibility in this case, of dialogue through writing alone. "As of a young age, the poor are so abandoned and so overworked that three quar-ters of them do not know how to read" she tells us, "and the other quarter does not have time to read. So to write a book for the people is like throwing a drop of water into the sea" [*WU*, 41-42]. If her target audience cannot read, then she will come to read her book to them.[2] Yet another layer of dialogue is added to the process through the diary, also called *Le Tour de France*, that Tristan kept throughout the trip, a personal journal in which we read a book about a book, essays about the reception of essays.

At the same time as Flora Tristan usurps the authority of the traditional masculine speaking subject of the essay, blurs the edges of a genre that was al-ready difficult to define, and confuses action and writing, she eliminates as well the distance between author and reader. Laura Strumingher puts it well in her book, *The Odyssey of Flora Tristan*: "Tristan did not try to maintain objective distance between herself and her subjects. She did not strive for the impartiality of the observer, but rather used something very much like the controversial feminist approach of the 1980s, trying to shrink the distance between the ob-server and the observed, to bring her subjects into the research process and to have them benefit from its results" [Strumingher, 76]. While similar to a more traditional conception of the essay, this method comes at the task from the op-posite end; instead of the writing subject offering itself to the scrutiny of the reader (something Tristan does in *Peregrinations*), in *The Workers' Union* the reader and writer merge through dialogue, as readers contribute publication costs to the author and the author travels to speak directly, and to listen, to readers, potential readers, and those who cannot read. Tristan, the self-proclaimed pariah of her autobiography, uses the same word—pariah—to describe workers in *The Workers' Union* and means to share with them not only her own narrative and experience as one of the oppressed but also the stories of their co-workers, spouses, and friends that she picks up in her conversations along the way.

Flora Tristan would agree with Montaigne that the essay is process rather than final product. "Let it be understood," she says, "that I am not claiming to trace a definitive unalterable plan. A plan totally spelled out in advance can never be realized. Only in the process can one appreciate the most appropriate means to achieve the enterprise's success" [*WU*, 99]. The process is also one of assuming her own voice in opposition to those in power. Self-knowledge as well as understanding of others come through the painful process of attempting to make her views understood and to understand them herself; her challenge to authority escalates as she continues to write. Within *The Workers' Union*, she brings into question not only the views of the dominant class but also those of her friends and sometime collaborators, the social utopians. In *Peregrinations* she separates herself from other feminist writers, George Sand in particular, by refusing to take a pen-name, insisting on personal identification and solidarity with other women, even at the risk of her life. (It was the book's publication that precipitated the attack in which Tristan was shot by her husband.) And as she continues her journey to publicize *The Workers' Union*, she records her activities in the personal journal published as *Le Tour de France*, expressing her defiance of the Church leaders who oppose her and the police and public prosecutors who have been sent to spy on her, and she makes the most of their opposition. Upon arriving in a town, she visits the authorities first, explaining her purpose, exposing her ideas, inviting them to her meetings while confessing in her journal that the very fact that she has been spied upon has been beneficial to her cause and "has had a good effect on the workers" [*Tour*, 68].[3]

The process of self-understanding, self-assurance, and knowledge of the other is evident in Tristan's challenge to authority on the one hand, and to the worker on the other. Early in the journal, Tristan describes workers as ignorant and incapable of learning. In doing so, she illustrates the difficulties of her kind of essay, one that has no protective limits between writer and reader: "From a distance I can accept ignorance, I see it, I discuss it calmly and without being upset by it—but close up I cannot control the irritation it causes me" [*Tour*, 68]. As she makes diary entries, she is forced to question the dialogic purpose of her trip as well as that of *The Workers' Union*. Her first meetings with workers teach her only that "it is insane to try to discuss their interests with them. One must present them with a ready-made law that will save them—what a good lesson" [*Tour*, 16].

I have suggested that Tristan's personal journal, *Le Tour de France*, is more than a record of her daily activities. The instability of genre limits becomes more evident as the journal becomes more like an essay and reveals not simply the details of a publicity trip for *The Workers' Union* but, more important, Tristan's examination of her own judgment and purpose, leading her to declare: "My mission is not to record facts, but more to seek the causes which produce them" [*Tour*, 89]. In this essay-as-journal Tristan is at the same time studying and passing judgment on herself. Contrary to the anger in the prefaces to the *Workers' Union*, against the aristocratic, patriarchal system in which she has no place and which she is forced to circumvent in order to publish her book, we see in *Le Tour* a more introspective view, mixed with an occasional lashing out at those in power. Through her writing, her reading, her meetings, and her travel, Tristan's conception of herself and her place in society is modified. She has moved far beyond the moment of her voyage to Peru (described in *Peregrinations*), when she tried to reestablish her birthright in aristocratic society, and she sees herself now as more than a pariah. Through writing and speaking, through acting instead of passively accepting, Tristan comes to view herself as not only outside but superior to those in power. What she has become, in her own eyes, is a variation of the Saint-Simonian female messiah; she is the "Femme-Guide," a mother to the working class.[4]

It is journal-keeping itself that makes her aware of this process of change. Her initial remarks indicate despair or defeat before having begun: "Who, tell me who, can serve these poor people, so crude, so ignorant, so vain, so disagreeable to associate with, so disgusting to view close up" [*Tour*, 28]. The answer, not long in coming, is the writer herself who embarks on "the beautiful and noble mission for which God [Dieux] . . . has chosen me" [*Tour*, 38].[5] Tristan's early moments of confidence come from rather simple and unflattering comparisons of herself with those she has set out to help: "I truly do not know how I manage when I speak to these men who are ignorant, fat, insolent, unapproachable by anyone; I am really quite wonderful!" [*Tour*, 40]. Yet this is not merely self-aggrandizement at the expense of the less powerful. In the first place, she admits the unfairness of asking workers to understand immediately what she herself needed twenty years to learn. Moreover, Tristan is testing and reflecting upon her own abilities in the face of a seemingly impossible task against all levels of society, the powerful as well as the weak. To her surprise, she discovers herself not to be wanting. Her strength is more than oppositional, and it is further modified as she continues to travel and to write and to understand her relationship with the workers she meets.

Although her growing confidence may seem egotistical and unrealistic (there are moments when she compares her own situation to that of Jesus being interrogated by Pontius Pilate), we must keep two things in mind. The reader of *Le Tour* is not the worker to whom she dedicated *Promenades dans Londres* and for whom she wrote *The Workers' Union*, nor is it the members of French society to whom *Peregrinations* was directed. The intended reader of *Le Tour* is Flora Tristan herself. Unrevised and unedited when she died, it is the writing of a woman talking to herself, holding a dialogue, as it were, with her other writings, delighted and amazed at her own force and willing, as one is in private, to indulge in a good deal of self-satisfaction.

But a more important aspect of the pleasure Tristan takes in her own accomplishments is that it is somewhat less self-centered than first impressions would suggest. Flora Tristan, in the tradition of the essayist, speaks of herself to the extent that she stands for the many. Just as Montaigne "had finally gained the supreme self-confidence to assert that the example of his own life—'a life ordinary and without luster'—could readily (and profitably) be applied to that of every other human being" [Fraser, 25], so Tristan achieved the same self-confidence and began to serve, in her writing, as model. But Montaigne's "every other human being" really meant every other upper-class literate male. Tristan more straightforwardly admits that her example serves only half of humanity—the half that has always been the excluded other rather than the subject or the model in the traditional essay. "What I am doing now, the results I am gathering, speak more in favor of the superiority of women than anything one could write or say on the subject. . . . Yes, it is a woman who was the first to come up with the very sacred idea of talking to the workers" [*Tour*, 71-72]. Indeed, after being told by an official (to whom she refers as a representative of men) that she will not be permitted to speak to workers because it is too dangerous, Tristan writes more generally of women in her journal: "Men believe that the word of life is dangerous—and there is the difference, women are driven to spread this word of life—woman is life and man is its limit—that is why woman is superior to man" [*Tour*, 72].

Although Tristan states early in *The Workers' Union* that language, i.e. writing, is insufficient and must be accompanied by action, she is aware that her writing is itself an act. The "word of life" in her essays not only replaces and displaces action, it produces it as well. While she claims not to use a literary style, her subtle shifts in vocabulary result in a powerful transformation of the ways in which the social world around her is conceived. The essay, as practiced by Tristan, uses language to favor women and workers whose marginalization has been reinforced by their very lack of access to writing. Not mere exhortation, these essays are a means of empowering women and workers by transforming the way in which they are described and named. When insisting on the importance of workers' representation, Tristan is referring as much to her own ability to represent them appropriately in her writing as she is to their need to have representation in government. She refuses the pejorative term "hospice" to describe the institution that will welcome, educate, and care for the working class; it will be called instead a "palace." And with the simple substitution of one word she turns forever the Saint-Simonian expression "the most *populous* and the *poorest* class" [*WU*, 48] into the vital necessary force that her country must acknowledge as "the most *populous* and *useful* class" [*WU*, 47].

Conscious of the importance of naming and labeling in the effort to constitute a working class, Tristan names and so brings into being (by virtue of her existence in Tristan's essays) the female worker, who has been invisible in pam-

phlets, treatises and, most important, in labor law. Recognition of male workers, Tristan notes, had already begun in 1789, again through language. Before
the French revolution, members of the proletarian class were referred to as serfs
or peasants. Suddenly they were named "the people" and referred to as citizens; finally, Tristan tells us, "they proclaimed the *rights of man* in full national
assembly" [*WU*, 77]. It is this redefinition of male workers that gives Tristan
hope for her own project—which is to undo what she calls woman's six thousand years of condemnation: "What happened to the proletariat, it must be
agreed, is a good omen for women when their '1789' rings out" [*WU*, 77-78].
Tristan's logic is that of present-day supporters of the Equal Rights Amendment; by inscribing women's equality in the essays of *The Workers' Union* (the
amendment), Tristan takes a first step toward inscribing it in law.

I noted earlier that Flora Tristan compares her own oppression to that of
workers by calling them and herself pariahs, as she repeatedly draws general
conclusions from self-observation. As the subject of many of her essays, she
clearly views herself as a model. Struminger points out that the course of
Tristan's life "was interlaced with a broad array of nineteenth-century wom-
en's issues" [Struminger, xi]. But she did more than live the typical story of
nineteenth-century women—she wrote it. Her preface to *Peregrinations* makes
it clear that she is taking the risk of publishing her own struggle against the
social order that constrains women in the hope that other women will have the
courage to imitate her model. In a slight variation, *The Workers' Union* is a
means of allowing individual, often anonymous and illiterate, workers to share
their stories with other unknown, isolated workers. *Le Tour* is more of a meeting, if not a confrontation, of the style of the other two books. While allowing
her own experience to serve as example, she writes introspectively of her growing self-understanding as she is touched by workers who are in turn touched by
her book.

It is through the constant interplay of her daily experience, her observations, and her writing that Flora Tristan takes for herself the authority to produce essays. While Montaigne drew on personal experience, reading, and observation, a good deal of that observation for him was secondhand. Though he
advocates foreign travel as an important part of education "to bring back the
characteristics of those nations and their manner of living, and to rub and file
our wits against those of theirs" [Montaigne, 204] some of his most insightful
cultural comparisons (In "Of Cannibals," for example) come from visitors
from the New World he met (or claims to have met) in France.

Tristan's essays, however, measure her life and her society against those she
visits and studies firsthand. Throughout her writing, we discern a movement
from the personal to the general and back. She begins with an understanding of
the economic status of working-class women, having grown up in the slums of
Paris, but she has no distance, nothing with which to compare the French context until she works as a maid in England or lives with the aristocracy and observes the peasants and slaves in Peru. Like her culturally diverse background,

Tristan's travels and her writing about them furnish her with a comparative view that allows more general comment on larger issues affecting women and workers in France and in the world.[6]

The Peregrinations of a Pariah is an autobiography that at times reads like a travelogue and a pretext for writing essays. Much of what Tristan writes here, from the first view of slaves to the lengthy descriptions of economic and social practices and the insightful depictions of women in Aréquipa and Lima, resembles the voyage literature so popular in the nineteenth century. Just as Flora Tristan's journal moved beyond the limits of its genre to become essay, *The Peregrinations of a Pariah* is as much essay as autobiography. In this work Tristan moves from recounting her own travels and experience to commenting on unfamiliar mores and customs. These customs afford her a pretext, a means of distancing herself from what she perceives and from what she has known, to make cultural comparisons that sharpen her view of the rules of her own society. In writing about different laws, customs, and expectations, she moves from her own life as model to personal comparisons and generalizations and finally beyond autobiography to comments upon the universal or contextual situation of women.

As she describes Peru in the pages of *Peregrinations*, Flora Tristan makes the tentative link between women, workers, and slaves that she will later insist upon in *The Workers' Union*. Although her first reaction to slaves is repugnance at their odor, ugliness, and stupidity mixed with sympathy for their plight, she becomes more aware of the situational nature of their degradation as she writes about them. Finally, near the end of the book, she reaches a point where she reads noble motives into slave infanticide, suggesting that the eyes of the imprisoned mother tell her "I would sooner have him dead than a slave" [*Peregrinations*, 286]. The argument Tristan makes in these writings is often indirect, and is particularly essay-like. She moves from observation to comparison to general musings on human nature. She links slaves and women through examples of ugliness that compounds their mistreatment, writing, for instance, of her cousin Carmen: "People found in the ugliness of the wife and the beauty of the husband sufficient justification for the plundering of her fortune and the constant indignities to which she was subjected" [*Peregrinations*, 101]. Tristan then brings the reader briefly back to the autobiographical nature of her writing by making a connection between her cousin's personal situation and her own (trapped in a marriage she has no means to end). Yet autobiography remains essay as Tristan uses herself as a model from which to draw conclusions for women in general: "Such is the morality which proceeds from the indissolubility of marriage!" [*Peregrinations*, 101].

Her observations lead Tristan to rail against the lack of education in Peru and the lack of concern expressed by the upper classes for the economic and instructional neglect of the poor and to decry hierarchy based solely on the degree of European origin. Yet Tristan is far more outraged, and her future far more affected, by the adverse legal position of women she sees in Peru. As the subject of this autobiography-cum-essay, she remains the model, a model she herself understands much better through cultural comparison and through writing, both of which offer her the distance needed to gain perspective on the social order. While she had protested earlier against the deplorable situation of married women in France, her indignation is now channeled, through the comparative optic of her writing, into larger issues. She will no longer be satisfied tinkering with laws on divorce, but sees all of human society in terms of force and enslavement, and she vows to fight to empower the heretofore tyrannized. "My cup of bitterness overflowed" she writes, "and I rose up in open revolt against a social order which sanctioned the enslavement of the weaker sex, the spoliation of the orphan" [*Peregrinations*, 174].

Nothing could sharpen Tristan's perception of society more than her desire to rebel against its injustice, for it brought into focus the stark contrast between her developing view of female superiority and her realization that women's societal situation remained most fragile. Her increased sensitivity to political life as well as to social inequities took a dramatic turn when revolution broke out in Peru during her stay. What is important for my purpose is not the detailed description of military activity, but Flora Tristan's conviction that she herself was more capable than anyone around her to lead the people of Aréquipa to victory. Her frustration arose from the knowledge that in action, as opposed to writing, she had to work through a man: "It vexed me exceedingly to have to rely on another when I felt capable of action myself, but I would have to find a soldier whose character and influence were strong enough to be of service to me, then inspire him with love, fire him with ambition and use him to risk the final throw" [*Peregrinations*, 174]. Though convinced of all the good she could do, she abandons her project for fear, she says, of the very power she seeks and the hypocrisy of the course of action necessary to achieve it. Power through destruction cannot be reconciled to her plans to ameliorate society. The ends do not justify the means, and Tristan hints here at the pacifism she confirms later when she refuses to allow soldiers access to the Workers' Union because they are knowledgeable only in destructive work. Her aim in writing has been to free women from the chains fashioned by society's laws, but it is writing itself, the exploration of her ideas and plans in an autobiographical essay, that convinces her that the only stratagem available to her at that time would transform her into the very kind of human who forges chains for others. "I feared the moral depravation which inevitably accompanies the enjoyment of power" she writes. "I feared to become hard, despotic—a criminal even—like those who were now in power. . . . Once again it took me all my moral strength not to succumb to the tempting prospect . . . I was *afraid of myself*. . . . [*Peregrinations*, 232].

The revelation itself, and her subsequent flight to Lima to avoid political entanglement, reinforce for Tristan her theory of the innate superiority of women, which she explores in different contexts throughout her work. She does this more openly in the autobiography based on notes she wrote to herself and in the journal meant for her own eyes. But she strategically hides the same message, as I will demonstrate later, in the more polemical essays of *The Workers' Union*, written from the beginning for a wide public.

In *Peregrinations* she is quite taken by the "rabonas," Indian women of Peru who follow the soldiers, live and eat with them, set up their camp, find and cook their food while at the same time raising children alone, since these women belong to no one man and are there for anyone who wants them. She finds the men of their race incapable of the courage these women exhibit. Tristan moves beyond description here and displaces herself as model by using the "rabonas" as striking proof of the superiority of women in primitive societies. Observations, examples, and generalization carry her to hypotheses she will later attempt to test in action as she now tests them in essay form in the autobiography, wondering if the same would not be true of people at a more advanced stage of civilization if both sexes received a similar education: "We must hope that someday the experiment will be tried" [*Peregrinations*, 180].

The aristocratic women of Lima evidence the same superiority over men as do the peasant "rabonas" of the countryside. Here Tristan meets women interested and effective in politics. And in Lima as well, Tristan finds reinforcement for her notion, later expressed in *The Workers' Union*, that the way in which women are perceived, described, or named makes of them what they are, supporting her hope in the efficacy of essay-writing. Language and experience interact as the strength of these women derives from what they are called; they do not take their husbands' names but keep their own.

Writing on cultural difference in an autobiography inevitably brings Tristan back to her own situation and fortifies her personal judgment that mental outlook informs character: "From what I have just written about the costume and customs of the women of Lima, it is easy to understand that they must have a completely different outlook from European women, who, from their earliest childhood, are the slaves of laws, morals, customs, prejudices, fashions and everything else. . . . In every situation the woman of Lima is always *herself*; never does she submit to any constraint" [*Peregrinations*, 275].

Tristan's own refusal to submit to constraint—her writing which will not remain within fixed limitations of genre, her publishing outside the system, her unaccompanied travel to reach the workers—regularly runs up against the aforementioned "laws, morals, customs, prejudices, fashions" imposed by French society. A continuing tension is visible in the more intimate journal writing of *Le Tour* between her repeated and unsubtle assertion of women's superiority and her realization that she herself and her writing, especially the more public *Workers' Union* essays, are sometimes rendered invisible by society's view of women. At the same time as she claims preeminence for her sex by being the first woman to talk directly to the working class, she admits that even many workers believe her "little book" is too well-written and well-thought-out to have been authored by a woman, and that she must be in the pay of "a highly intelligent man" [*Tour*, 66] afraid to make himself known.

This social reality that forms a horizon for Flora Tristan may well be what precipitates the problematic treatment of women's subjectivity in her writing.

The Workers' Union is striking in this respect and most revealing in its relation to the reader. The "little book" is dedicated to, and written for, the workers themselves in the belief that they must be responsible for their own emancipation: they must, in constituting themselves as a class, constitute their own subjectivity. Yet the chapter "Why I mention women" is, by contrast, addressed to men. In the same chapter, when Tristan claims repeatedly that woman is everything in the life of a worker, one wonders, on a first reading, if she conceives of woman here as subject or object. One way to read the chapter is as strategy. Men—even working men—enjoyed civil rights and had formed organizations that had at least some political power, whereas women had none. Tristan's argument must convince men, not women, of the necessity for women's equality and it is carried on in such a way as to appeal to the self-interest of the male. In an attempt to reach the male reader, Tristan portrays women as wives, mothers, and sisters to the extent that, in these roles, they can benefit or handicap the men in their lives. They are depicted as the moralizing agent in a man's life and the educator of his children. Rather than writing in the name of women's superiority, she claims to do so in terms of their social individuality.

Yet while the appeal is couched in terms of men's self-interest, its goal is the one advocated more openly in the less polemical, more personal works and stated occasionally even here—that of placing women "on a footing of absolute equality with men to enjoy the legal birthright all beings have" [*WU*, 83]. It is the blurred boundaries among Tristan's different works that permit us to read beyond her strategic appeal to men in *The Workers' Union*. Readers of *Peregrinations* (which is a discovery and recognition of her own and other women's "social individuality") or *Le Tour* (which clearly places women's capabilities above those of men) will read skeptically any denial in *The Workers' Union* of women's superiority and will suspect that Tristan is simultaneously (if surreptitiously) addressing the women who are the subject of this essay.

Permeable boundaries are a constant within and among Tristan's various writings and reflect her overarching desire for unity. For while she recognizes women's individuality, she writes of the bonds that unite them and, in one case, even sees a disappearance of any limits between two women: herself and her disciple, Elléonore Blanc. "Elléonore lives in me" she writes, "because I have had the strength to incarnate myself in her—what a feat! My soul taking possession of another without taking any account of the envelope" [*Tour*, 120]. Looking at Tristan's writing from a twentieth-century perspective, we can speculate that she, like most females in Western society who have been raised by women, does not perceive boundaries as separating forces the way males tend to see them but as tentative limits constantly crossed, as lines easy to dissolve.

Does this mean that women are more likely than men to preach unity or union, rather than individuality? Are they more likely to write in such a way that genre boundaries are less stable, allowing separate works to form a kind of "union"? These questions are not unrelated. The works studied here retain the mark of different genres—essay, journal, autobiography—while they all function as essays. To Tristan's mind, people must also dissolve the rigid boundaries between them and begin to work together, though by doing so, they need not completely submerge individuality. She respects difference but plays down its separating effects in movement toward a common goal. The same push for convergence of groups is brought to bear on men and women as Tristan alternates, combines, and finally blurs the two in a joint aim. In the chapter, "Plan for Universal Unionization" of *The Workers' Union*, Tristan addresses all women, calling on them to unite. Her union of workers was the first, she insists, "to recognize in *theory* women's rights. Today its cause and yours are becoming one and the same" [*WU*, 111]. More remarkable still is the way in which she calls upon wealthy women to use their power of influence and protection for men, for male workers "who have only numbers and rights to make them strong" [*WU*, 111]. In turn, she promises, those men will lend their strength and support to the cause of women's rights. Reciprocity, blending of goals and aims, alternating among the needs and desires of each group, seeking common cause, this is what Tristan sees as the strength of the Workers' Union. And this strength can only benefit women by becoming the espousal of their cause. Tristan believes with Fourier (and later Engels) that the status of women is evidence of the evolution of society.

Indeed joining, combining, and blurring borders seem to be a trademark peculiarity of Tristan's way of thinking. The essay, so fitted to her style because it is an intersection of the public and the private, is more than a form for Tristan's thoughts; it serves as well as their model. Her view of women, like her choice of literary form, joins the public to the private. Strumingher points out, for example, that the utopians and Marx assumed the family would wither away but that Tristan makes it a central focus of the discussion [Strumingher, 148], insisting on the link between intimate family life and the more public workplace. To improve the life of the worker, she seeks change in patriarchal structure, and the basis of that change has to be the education of women. But she considers the family itself vital to the life of the worker, male or female.

Still, the kind of family promoted in her essays is not isolated from the public sphere and was, in fact, already undergoing transformation. Working-class women did not remain in the home, isolated from the world of labor, providing a private life in which a working man could seek refuge from the demands of the public world. Tristan recognized that women were and always would be a part of the public world, and the structure of the family had to reflect that reality if it were to continue to exist. Family is politics, she believed, and women must be concerned with political, social, and humanitarian affairs: "I will show them" she writes, "that the political touches everything, right down to their pot of stew" [*Tour*, 78]. Yet it is not simply that working life slips over into the realm of the family. Family life itself serves, in Tristan's essays, as a model for the work-place. First, blurring the distinction between boss and worker, she claims that the better "chefs d'atelier" in Lyon are also workers and make common cause with their employees. Moreover, in the best-run workshops, they all live "en famille," sharing meals and sleeping in the workshop where each is treated with absolute equality.

It is private thoughts that make the public book, family life that forms that of the workplace, and it is the status and the experience of women that measure society. It is that very status and experience that Tristan means to change through her essays. In *Peregrinations* she offers herself as example; in *Le Tour* she develops her most personal thoughts on women's position; and in *The Workers' Union* she spells out the means to the change so necessary for society. Not interested in merely improving life for the workers—alleviating misery will not destroy it—Tristan writes to effect radical change in their material and moral position. It is education that must form the base of every change Tristan advocates in the social fabric, and here again, action and writing coincide in these pages: her essays themselves serve to educate the literate working and upper classes while at the same time they advocate education for the illiterate.

My final comments refer to the chapter "Plan for Universal Unionization" in *The Workers' Union*, in which Tristan develops her theories of education. I return to the book I began with because *The Workers' Union* offers the clearest view of the importance of Tristan as essayist and of the changes in the genre wrought by her writing. Flora Tristan's conclusion that education must be the means to change society is not new. Indeed, it is a fairly conventional essay subject. What is new, and most indicative of Tristan's molding of the essay to her own purposes, is her treatment of the dialogic nature of the genre. The change in this dialogue and in the writer's relation to the reader has a far-reaching effect on the essay which, thanks to Tristan, is taken over by those who were never meant to read it in its earlier form. Montaigne's famous essay on education was written for the soon-to-be-born male child of an aristocratic friend who was "too noble by nature to begin otherwise than with a boy" [Montaigne, 197]. "Learning" he claims, in the same essay, "is of no true use in mean and low hands" [Montaigne, 199]. This passage is selected not to criticize Montaigne for being a product of his times but to observe that Flora Tristan was more progressive than her own. Her essays are specifically directed to those without fortune, and they are written intending to educate the reading workers as they call for the education of those who cannot read. For Tristan, it is denial of education that makes the workers, particularly female workers, "mean and low." They are brutal not by nature, she claims, but because they know nothing but brutality. The education of these "low and mean" minds is society's only possible salvation, and their education with other classes its best means to that end. Tristan—as she does with different forms of writing, as she does with different kinds of workers—would bring children together, boys and girls, French and foreigners, old and young, working class and bourgeoisie (who could attend for a fee), all in the workers' palace. In education, as elsewhere, Tristan's aim is to undo limits, deny separation, and blend the different.

The essay has traditionally set itself up as a model, presenting examples that instruct the reader in the art of living. Usually the essayist offers herself or himself as example. Secondary examples or models are abundant in this kind of writing, and Tristan's essay on education is no exception, with the kind of example chosen indicative of gender equality and inclusion. As usual, Tristan's models manage to retain individual diversity within the unified groups she encourages them to form. She writes, "I would also like each palace to offer its hospitality to a dozen persons (six men and six women) who would have as their title *palace guests*. They would be selected from among elderly (not to be admitted before the age of sixty) artists, professors, scholars, and writers lacking resources. Foreigners would receive preferential treatment. The guests would occupy seats of honor at all the ceremonies; this would be morality in action, to teach children respect for talent even when its circumstances are impoverished" [*WU*, 123].

The model is, in many ways, indicative of the evolution of the essay. Montaigne suggests that his life, though ordinary, can illustrate that of man in general. In some way, he himself can represent all men. Flora Tristan has multiple models. Even when she casts herself in that role, it is not so much that she sees herself representing all women. She sees, rather, that women, herself included, can serve as a model for men and for society in general. Throughout her writing, autobiography, journal, and essay merge to offer their subject, women in general and specifically Flora Tristan, as an example to be discussed and debated by the reader. The reader of her essays, the other half of the dialogue, is asked to understand both halves of humanity in order to comprehend Tristan's social vision. It is in the elimination of crisp boundaries between reader and writer, as well as those that distinguish genres, that Flora Tristan offers us a new model for the essay—a model more intimate, less distant than even the personal essays of the past. Every reader is invited to join the Union, to be a partner in publication, to continue the conversation, and to share in, and profit from, the life and writing of Flora Tristan.

NOTES

1. On the status of women, subjects, and souls, Flora Tristan ironically notes that in answer to the question, "Do women have souls?" the Council of Mâcon deigned to decide in favor by a margin of three votes, and she adds, "Thus, with three fewer votes, women would have been seen as belonging to the realm of beasts, and this being so, man, the lord and master, would have been obliged to cohabit with the beast! That thought makes one shudder and freeze in horror!" [*WU*, 89].

2. Once more inside and outside merge. Tristan's need to travel in order to read to the illiterate reinforces the arguments of a major chapter in *The Workers' Union*, treated later in my article, advocating education for boys and girls of all classes.

3. All translations from *Le Tour de France* are mine.

4. Tristan's notion of the "Femme-Guide," the strong woman who is no longer obedient or passive and whose mission is to lift men above the petty concerns of the world, is best explained in her novel, *Méphis*.

5. Tristan consciously chooses the plural spelling to express God. Puech, citing l'abbé

Constant and Elléonore Blanc, says that, for Tristan, "Dieux" is the father, the mother, and the embryo, represented in the form of a triangle [Puech, 390, note 2].

6. Indeed, Tristan's understanding of France's foibles and its strengths stands in stark contrast to another collection of essays about the working class, *Le Peuple*, written only a few years later by Tristan's compatriot, Jules Michelet. To Michelet, the way to help the working class is to eliminate the more blatant distinctions among classes, which can only be done through a common hatred of foreigners and a strong notion of the superiority of France and the French. Blame for the sorry plight of workers can be placed first on England, then on any other foreign power, then on wives and mothers who debilitate and corrupt the strong, nationalistic, militaristic French peasant. Tristan began in a somewhat similar frame of mind. But by the time she wrote *The Workers' Union*, she advocated preferential treatment of foreigners in the workers' palaces. In the first pages of *Peregrinations* she tells us, "I must admit that in 1833 I was still very narrow-minded. I thought only of my country and hardly considered the rest of the world at all. I judged the opinions and customs of their countries by the standards of my own: the name of France and everything related to it had an almost magical effect on me. At that time I thought of the English, the Germans, and the Italians as so many *foreigners*" [*Peregrinations*, 12].

WORKS CITED

Fraser, Theodore P. *The French Essay*. Boston: Twayne, 1986.
Michelet, Jules. *Le peuple*. Paris: Libraire Marcel Didier, 1946.
Montaigne, Michel de. *The Essays of Michel de Montaigne*. Trans. George B. Ives. New York: Heritage Press, 1946.
Puech, Jules L. *La vie et l'oeuvre de Flora Tristan, 1803-1844*. Paris: Marcel Riviere, 1925.
Schneider, Joyce Anne. *Flora Tristan: Feminist, Socialist, and Free Spirit*. New York: Morrow, 1980.
Stanton, Domna. "Autogynography: Is the Subject Different?" *The Female Autograph*. Ed. Domna Stanton. New York: New York Literary Forum, 1984. 5-22.
Strumingher, Laura S. *The Odyssey of Flora Tristan*. New York: Peter Lang, 1988.
Tristan, Flora. *Méphis*. Paris: Ladvocat, 1838.
———. *Nécessité de faire bon accueil aux femmes étrangères*. Paris: Delaunay, 1835.
———. *Pétition pour le rétablissement du divorce*. Chambre des Deputés, no. 133, Pet. 71 (December 20, 1837). Pamphlet in Archives nationales, Paris.
———. *The Peregrinations of a Pariah, 1833-1834*. Trans. Jean Hawkes. London: Virago Press, 1986 [*Peregrinations*].
———. *Promenades dans Londres*. Ed. François Bedarida. Paris: Maspero, 1978.
———. *Le tour de France*. Preface de Michel Collinet, notes de Jules L. Puech. Paris: Editions Tête de Feuilles, 1973 [*Tour*].
———. *The Workers' Union*. Trans. Beverly Livingston. Urbana: University of Illinois Press, 1983 [*WU*].
Zucherman, Phyllis. "Ideology and the Patriarchal Family: Nerval and Flora Tristan." *Sub-Stance* 15 (December 1976): 146-58.

CHAPTER FOUR

Between the Lines

On the Essayistic Experiments of Hélène Cixous in "The Laugh of the Medusa"

MARGRET BRÜGMANN

MIRROR GAMES

When I was small, I knew a magic place. When I was alone, I would go into my parents' bedroom and stand in front of my mother's dressing table. It was a familiar piece of furniture which aroused associations with the hall of mirrors at the fair and an altar in the church. Comb, brush, perfume, manicure set were all carefully laid out on the glass tabletop. I used these forbidden objects to experiment with who I was, what I could be, to see what variations on the theme of "me" were possible. I turned to the mirror to see the results. The mirror had side wings you could adjust so you could see every angle of yourself. The most wonderful sensation of the mirror game occurred when I placed the mirrors so that I could see unending reflections of myself and the area around me. When I moved the side wings, I was engulfed in an infinity of dancing girls stretching into endless space.

This image returns to me as I read Hélène Cixous' masterly, witty essay "The Laugh of the Medusa." As with Cixous' other works, this piece survives many rereadings for me, each reading opening new panoramas of insight. And yet at the same time, it leaves me disturbed, with mixed feelings about what it is that Cixous is presenting us with. Her articulation of how game and reality are interwoven is exquisite. In "The Laugh of the Medusa," she writes on the one hand of the historic, mythical, and social situation of women, and on the other she leads us through her utopian vision of possibilities that can and must be imagined and developed. Cixous blends these two sides in all her work. It is hardly surprising that she so often chooses the novel or play as her medium; in both aesthetic forms she is free to use unscientific, nonempirical methods to describe the so-called truth of women's lives. Although many texts have grown out of Cixous' readings and lectures, she has produced relatively few essays.

It could be that this is not coincidental but rather indicates an extremely delicate balance and "delicate difference" in the way that women express themselves publicly in their speaking and writing and the way in which femininity is valued in our society. Let us begin with a historic dilemma: In past centuries when women were openly involved in intellectual debate, it was mainly through letter-writing or in hosting a literary or political salon. The female voice was mainly placed and kept within the private sphere, as the advisor, the listener, or the inspirational muse, being regarded in all cases as subjective. Although subjectivity was linked with women, men could also legitimately express their subjectivity. Within mainstream literature the essay form developed as a subjective form of expression relatively free from the constraints of academic argument. In traditional classification systems, poetic language was (and is) associated with femininity. In the course of the nineteenth century, elements of "the feminine" were annexed by art, in the so-called "decadence" and later the avant garde. Forms of spontaneous creativity (and not academic commentary) that until then were attributed to women, found their place in the essay and are surely a reason for its popularity in the dominant discourse.

As always, when women have the chance to be published and enter into the intellectual debate, they express an ambivalence towards the dominant tradition. On the one hand, we find women who use their academic space to write weighty tomes laden with a surplus of footnotes aimed at reinforcing their academic validity. On the other hand, we find women who make use of the existing, dominant models of recalcitrance, such as the essay, to express their strength and vision. It is a balancing act, this use of existing forms in an attempt to create new meanings. In my opinion, Cixous is one of this latter group of writers.

When I try to place Cixous' writing, I think of the theoretician Theodor W. Adorno. Adorno, a rebellious spirit and an outsider (as a Jewish intellectual in Germany), saw the essay as political dynamite in the academic world. Before I go further into Cixous' particular use of the essay form, I would like to comment on the special form and the possibilities of this genre. I draw largely on Theodor W. Adorno's inspiring writings on the essay. I will then use this theoretical perspective to examine Cixous' "The Laugh of the Medusa."

THE MUSICAL LOGIC OF THE ESSAY

In "Der Essay als Form" ("The Essay as Form") Adorno champions the distinctive mixture of media he defines as the essay. According to him, scientists distrust the essay form because the essay can choose to approach the whole mountain of knowledge from whichever angle it chooses, beginning and ending wherever it pleases. This goes against the "rules of the game" of disciplines which like to see themselves as scientific or scholarly. The essay can speak with several voices at one time and in that way is reminiscent of a work of art, which can present a number of different—sometimes even contradictory— statements. In this way, the essay is surely a superior medium to an academic discipline that presumes to pigeonhole reality into easily controlled concepts and ordered definitions. Rather than proceeding from definitions of axiomatic assumptions, the essay uses existing concepts as they are without necessarily redefining them. In an essay, concepts are given new and original meanings through the contexts in which they are placed and the connections made by the author. In this way, the essay can present new possibilities for existing concepts that are currently unexpressed and/or hidden. Adorno contends that the essay plays with concepts, in what he describes as a "systematically unsystematic method." It is not scientific definitions or dictionaries that help our understanding when we read an essay. "When the reader reads the same word in a variety of contexts thirty times, they will understand the meanings better than if they had looked up the different meanings in a dictionary, because they are often, in context, either too narrow or too vague" [21].

The essay is, then, not an analytical construction but a movement of interweaving concepts that demand neither origin nor end, completeness nor continuity. The essay recognizes that there is no single reality but rather realities that are discontinuous and brittle, and that people are not 'lords and masters' of creation. The essay frequently employs parody to emphasize this. The more the essay offers a critique of an essentialist concept, the more clearly we can see that some concepts seen as natural are in fact cultural constructions. The essay addresses the relationship between culture and nature by playing with apparently unshakeable convictions. This playing and the very enjoyment of the game lead "serious" scholars to brand the essay form as flippant. This joy of thinking, and the imagination of the new, the utopian, are given room to move in this medium. Cross-connections can be brought to light precisely because it is not necessary to argue within an accepted scientific paradigm. This goes against Cartesian thought. "Wherever a word has more than one meaning, the various meanings are never completely different from each other, but sometimes show how deeply hidden some connections between things are" [32]. Adorno concludes that the essay can be seen as a sort of heresy within the sciences, because it brings to the surface issues that science and philosophy are blind to, and that traditional concepts fail to recognize.

In his analysis of the essay, Adorno describes the possibility of breaking through the prevailing academic discourse to generate new meanings. For me, the attractiveness of the essay as Adorno describes it lies in the flexibility he gives it: it gives us the possibility of introducing new meanings and ways of thinking without necessarily having to be prescriptive. Unfortunately, Adorno did not further examine the implications of a text's subject matter for contextual meaning.

WOMEN'S WRITING: A NEVER-ENDING ESSAY?

If we apply Adorno's comments on the essay to feminine aesthetics and women's writing a number of observations can be made, particularly when we look at *écriture féminine*. Like the essay, this way of writing can be criticized as elitist and hermetic. If the writers of *écriture féminine* come from the academic world, and this is expressed unhesitatingly in their work, the label elitist certainly applies. These texts also often exhibit an unwillingness to explain concepts in lay terms and to make their political standpoints and directives explicit. The use of terminology and concepts from psychoanalysis and French postmodernism adds to the difficulties of translating the meaning of these works directly into feminist politics. The writers' standpoints are not always unambiguous. They employ concepts and definitions from psychoanalysis and literary criticism of male theoreticians at the same time as they criticize them or present their work parodically or ironically. The "I" in the text, which is so often in the foreground in the essay as the manifest opinion of the author, is frequently withdrawn into such a maze of varying textual styles and voices that the reader is left not knowing where she or he stands. The text plays with the reader: to join in the game readers often must be prepared to let go of their traditional manner of reading. This is not always easy: many of us are used to choosing texts that comply with our way of thinking, that are supple in fitting themselves to our reading needs.

Such a master/servant relationship does not apply to the reader and some texts, Cixous' among them. These texts demand to be approached with care, and without too many prejudices. They require time if one wants to get to know them; the reader must become acquainted with them calmly and gently, often through more than one meeting. The reader must "travel light"—these texts cannot be approached with literary or intellectual baggage. Moreover, it is not important whether you begin in the middle or at the beginning. "The Laugh of the Medusa," for example, is comprised of many small, independent pieces that can each stand on their own. But it is only when you can see the text in its entirety that you discover that the game of the never-ending mirrors is being played, where each new reading offers new perspectives and meanings.

This way of reading is made possible by the flexible form of the essay. And this flexibility suits the needs of the woman who writes about, for, and through women. The "I" of the author mirrors itself in the existing theories, myths, and clichés about women, turns these around, places them in shifting contexts, permits a normally unpermissible mingling of discourse levels, so that the text buzzes and sings in the reader's ears. The essay is constantly assailed by feminine identities, which explode and multiply in the text until the reader loses her way in this maze of identities. By "playing" with the inadequacies of concepts and definitions of femininity, Cixous creates the thought-space necessary to realize new possibilities.

This inherent possibility of the essay as described by Adorno, which is generated from the subversion and splintering of concepts and thought structures, has much to offer feminist criticism. At the same time, in my opinion, it can be quite risky. The deconstructionist style that precludes redefinition and limits us to playing with the existing discourse cannot offer us an answer to the question of feminine identity or address the socio-political concept of societal change. If a woman writer strictly follows Adorno's form of the essay, her voice and her

"I" will be splintered, and she will be in danger of rendering herself dumb, without her own melody, when she herself comes to speak. It is clear that if a woman writer wishes to avoid the trap of essentialism (false definition) and the pitfall of identity-crushing deconstruction (losing all self-relativity), she must bend and mold the enticing medium of the essay, draw it to herself, and fit it to her own needs. In "The Laugh of the Medusa," Hélène Cixous risks this experiment.

THE FUTURE MUST NO LONGER BE DETERMINED BY THE PAST

In a series of seven sequences, Cixous leads us at a furious pace through woman's history and future, her shortcomings and possibilities. The overriding imperative of the essay is: "Woman, write!" But it also demands of us that we live—live out our own lives, determine our own history. "Write" is used in its original meaning of *inscribere*—she challenges us to make a notch, make our mark on the traditional culture. Woman is continually addressed, even accosted, as a principal actor in this process. Cixous sees that this meaning-giving process has to follow a ruptured, circuitous route.

In the first sequence, Cixous addresses herself intimately to all women readers: "I write this as a woman, toward women. When I say 'women,' I'm speaking of woman in her inevitable struggle against conventional man, and of a universal woman subject who must bring women to their senses and to their meaning in history . . . there is, at this time, no general woman, no one typical woman" [875–76]. She shows us immediately that woman and women cannot simply be lumped together in one convenient category. On the one hand, she examines the concrete, everyday struggle against traditional man. She links this to woman's need for a subject construction different from that of man. Cixous concedes that there is no symbolic, autonomous, female subject existing in our culture. She searches for the reason for this absence and sees it in the fact that from the time she is a small girl, woman is deprived of her sexuality, her energy, her imagination. If a girl is deprived of her potential for sexual pleasure, she is deprived of her joy of discovery, her own writing, her own eloquence. "The little girls and their 'ill-mannered' bodies immured, well-preserved, intact unto themselves, in the mirror. Frigidified. But are they ever-seething underneath! What an effort it takes—there's no end to it—for the sex cops to bar their threatening return" [877]. We find this text movement returning throughout the entire essay, a form of militant analysis coupled with an encouragement that anticipates the future.

It is hardly surprising to find that the second sequence begins by ascertaining the continuing presence of women. "Here they are returning, arriving over and over again, because the unconscious is impregnable" [877]. Cixous does not identify woman with the unconscious, as is often done in postmodernism. Rather, she sees that everything that has to do with her own life, everything coupled with the lives of others, is supplanted by self-hate: self-hate generated

by the fact that she is not a man. Cixous briefly mentions the link between
Freud's metaphor of women as "the dark continent" and the struggle of blacks
against oppression by whites. According to Cixous both have been pacified and
made silent by white men. She contends that because of this oppression, there
is still no real women's writing. Women who have written have "obscure[d]
women or reproduce[d] the classical representations of women [as sensitive-
intuitive-dreamy etc]" [878]. Cixous deliberately labels this masculine writing
and claims that the dominant libidinal and cultural economy works hand in
hand with women's oppression.

In the third sequence, Cixous links "factual" history with the history of
writing, presenting both as being thoroughly permeated with phallocentric
thought. She makes some minor exceptions: a few—very few—male poets
have shown a glimpse of the feminine in their work (Heinrich v. Kleist, E. T. A.
Hoffmann, Jean Genet) in that they broke with social codes and structures that
deny women. It is precisely this step that Cixous demands of woman. She has
to step out of man's shadow, out of her passive, servile role, and actively speak
out. Cixous does not deny the difficulties involved. Often the only female
voices that are heard are those that speak in a traditionally acceptable manner.
But women must be able to withdraw from and reject the disconnected discourse of so-called logicians. We must be able to go further than merely mas-
tering the discourse for its own sake. We must mix, mingle, interweave levels of
discourse in order to create new levels of understanding.

Cixous asks that women include the primary experience of contact with the
mother in "male causal symbolism." In contrast to Western cultural thinking
that denies and/or abhors the many variations of early bonding with the
mother, Cixous sees this as a chance to reestablish an unsublimated, unre-
pressed enjoyment of the body and to regain the music, sound, and language
that are connected with this. "Even if phallic mystification has generally con-
taminated good relationships, a woman is never far from 'mother' (I mean outside her role functions: the 'mother' as nonname and as source of goods). There
is always within her at least a little of that good mother's milk. She writes in
white ink" [881]. This deeply poetic and highly suggestive passage concludes
with the women writing in "white ink."

It is always dangerous to write about women in terms of anatomical
metaphors—we are still fighting to free ourselves from the dualistic association
of women as purely physical beings with no connection with the intellectual,
the spiritual, the non-physical. But Cixous chooses this direction to emphasize
that it is not the role of the mother that she means but the experience of an
intense and loving physical enjoyment that is presented to us both as reclaimed
memory and future possibility. Taking the metaphor of the "white ink" further,
we can associate it with secrets or a secret code (writing in milk). In each instance the image is diametrically opposed to what is visibly written. Maybe we
can see it as the space between the letters that is free for anyone to fill in at their
own discretion according to their own imagination—"writing between the
lines."

Cixous spins out the mother metaphor further in her fourth sequence. She recalls for us the bodily contact linked with mothering (and being mothered), the caresses, rhythms, songs, joys, and passions of the phase where you are being encouraged to come "out of your heart into language." Cixous sees this motherly affection and encouragement as an economy of unselfish distribution, in contrast to the classic economy of giving only to receive. As this female economy becomes more significant in social and political terms, traditional structures and codes will undergo fundamental changes. "As subject for history, woman always occurs simultaneously in several places. Woman un-thinks (*dépense*) the unifying, regulating history that homogenizes and channels forces, herding contradictions into a single battlefield. . . . As a militant, she is an integral part of all liberations" [822]. This militant position will lead to a changing, rather than a changed writing form, a female form that is neither definable nor theorizable. "[I]t does and will take place in areas other than those subordinated to philosophico-theoretical domination. It will be conceived of only by subjects who are breakers of automatisms, by peripheral figures that no authority can ever subjugate" [882]. Here Cixous broadens the concept of women in an interesting way. She begins with woman as a subject from history and gives her a revolutionary function in all historical change. Finally, she equates the feminine in writing with anti-authoritarianism and the nomadic situation of marginal figures in general. In this way she shows us that it could be possible for men also to articulate the feminine.

From this position, Cixous continues her ideas on writing in her fifth sequence. She differentiates two economies of writing: an open, revealing, feminine style, and a conservative, phallic, masculine one. Cixous rages against the classic constellation, whereby under the primacy of the masculine symbolic and libidinal economy, the feminine as other is appropriated. (Think of male artists who claim to "give birth to" their works of art.) Cixous' vision is of another type of difference, another type of "bisexuality": ". . . that is, each one's location in self (*repérage en soi*) of the presence—variously manifest and insistent according to each person, male or female—of both sexes, nonexclusion either of the difference or of one sex, and from this 'self-permission,' multiplication of the effects of the inscription of desire, over all parts of my body and the other body" [884]. Although Cixous frequently disparages psychoanalysis, in the passage quoted she cites Freud's theory that every person is in principle bisexual, and it is only through cultural conditioning that one of the sexes is closed out or repressed. Cixous sees the theoretical constructions of Freud's castration complex and penis envy and Lacan's "lack" as ways to present and reinforce the feminine as the negative, the dead, the inadequate in our culture. With a hint of the Medusa myth and an idiosyncratic interpretation, Cixous refuses to negate the feminine as lack. She pleads with us to embrace the masculine and the feminine in each person, so that both poles can be present and active, each attractive in their differences. This gives us a starting point to deal with other aspects of multisexuality. This circulation of desire should also have its effect on texts. Cixous suggests that under this libidinal economy genres will become interwoven, linear logicians undermined. An unending, circular text production will begin.

In the sixth sequence, the disturbance of order within syntax and culture is further spun out and radicalized. Cixous refers to the strength of the protest of the hysterics. She calls Freud's Dora the Signifier's mistress (a sophisticated word play): Dora, papa's little darling, whom he misuses as a pawn in the adults' sexual game-playing. With her self-confident appearance and her precocious background, Dora is Freud's teacher in hysteria analysis. Dora, who masters the discourse, remains closed throughout Freud's analysis, breaks off the analysis, and refuses to be molded into the traditional female role. We see here how many layers one sentence, one metaphor, can generate. How, connected with other sentences and passages, it can say everything that the text can accommodate. We see it romping, cavorting, playing in and with the white ink!

Cixous creates for us another of her favorite metaphors in this passage. She use the verb *voler* in its double meaning of flying and stealing to show the ways in which women relate to the Law, to the cultural order. Cixous compares the woman to a bird and a thief. Thieves take what they want, and disturb the order of the house. Birds fly overhead, flying away from where they don't want to be, flying to where they do want to be. Because woman has learned not to be scared of anonymity—she so easily loses her titles (as spouse) or her property (of her spouse)—she will, like a thief, throw the property relationship between the sexes into confusion. This "lightness of being" means she can flit swiftly from one place to another; Cixous calls her an "airborne swimmer, in flight, she does not cling to herself" [889–90].

In the seventh sequence, Cixous returns to earth with her extremely personal flight through many aspects of meanings and meaningful elements. She summons women not to preclude themselves nor to allow themselves to be precluded from any single thing that they want to do, even when it comes to the precarious area of motherhood. Earlier in her text, she emphasizes that she is not talking about motherhood as a social role, yet here that is exactly what she means. She places motherhood in opposition to psychoanalysis, where a child represents a surrogate penis. She thunders against the "necessity" of seeing the mother-child relationship in terms of family structures. She encourages the pregnant woman to go on with her pregnancy as with her life—to "live" her passions, her language, and her intellectual and spiritual autonomy. Pregnant women are always suspect—their bulging bellies irrefutable evidence of the sexuality, the base physicality of women. But they are also unique here—giving birth means neither an increase nor a decrease in their body—they do not fit into the masculine economy. This sequence ends in increasingly shorter emotional statements on the importance of writing and the longing for the other. It tells us of the renouncing and yet the simultaneous use of symbolic meanings to radiate an image of love. A love that constantly experiences the similarities and differences of the other, that even surpasses all expectations, a love that, in this text, does not differentiate between text, erotic, self, other, meaning, and subconscious, and that withdraws from articulation: "This is an economy that doesn't have to be put in economic terms" [893]. But then, why should it? The starting point was always: "The future must no longer be determined by the past" [875].

WHO IS STILL LAUGHING?

If we start with the assumption that the form of the essay is not fixed, that it offers the author complete freedom, then it can be difficult to define what is innovative or experimental. Everything is permissible in terms of style and theme, even if it is only a small, recalcitrant work of art. Yet I want to return to what it is that makes the aesthetic form of Cixous' essay so exciting.

Cixous tends towards an openness that is at home in the essay; she moves from a personal statement and expands it into generalizations — one of the major elements of the essay. Now and then she broadens her considerations in directions which include men. Here Cixous deviates from the usual essay that assumes a male author/narrator who is placed against a self-evidently male-dominated cultural background. This, however, does not automatically make Cixous' essay more experimental than many other essays. What makes Cixous' essay special is that she positions herself clearly as a female author writing for a female public, with only some of her assertions being valid for men as well. She deviates from the standard essay form that addresses a public that is automatically coded as masculine.

It is worthwhile examining some of Cixous' structural elements of style. Cixous divides her text into seven sequences; in the first, she presents us with her paradigm that the future must be anticipated. At the end of the final sequence, she leaves us with "In the beginning are our differences" [873]. With this structure, and this final passage, Cixous parodies the seven days of the Creation. She recreates the universe out of the chaos of male disorder. She brings into being a new, renewed, and renewing female creation. Her often hymnal tone, her utopian encouragement, her prophetic visions blend with her critical-historical analysis to emphasize this image. Her heretical amendment of the first line of the Creation is feminist and provocative. Here again, Cixous challenges us to test the intertextual connections. My reading of the essay takes the following line: Cixous places the proclamation "In the beginning are our differences" at the end of the seventh sequence — metaphorically speaking, on the seventh day. This is the biblical day of rest, when God admired his creation with satisfaction, Adam and Eve were already created, the Creation was in complete harmony, and God was the Father-by-projection to whom the world owed its existence.

Cixous revises the Creation. She begins on her first "day" of creation by telling us that we must not allow ourselves to be restrained and blinkered by what has been when we set ourselves the task of imagining what could be. She calls up the world — she is a second creator of a universe that partly supersedes the present one and is partly still being elaborated. She plows relentlessly through the universe with open, searching eyes, both admonishing and encouraging us. Then comes her seventh—one of the oldest sacred numbers—text fragment, which is both the most personal and the most utopian. It could, at the same time, be read as the first fragment, as the beginning. In the beginning there is not the Word (as in the Bible) or the Deed (as in Goethe's *Faust*), but the Differences, our differences. The basic premise of Cixous' re-Creation is humanity as it exists, with no ontologically defined essential characteristics. There are only Differences. People are different from each other, and we also change from one moment to the next, becoming "different from ourselves" as we were.

This fundamental supposition of the Creation à la Cixous implies that all ordering must be rethought and that no one has any prior claim to any particular form of existence by virtue of their sex or status. This means, too, that all symbolic systems are both provisional and flexible because nothing can be invoked on the basis of concrete, unchanging attributes. The primacy of difference will always modify symbolic forms. Above all, this means that all existing stories, canonized theories, and myths exist by the grace of the Denial of Difference. Cixous once again uses fragments of myth in her essay (and her literary work) to show us that this masculine story-telling tradition has generated a world that is very different from the one that would come into being through feminine myth-making.

A female retelling would be another story: it would consist of other stories, with different aspects of the tale honored and valued. The collected stories that have sprung from the resistance to male fear and female self-hate, and vice versa, stories of death, love, conquest, would, in another economy, lead to other myths. Cixous uses the image of Ariadne's thread to show another way of handling myths. She builds no cathedrals, no symbolic buildings with matriarchal precursors. Rather, she spins her yarn, teasing language into new and unfamiliar chains of association. The Word is not, in the figurative sense, used as a metaphor; rather, the metaphor is taken literally and returned to its original image. Here *prendre la parole* is no symbolic deed—it is spun out through the sound, the music, the orality, the mouth, the body that speaks, she who speaks, she who is spoken to, what it is that speaks, what she speaks about, what she could speak about, why she stays mute. A word, a thought, chases other thoughts in an interior monologue that is orchestrated so that the reader can insert her own part. This spontaneous concert may well seem chaotic from the outside. But there is a melody line, and that is the theme "woman," in all her many and varied synonyms, in all of her resonances, assonances, fugues, codas, and echoes.

We return finally to the beginning that is no beginning. We return to the story of creation—one of the finest myths there is, the myth that functions, as Northrop Frye put it, as the "Great Code" of western society. Cixous is bantering with this code, all the while taking a position as a speaking "I" in the text that is reminiscent of the Creator, here recreated in female form. Cixous loves her creation and her creatures, most certainly those of the female variety.

What sort of guiding light do we have before us? Who is this seductress who is raging and wild, magnetic and compelling? In other words, I must ask the question: Where do you stand, Hélène Cixous, in your own Creation?

Jane Gallop tells us, with considerable irony, that Irigaray never actually comes to grips with the question of the daughter who seeks affection and understanding from the father. And Gallop finds that Kristeva's brilliance and authoritarian voice demand the position of the phallic mother. So where should we situate Cixous? Two pieces from Cixous' text haunt me. At the end she says "I want it all." This is a valid wish, and in itself is not extraordinary. But if it is linked with her vehement plea of a fundamental bisexuality, and her statement that no woman has essentially broken her tie with her childhood, which is supported by her almost mystical veneration of the mother, then I receive the impression that she places woman in her most original stage in this childhood, after which cultural patterning robs her of her originality. In this phase of life, children play with and try on for size all the roles and rituals that they are offered, not critically, but acceptingly, so that they can find their place in their environment and deal emotionally with events in their lives. This "child's play" is often played in deadly earnest and is not wanting for aesthetic beauty. Children do not yet reflect their history — or a history. They are working on finding a place for themselves in history.

Adults look indulgently upon children's games. The innocence ascribed to children comes from the fact that they don't yet have their "place" in history. This cultural attitude is reflected in the New Testament; people must enter the kingdom of heaven as if they were children. I am inclined to think that Cixous sees this naïveté as either an imitation, or a source of, female creativity. This would explain her avoidance of "political statements," and why, when she does make strategic feminist statements, she takes refuge in poetic, mythical, ageless description. Perhaps these distractions are consciously laid out by the author to preclude a new theory or concept of femininity from being distilled from her text. The result is a curious paradox: on the one hand, her "I" in the text continually encourages her readers, obstinately and unequivocally, to realize — in both senses of the word — an existence in language, culture, and history. On the other hand, just when the reader wishes to take up the challenge and seeks a concrete directive, a solid standpoint, the subject of the text withdraws itself as a leading or advisory figure. It would be sufficient if the challenges the author so enthusiastically presents were linked with an occasional personal experience, even assuming that such challenges could not be representative of all women. Cixous' writing style creates an enormous distance between herself and the reader, even though she speaks constantly of closeness, intimacy, giving, of the physical. It throws suspicion on whether her postulation of the unselfish giving of the feminine economy is perhaps merely a noncommittal postmodern mannerism, or whether it can only be realized in the hereafter. In her argument, Cixous combines the promise of an experienced friend, of a mother, with the experimenting fury of a small child. The one looks at the other over her shoulder in the three-sided mirror. Perhaps because of that, she has forgotten that there are other rooms in the house. In reading Cixous' "The Laugh of the Medusa," that leaves me with no inclination to laugh.

Nevertheless, Cixous' text remains an interesting experiment with the essay form. Cixous mixes different discourse forms to illustrate the complexity of the concept of femininity, without insisting on a new definition. In this way she works within the style of the essay as Adorno describes it. Still, she alters the form in two ways. First, she pours her associative style into the relatively strict structure of seven sequences in an analogy of the creation myth. This evokes associations with a play or a mythical essay-telling and gives a solidity usually missing in the essay, at least according to Adorno.

Secondly, in her narrative perspective, Cixous brings out the position of the subject of the text as problematic. Cixous refuses to recognize the masculine subject/narrator as taken for granted. Sometimes she is dominantly present, and sometimes she disappears behind her descriptions of historical impediments or her visions of the future. This can be irritating to the reader, yet this subject position can also be read as an indicator of the place that the female voice takes in the intellectual, masculine domain. Her voice rings out as she analyzes the historical position of women. She sounds hopeful and strong as she encourages change, but the female voice becomes uncertain when it comes to describing her visions of possible futures. With this change of tone, Cixous shows us the difference that exists between the taken-for-granted male critical voice in the essay and a new and critical female perspective that is trying to articulate itself. This is not a one-dimensional endeavor; it is happening in different ways and on different levels at the same time. And it lies with us, her readers, to develop this further, on the multitude of levels offered to us. The essay is but one of these levels.

TRANSLATED BY DEBBI LONG

WORKS CITED

Adorno, Theodor W. "Der Essay als Form." *Noten zur Literatur*. Frankfurt am Main: Suhrkamp Verlag, 1974. 9-34.
Cixous, Hélène. "The Laugh of the Medusa." Trans. Keith and Paula Cohen. *Signs* 1, 4 (Summer 1976): 875-93.
Frye, Northrop. *The Great Code: The Bible and Literature*. New York: Harcourt Brace Jovanovich, 1981.
Gallop, Jane. *Feminism and Psychoanalysis: The Daughter's Seduction*. London/ Basinstoke: MacMillan, 1982.

The Conscious "I"

Authority and Ambiguity
in Women's Essays

CHAPTER FIVE

Woman Taking Speculation into Her Own Hands*

BARBARA SICHTERMANN

Satirists have already commented on the tendency of feuilletons, blurb writers, and freelance writers to upgrade reflections on this or that subject by subtitling them essays. They claim that too much that is arbitrary or worthless has been elevated in this way to the level of the experimental, and they think that this trendy failing should come to an end: whoever has something to say should address the issue directly and not beat around the bush essayistically. And it looks as if the inflation of essays that occurred in recent years, since the early eighties, when every other text was really somehow tied to the family of the essay, has come to a stop: whereas the good old composition,** the pale but worthy article or contribution, the treatise and the gloss, the pamphlet and the commentary have returned to prominence, whereas even observations, suppositions, probings, and approaches, forms that were in real trouble in the sixties and seventies, are daring to re-emerge. The essay is recovering from its all too great popularity and will soon perhaps, after a deserved rest, show its true character again.

But what precisely is that character? It is probably not inappropriate to point to its resemblance to the scholarly treatise, its willingness to play with literary forms, to emphasize the role of the argument, of discussion, of the anticipated counterargument, and finally to reassert the right of subjectivity to express itself, the right to pure opinion ("I can do nothing else, so help me

---

* "Die Frau beim Grübeln auf eigene Faust." *Wer ist wie?* (Berlin: Klaus Wagenbach Verlag, 1987). 95-104. This essay is a revised version of Sichtermann's acceptance speech upon being awarded the Jean Améry Prize for essay writing (Berlin, November 1985). Born in 1912 as Hanns Maier, Améry was an Austrian Jew who fled Austria in 1938, only to be arrested in 1943 and deported to Auschwitz for working in the Belgian resistance. After the war, he assumed the French name and worked as a journalist in Brussels. He committed suicide in 1978. Though he spent a large part of his career as a journalist, he is remembered primarily for his later philosophical essays. The Jean Améry Prize has been awarded annually in Germany since 1982.

** The German original uses the word "Aufsatz," distinguishable from the other German term "Essay" by its connection with the academic practice of writing a "paper" or a scholarly article.

God") as a freedom granted to the essay. But in the midst of all these determinates there is a sense of indeterminacy, a deliberate vagueness: we can only definitively grasp the essay by trying. And even this is to no avail; it seems to want to remain incognito. Its indeterminate character has no doubt contributed to its attractiveness, to its label being sold off cheap. On the other hand, its indeterminacy is also somewhat brusque, even intimidating, as if there were a warning: "Caution—experimental station! Proceed at your own risk."

I want to say something about the difficulties the essay creates, the fear that it can create precisely because one doesn't know exactly how to do justice to it. I have a particular subjective premise. Ultimately I shall shift over completely to that premise, a step which, I hope, the essayistic framework of this piece allows me to take.

When my first publications produced their first echo a few years ago, a well-meaning colleague said to me: "You are lucky because you've found a fashionable topic." He meant feminism. I agreed with him absolutely at the time, completely wrapped up in the modesty of the beginner who only too willingly views the attention she gets as chance and tends to be more fearful than happy at the prospect of its continuation. Women are interested in fashion—why not in fashionable topics? In terms of public attention they are the momentary sex. Resonance that occurs only in the context of a passing fashion seemed to me to be all that I as a woman could expect.

But like every other human being I was not only a gendered being—there were other fundamental concerns such as inclination, profession, reproduction, and other demands that went more or less above and beyond gender, and so it happened that I continued to write. I tried to get away from this tiresome, fashionable topic. I focused on my academic qualifications and attempted to concentrate on business management and labor market problems. But no matter what I did, the thing kept acquiring this fashionable veneer. I ended up with questions of women's employment and the conflicts of working mothers.

My further efforts to become more respectable bore little fruit as well: the fashionable topic pulled me toward it, as if by magnetic force. In this story the women's movement was in more ways than one the hedgehog: prickly, cunning, and always present.* For safety's sake I should add that my fruitless flight from feminism was carried on by only one part of my professional self; in no way did I want to withdraw from the women's movement, quite the contrary, but I wanted to write about other things as well, not to tie myself down, but to demonstrate my versatility, all those well-known requirements of a proper professional profile. But I couldn't get away with it. The topic of women almost always caught up with me: it set the decisive tone even in my work that had

---

* The fable of the hedgehog and the hare, well-known in Germany, is akin to the familiar tale of the tortoise and the hare. The hedgehog and his wife (!) outwit the hare by positioning themselves at two different entrances to their burrow; hence, when the hedgehog and the hare race from one hole to the other, the hare is dismayed always to find the hedgehog there ahead of him.

originated in completely different things, like overpopulation or shortening the work-day.

In the failed attempt to tie myself down, I was able to learn how contemporary history makes people like us dance to its tune; how, even if it doesn't provide us with topics, it nevertheless gives us an index; how it directs thoughts via remote control, as it were, so that they merge again and again with its concerns. In the meantime, I have given in and still have a better conscience than I did before. Women's emancipation is no longer a fashionable topic—on the contrary, most intellectuals tend more often than not to react politely if a woman admits interest in it—and thus, women's emancipation achieves a status that carries a certain grudging honor. The colleague I spoke of earlier no longer talks about the luck I had—he finds that I should now prove what is in me and begin talking about serious matters. But what can I do, the hedgehog is already there, time saddles us with worries, history guides our thoughts by remote control. Sometimes a historical trend dresses itself for awhile in fashionable colors, and the whole world turns its head to look. Later it becomes more difficult to keep one's attention focused steadily on that trend and the problems that it raises.

For my part, I take the liberty of repeating that I no longer believe in a free choice of my topics, that I have surrendered to the craftiness of the hedgehog and, as it were, am now available for women's issues.

My efforts to escape feminism as a writer also had something to do with the *form* in which I was writing. The essay, a form that appealed to me because of its relative lack of rules, somehow didn't seem to be appropriate for women's issues. Women's issues were (and are) extremely sensitive and unresearched and belong completely under the wings of a more meticulous and (in a positive sense) more ponderous science, I thought. The playfulness that the essay presumes does not do justice to the existential dimension that women's issues, in all their breadth, might occupy; opinions, impressions, and other subjective means of transmitting ideas and theses seem too light, too fragile for the cargo of feminist ideas.

Now and then essay-like insights have come over to us from England and America, but perhaps there is an international division of labor here: the Anglo-Saxons take over empiricism and carefree reasoning, and people like us have to carry the burden of theory. But then I found a compromise between my desire to let loose and write and my fear that questions of women's emancipation would not be able to stand that: a compromise between speculating at my own risk and feminism's entitlement to rigorous analysis. I don't want to go into this compromise. But what does seem worth noting is the relationship between women's issues and the essay or, in more general terms, the relationship of women to speculating at their own risk.

Women don't like to write essays. If I look at feminist work in Germany, scholarly investigations are at the head of the line, no matter how narrowly defined the object of investigation, no matter how modest the results. In addition, news stories, commentaries, and features, i.e. journalistic contributions in

a broader sense, are probably just as numerous. Independent feminist speculation that is not dedicated to a project, a study, or a series of lectures but rather
only to personal opinion and partisanship are relatively rare outside of daily
journalism. Why is this so? Countless causes can be found and interpreted. I've
selected the following.

Whoever dares to enter the public sphere with nothing but a personal view
of things depends on being heard by the public because he is who he is. Women
generally do not have such firm faith in the extensiveness of their personal
aura. It is quite a different matter when women express themselves as a part, a
member, a representative of an institution like, for example, a university, a research group, or the editorial staff of a journal. The institution, the group with
its specific habits, its rules, and its reputation, supports women and offers protection; appearing in public under the protection of such a superstructure is
less personalizing. But the essay exposes its author; she alone is its creator; no
scientific community, no editorial collective stands behind her. She identifies
herself neither by her academic degree, her research contract, her method, her
theoretical school, nor by her institutional affiliation, actually not even by her
name, but rather by her own idiosyncratic nature. And what would that be? In
any case something undependable. And women in particular don't like to sell
themselves in that way.

Male authors also face the choice of either speculating at their own risk or
placing themselves under the protection of an institution, and probably most of
them choose the latter course of action. Still, it is likely that considerably more
women than men shrink back from the warning sign that says "Caution—
experimental station." But not because women are by nature more hesitant,
and not because their socialization, widely recognized as disadvantageous, has
severed their courage, but rather because they have seen it all before. Generally
speaking, when they speak up without institutional legitimization, women are
not heard. When they take the floor in their own name, women are heard more
seldom, more poorly, imprecisely, and fragmentarily than men.

Luckily, modern linguistics has meanwhile proved this through a series of
tests and analyses, so I don't have to refer at this point to something as ques-
tionable as my personal impression. No, the notorious *mulier tacit in ecclesia*
(woman should be silent in the community) is somehow still present between
the lines of public address, whether in parliament, in a university lecture hall,
on television, or on the occasion of an awards ceremony.

The reasons I have found for this discrimination all seem to me to be un-
satisfactory. The tautology is repeatedly raised that women are heard less well
because women are, after all, worse off everywhere, or reference is made to the
famous misogyny that seems a virtual mental illness of modernity. More realistic to me are observations that point to the unfavorable pitch of the female
voice. But in all seriousness, it is difficult to find an explanation for the peculiar
phenomenon of women's being heard less that does more than rephrase the
question or trivialize it. I don't know whether or not the explanation that I am
presenting avoids these two pitfalls.

In the course of what we call the history of the Western world, I assert that male approval has created an institution that regulates the division of public attention. If we generalize and call it *Meaning*, if we view it as gender-specific, then we can determine that women are almost entirely excluded from the privileges that it guarantees. In connection with public attention and all that it brings about and sets into motion in the field of politics, women are the sex that lacks Meaning; at least they have been until recently, and the fact that they are now shedding their old lot of being meaningless is not yet widely known. Certainly, other factors completely separate from gender still play a role in obtaining the public ear: education, for example, eloquence, a talent for diplomacy, etc. One could also discuss the problem along class lines; the barrier of gender, however, is the most solid by comparison, for the least educated, least clever, and least eloquent man until very recently has had a better chance to be heard than a woman, no matter how learned she was.

Thus far, all in all, it's familiar. As far as the unequal distribution of Meaning between the sexes is concerned, it seems to me that some of its implications have yet to be discerned. The fact that Meaning and its by-products—expectations, favored status, a willing audience—are so obstinately bound up with masculinity must have something to do with a division of labor between the sexes that women could also accept. It seems to me that women have been issued the historical mission of freeing both sexes from the burden of Meaning altogether or at least temporarily. In their life outside of Meaning, women have shown that it is possible to get along without it, and by gossiping, chatting, singing, and cooing meaninglessly for man's comfort and delight, they have freed him again and again—to the extent that he was inclined to join in—from the oppressive norm of his own privilege.

Indeed, there needed to be someone who was convinced that the emperor was not only naked, but that this entire exhibition that is called the exercise of power was not at all necessary. Only thus were men forever able to sing countless praises befitting their importance to the imaginary wardrobe of power. Someone had to stand outside the hierarchy and nevertheless be human so that the agony of ambition, rank, and competition of Meaning could remain bearable. By remaining silent in public, women thus obeyed not only a command but also the demand to relativize Meaning itself—not to relativize man as such but certainly his tone, his pose, his arrogance. They did this by making a display of meaninglessness in connection with the performance of such vital tasks as bearing, feeding, and caring for human beings. According to this reading, women would then be the real clowns of written and publicly discussed history, in contrast to the court jesters, who, after all, offered merely a travesty of Meaning.

Of course, this interpretation puts the situation of women in too favorable a light. Naturally, women were also the sex that was gagged and muzzled, that repeatedly fought for its right to speak and share in Meaning. But today, as these attempts are crowned with increasing success, it seems all the more important to me to make reference to that subversive function that the meaninglessness of women must also always have had. Women must indeed still work hard to gain authority, and people often don't want to hear them—that has already been said. On the other hand, we can clearly see how positions are set in flux, how men no longer manage to claim the cake of Meaning for themselves alone, how women are demanding their share, and are in fact already enjoying their first bites. They are speaking in parliaments and universities; they are writing in essayistic forms. They are engaging in politics, science, literature.

In the face of these achievements, for which we can thank the women's movement, or for that matter democracy understood in the broadest sense, it must be pointed out that Meaning is a cake whose digestibility is open to question. When asked where she would locate the primary difference between the behavior of men and women, Simone de Beauvoir responded by saying that men tend toward pompous self-staging and grotesque self-importance, which are fortunately found much less often in women. Here we have it: the happy inheritance of meaninglessness. Women, as the meaningless sex, are not only the rhetorically inferior and envious sex but also the more laconic and level-headed sex. Their centuries of meaninglessness, their task of criticizing Meaning subversively, sharpened their eye for nakedness—even the emperor's.

But now, as Meaning becomes a thing of which women avail themselves as well, the danger exists that the value of Meaning itself will be increased, and thus that Simone de Beauvoir's flattering description of women as the less pompous sex will no longer have a basis in fact. We could, of course, try to differentiate between presumptuous and deserved Meaning, or between true and false Meaning, between seriousness and fraud, but that would overcomplicate matters. Perhaps we can agree that even the most well-founded and praiseworthy Meaning does not escape entirely without affectation, and that this is also not necessarily objectionable: *any* expression of superiority must be careful not to go too far.

This means, then, that there is and can be no completely acceptable form of authority, no status anywhere in public life that garners attention without some degree of embarrassment. Thus, the pursuit of Meaning demands great courage precisely from that sex which is particularly sensitive to the ambiguity of the hierarchy of Meaning because of its own historical exclusion from it; it is important that this courage not be taken away from women. In their reach for Meaning, it may be expected that women reenact a part of their old function, that, while they take what they are demanding and make themselves at home in it, at the same time they also denounce it a little—and not just according to men's desires. The fuss about Meaning that somehow is part of the mechanics and expression of public life is in itself already idiotic. Women ought to know how to make that clear without refusing to participate themselves.

I said above that women avoid the essayistic form because they can't count on being heard when they speak in their own name. It is proof of society's deafness that when a woman, as a representative of the sex that lacks Meaning, speaks publicly, she is inviting everyone to whisper, to read the newspaper, or to let their mind wander. This situation is changing. Women are not only appropriating words but Meaning as well, an incomparably more difficult task. My concern is that in the execution of these long-overdue operations, Meaning as such does not come off well. At the same time I am optimistic, since I cannot imagine that, after demonstrating the existential superfluousness of the dignity of office for such a long time, women will now set about donning this gown of dignity without tripping over its train. The humor of the situation must become clear to them, and their giggling may be just the thing for making visible the ill fit of Meaning itself, that stiff gown with the train that may or may not have been provided by its tailor.

Women prefer to enter institutions because they are heard more clearly there, and we can assume that they are inside to stay. The subversion of women is especially good for the big mind-and-intellect factories like universities, publishing houses, and the media, as these places are so weighed down with Meaning that they can hardly move. So it's not really a bad thing anymore that the essay is a male domain. But to the degree that women no longer need the protection of institutions, that too will change, and the sign: "Caution! Experimental station!" will strike them rather as an invitation.

This presupposes that female speakers will be heard, even when they appear publicly in their own name alone, and here it again will be necessary to find female speakers who are already equipped with a certain respectability. Because Meaning is a so-called cake that can be, at the very most, sliced differently but never made bigger, the competition for its pieces will become greater as women enter the game. But let's put these less cheery aspects aside for now. What is vital to me is that someone recognize and take up the task that women have managed on the side until now—almost naturally—namely, the denunciation of importance.

It is clear that once Meaning is no longer parceled out according to gender, its critique can no longer be bound to gender. Thus, in the future women will be subject to a double burden in these matters as well: they will want simultaneously to possess Meaning, to attain it, and to approach it critically. As carriers of Meaning, men too will have to face the fact that the essence of that which bestows skill and responsibility upon them no longer goes unchallenged. It is time we admit that men too have long been immanent critics of bluffing and boastfulness. While putting their shoulder to the wheel of Meaning, men have at the same time known how to demonstrate that form, forms, and formalities are often hollow inside—as indispensable, impressive, and beautiful as they may be—and that even when they are not hollow, even when they are uplifting or pleasing, they nevertheless create scales of Meaning and thus classify, degrade, and oppress.

Jean Améry provides a meaningful example of this kind of self-critical journalism. I have approached him from a side street because I don't feel capable of a direct *ad personam*, for various reasons. What matters is that Jean Améry was one of those rare writers who was unable to abide Meaning in the sense I have given it here, and who managed to desire the status of an "unfamous person" without a trace of coquettishness. The question of the effect of one's own writing, as well as of one's demeanor and self-expression in general (which is a legitimate and sometimes necessary question) seems in Améry's case to have disappeared entirely behind the "what," the material, his story. His essays are so severe, so bare and free of any ornamentation in their earnestness, so mistrustful of anything that is not clearly essential, so (if I may say so) mercilessly unvain, that there is no room for the resonance of any bit of pride that could be construed as Meaning.

Jean Améry wanted neither an award nor an academic title. He was a demystifier, a head-shaker like the child whose famous, unswerving gaze remained fixed on the emperor; we have Améry to thank if the essay as a literary form, with its determined-undetermined character, has been able to shield itself from the fuss about Meaning that has existed since the time of its inventor, Michel de Montaigne. How easily one can do without importance while letting oneself be heard in a medium that nevertheless presupposes that the speaker is assured of that minimum of Meaning ultimately necessary in order for dialogues or controversies (that exchange of ideas and critique that keeps the essay alive) to occur; how weightlessly that proper economy of Meaning can be achieved. Jean Améry demonstrated this as only very few have.

The critique of self-importance is naturally not a question of gender. Women have a historically greater chance to connect this critique to their own process of becoming more important, that is all. Men too have many reasons to argue against the necessity of this critique. But a few have always practiced it in their self-expression, and one of them was Jean Améry. He did it in the most effective way: not proclaiming bluntly but rather implicitly and in passing. Maybe I, maybe we, will also reach that point.

TRANSLATED BY RUTH-ELLEN B. JOERES AND ELIZABETH MITTMAN

CHAPTER SIX

Christa Wolf's Signature in and on the Essay

Woman, Science, and Authority

ELIZABETH MITTMAN

How is authority constructed within the essay?[1] How does the narrating voice establish its authority to speak, and how does it make itself heard within a given cultural and historical context? As numerous critics have pointed out, this genre is closely linked to the formation of the individual humanist subject in the sixteenth and seventeenth centuries: the appearance of the self-contained individual coincides with a new nonfictional genre marked by its own self-containment, its authority resting solely on the voice of a speaking/writing self [Good, Mowitt].[2] In other words, in a space that possesses neither the institutional legitimacy of a scientific treatise nor the cover of traditional generic conventions (lyric, epic, dramatic), authority is intimately tied to the author. This unique relation of author to text raises interesting and important questions for any discussion of women and essays. While the essay clearly belongs to a male-defined tradition [see Sichtermann, also in this volume], it has evolved and been used not only by the sons of Montaigne and Bacon, but also by women and other dispossessed people, and calls for a discussion that would take dimensions of materiality and history into account. Given the history of essays as written by those who already possessed authority, we must ask how women and other historically "unauthorized" writers assume authority for themselves within this genre.

Christa Wolf, the most prominent literary figure in the (now former) German Democratic Republic (GDR) since the late 1960s, is most famous for her ground-breaking novels (among them *The Quest for Christa T., Patterns of Childhood, No Place on Earth*, and *Cassandra*). Wolf's fictional writings—novels and short stories—are widely discussed for their autobiographical elements, for the ways in which she blurs traditional boundaries between fiction and reality, between author and narrator, as she takes pieces of her own life history or experience and inserts them into the lives of her novels' protagonists. Since the late 1960s, her writing has continuously and explicitly addressed "the difficulty of saying 'I' " [*Quest*, 169-70]. However, by explicitly formulating the problem of a new subjectivity within her texts, Wolf simultaneously controls that "I," sets its parameters. In addition, she organizes her apparent blurring of fictional boundaries around the stabilizing term(s) of the "I," a move that can ironically be read as serving to close her texts around "Christa Wolf" as both author and subject of her own texts. The connection between author and work takes on a kind of organicity, the one containing the other.

Wolf is also recognized as an important writer of essays, which are most often reflections on her own fictional texts or readings of other authors' works and lives. Her prolific essay production bespeaks not only her initial university training as literary scholar and her later work as editor of a literary journal but also an affinity for the mode of reflection the essay offers. But despite her own acknowledged blurring of boundaries, generic and otherwise, discussion of Wolf's notions of identity and subjectivity has centered almost entirely on her prose fiction. Thus, her essays are read as nonfictional documents that can shed light on her fiction.[3] I intend something different here. By shifting the lens and focusing on Wolf's essays themselves, I will try to disentangle "fiction" and "nonfiction" a bit, to tease out the strands of identity that together form the thread holding her texts and their readings together. An exploration of the narrative strategies Wolf employs in her essays is a useful starting point for both a discussion of genre-specific issues inhering in the essay and a questioning of the construction of "Christa Wolf" by herself, her readers, and her texts.

In particular, I will explore that space around the signature, what Peggy Kamuf calls a place that "is not a place at all, but an always divisible limit within the difference between writer and work, 'life' and 'letters.' Signature articulates the one with the other, the one *in* the other: it both divides and joins" [Kamuf, viii]. In other words, the signature is like a seam that both separates and connects the author, as the "real" person who exists outside of the text, and the disembodied authorial voice within the text. I would argue that the essay as genre is the site where the signature, in Kamuf's sense, is most clearly visible. The author's signature is perhaps the single-most important convention that governs the essay, a genre lacking the guideposts of other literary conventions such as plot. The essay exists as a unique discursive mode because of and through the seemingly transparent presence of the author both within and outside of the text; the author's presence becomes, in a sense, the essay's narrative structure. When we read an essay, the author's signature above the text is the ground of authority; the name gives us everything we need to know in order to read the text as an essay. "It is this double-jointedness of signatures that will be lost to any discourse that continues to posit an essential exteriority of subjects to the texts they sign" [Kamuf, viii]. For my purposes here, I read this to mean that, while the author outside of the essay is generally unproblematically identified with the narrative "I" within the essay, a politics of the essay demands that the constructed nature of that signature be explored. And in the case of Christa Wolf, signature is everything.

Before moving on to a detailed consideration of these formal issues, it is important to keep in mind the multiplicity of intersecting vectors at work here. Christa Wolf is historically situated in a country that was founded as she entered adulthood and disassembled as she entered her sixties.[4] This is a fact of no small significance as we consider, on the one hand, the struggle of that state to establish an identity of its own and, on the other, Christa Wolf's ongoing project of situating, creating, forming and reforming, analyzing, and sometimes celebrating an identity of her own. This identity is intended not merely to anchor her own self as Christa Wolf but to serve as a paradigm, a model for her society, for other Selves, for an ideal human Self. In this, we can trace a kind of identity between Christa Wolf and the GDR. Simultaneously, Wolf's writings have constituted a moment of resistance to that state. Literature in such a society serves a unique compensatory function in the face of little or no open public debate on pressing social, moral, political issues; it provides a space for difference, a different language than the flat, closed, official tongue. From this perspective, too, Wolf becomes a figure larger than herself—an agent for the silent and the silenced, a voice of authority for those who would escape, subvert, dislodge, or undermine the State's authority.[5]

All this, and yet there is more. She is a woman. It is vitally important for feminists to examine with care and caution the notion of subjectivity that explicitly or implicitly shapes Wolf's works and to recognize at the same time that subjectivity is perhaps the single most loaded concept for feminist literary critics and theorists. Her own particular project foregrounds the importance of establishing a kind of subject, or form of subjectivity, that could both resist and help to overcome societal problems. Western feminists have drawn upon this aspect of her work as important for their own projects involving the establishment of a new female subject or, alternately, a new human subject that would escape the ideological bonds of patriarchal or phallogocentric thought systems. Wolf's framing of political, moral, and aesthetic issues did indeed become consciously gendered in the late 1970s and early 1980s, and it is easy to read her work in terms of a paradigm shift, from Wolf-the-socialist to Wolf-the-feminist [see Kuhn]. Yet what happens when we impose such a model of development upon Wolf's textual production? How are identity and difference figured in the authorial first person, and what is their relation to gender? How does Wolf's particular political, cultural, and historical positionality write itself into her texts, and what does her textual practice in turn tell us as an interpretation of that positionality?

For my discussion of the ways in which Wolf's authorial voice takes shape, I have chosen to focus on four central essays and one short story, all written between 1968 and 1981. While her rhetorical strategies change with the shifting content of the essays—in particular her increased attention to feminist issues—certain structuring elements remain constant. Most importantly, I will trace the evolution of a binary oppositional structure within which Wolf positions the "I." The individual subject is at times equated with prose writing, women, or the ideals of socialism, while the other "half" of this dualism is most often played out in the thematics of a critique of science. I will briefly leave the essay form in my discussion of "Self-Experiment," a short story that

explicitly articulates the opposition of Woman vs. Science, in order to explore
this persistent dualism and questions of genre from a different angle. Within
this fictional text, the "essay" is staged as a genre with gendered implications.

"The Reader and the Writer" (1968) is a programmatic piece that Wolf wrote
in part as an explication/justification of her controversial novel *The Quest for
Christa T.* It is an interesting essay for the ways in which it exploits the position
that the genre occupies between fiction and nonfiction; it is important as a moment in which Wolf sets out the coordinates for much of her future work. Engaged
in a struggle against the tradition of socialist realism, Wolf confronts issues of fiction and truth, locating the ultimate goal of prose writing in the communication of
truths in fictionalized forms. For Wolf, this can only occur through the insertion of
the author's "subjective authenticity" into the process of writing: "[He] decides to
tell, that is invent, truthfully on the foundation of [his] own experience" [*Reader
and Writer*, 193].[6] And later: "Literature and reality do not stand face to face like
a mirror and what it reflects. They merge in the author's mind. For the author is an
important person" [206]. Wolf's insistence upon the primacy of individual experience makes her use of the essay form particularly interesting. The essay as such is
indeed characterized by its self-presentation as subjective, personal truth, and is
shaped by the "signature" of its author.

Generally speaking, however, the constructedness of the author/narrator es-
capes analysis, since the essay's "I" is assumed to be identical with the author.
This moment of illusion serves Wolf well as a strategy in her attempt to reunite
"literature" and "reality." For her, reality has been taken over by the overwhelming objectivity-worship of Science, leaving literature with what she considers to be the dubious function of entertainment. In "The Reader and the
Writer," the author as a category is created as the site of reconciliation between
the two, and absolute subjectivity replaces absolute objectivity as the path to
truth. As such, an essential function of the distinction between essay and prose
fiction is erased: the author presides over both, imparting truths to the reader
in both genres. Yet while both of Wolf's primary avenues of expression—essay
and prose fiction—are read with regard to their truths, it is seldom if ever that
we find a discussion of the fictionalized forms in and with which they are figured. I read Wolf's collapsing of "literature" and "reality" under the sign(a-
ture) of the author as an invitation to explore the terms of that collapsing of
artifice and authenticity, of life and letters—not assuming that "form follows
content," but that form creates, shapes, is content.

In "The Reader and the Writer," we find that the "I" cannot be unproblematically equated with "Christa Wolf" and in fact that the "I" itself does not
remain constant. As we shall see, the succession of at least seven distinct subjects throughout the essay's nine separate sections under the single name of "I"
functions as a rhetorical device, channeling the reader's attention in a very specific direction. It is also difficult not to notice the exclusive use of the generic
masculine for the writer, the reader—indeed for any of the "I"s—throughout
the essay, particularly in light of Wolf's later work on issues of gender. While it

can be argued that Wolf is simply adhering to the conventions of the time, her use of the generic masculine within the essay is in some measure a reflection of its gendered nature: as Wolf employs the essay's traditional authority, she can be said in one sense to be writing as the generic essayist, i.e., as a man.

The essay opens with an ostensibly personal narrative about a trip taken by the first narrator, the Writer, to the Russian city of Gorki. This personal description of experience is embedded within a larger set of questions about the possibilities of writing when old coordinates by which one lived and judged the world are rendered invalid by experience. The narrator wants to establish a new set of coordinates between self, life, reality, and truth: " . . . tremendous efforts people make to grow beyond themselves or, perhaps, to reach up to themselves. This may be the meaning and task of depth in our consciousness" [181]. For the writing subject here, depth is the key to the way in which we make sense of the world and is simultaneously the unique property of prose: memory, experience, projections all combine to create a site from which to describe the world "authentically." The narrator demonstrates this mode of description in "his" sketch of Gorki, which is written in the present tense, as if "he"/Wolf were actually writing this essay in the moment of primary experience: "I am writing this sitting at the dusty desk in my room in the Hotel Rossiya" [180]. In other words, Wolf carefully constructs a writing subject who pretends, among other things, that only five minutes lapse in the writing of the passage: "The five minutes are over. On this journey I have not the time truly to describe them in prose" [181]. This is all quite clearly an example, a means by which Wolf wants to illustrate literature's capacity to transcend the superficiality of the moment through reflection and "depth"; yet she makes this point by means of an interestingly unreflected fiction of temporality. The constructedness of the narrator and the narrator's time is hidden behind the veil of authenticity that accompanies the signature in the genre of the essay.

In the third section of the essay, "Tabula rasa," the writing subject is replaced by a reading subject to whom the author's truth can be conveyed, and for whom prose is to be saved.[7] Here, the "I" or "Wolf" as reading subject leads us through a narrative of personal development: reading is the site of the formation of moral consciousness; books are the primer of civilization. One of the most interesting aspects of this section is the fact that it is written in the form of a negation: what if I had never read a book? Who would I be? The reading subject answers that "without books I am not I" [190]. This move is morally powerful, particularly as Wolf draws on the memory of Nazi book burnings. But it is at least interesting, if not problematic, given Wolf's own historical and political context, that her narrator invokes bourgeois traditions as a model for a more humane socialism. The entire premise here—that subjecthood, civilization, morality, and reading are all basically the same thing—is in some ways a quite conservative one. And the same dynamics of a unified subjectivity that informed her writing subject inform the reading subject as well: "comparing, testing, looking on from outside and gradually learning to see [. . .] oneself" [189].[8] The argument in this section is remarkably binary: "I" becomes synonymous with "good," and the assumption follows that "not I" is not simply something different but an absence, a lack that is "bad."

The notion of reading is clearly limited to the reading of (primarily canonical) literary texts; literature occupies a privileged position in relation to truth, morality, etc. Perhaps Wolf is really creating a moment of political resistance here, books being equated with freedom, with resistance to externally imposed norms. But the resistance is structured by the erection of a new moral authority, namely the author himself [sic]. The signature above both "Observation" and "Tabula rasa" is the same, the "I"s that begin to layer themselves here take on the form of omniscient narrator. Does all of this, on some level, fly in the face of "subjective authenticity"? Or is the omniscient narrator the ultimate "authentic subject"? Seductively, the "I" that this essay would have us accept as individual, particular, limited, in fact reaffirms that universalizing, paradigmatic dimension that is part of the conservative side of the essay and its tradition.

Indeed, in the following four sections of this essay, Wolf employs the authority she has established with the trinity of reader, writer, and text to drive home her moral point. Using again the "I" of the Author, she engages in a series of polemical discussions: against a "filmable prose," that is, one which would communicate only a set of fixed, predetermined meanings; against the novel as a genre that has become degenerate, lifeless, formulaic in its narration; against the French writer and theoretician Robbe-Grillet for questioning the authority of the author. Here, the personal, biographical "I" becomes increasingly fused and confused with a universal writer, and the voice of the essay becomes increasingly dense and powerful. When we look at the construction of this essay as an essay, the globally unifying nature of Wolf's own notion of subjective authenticity becomes clearer: the convergence of "I's" in one speaking subject creates the authorial power that is necessary for Wolf's program to function. Rather than opening a multiplicity of perspectives, the shifting of "I's" every few pages actually produces the effect of a single, unified subject under the signature of "Christa Wolf."

This becomes even clearer in the final sections of the essay, in which the personalized "I" author is replaced by a paradigmatic "he," while the narrative voice joins with the implied reader to form a collective first-person "we": "The writer we are talking about does not, therefore, let himself be pushed into the position of an outsider. . . . " [208]. Both of these moves reinforce the authorial position I have delineated above and underline Wolf's insistence upon her utopian vision: "The writer we are thinking of is profoundly uneasy about man's future, because he is concerned about it. . . . His optimism can be solemn or angry, but never indifferent. As he knows, it is only then that he is entitled to say 'I' from time to time" [209]. As we have seen, this supposedly tentative "I" is actually anything but tentative, being embedded both within specific ideas about subjectivity and within the specific discursive practices of this essay.

It is only in the second section, "Lamento," that the essay's authorial "I" retreats entirely, allowing literature itself to take center stage. Prose "herself" is the subject (or is it object?), a genre that "fights for [her] life . . . This means that [she] has drunk of the poison of self-abandonment" [185].[9] It is significant that this section, the only one in which Wolf declines the use of the first person for her narrator, is also the one that deals most directly and thematically with the notion of the individual subject. In the eyes of this disembodied, narrating subject, prose is the place where the subject, the individual, finds and expresses itself. She—prose—is figured as a moment of resistance to that which threatens her: technology and science. Personified, prose "has a prospect of survival only if it can do something that all the powers massed against it [literally, that press up against her body—*die ihr zu Leibe rücken*] cannot do" [185].

This is the first text in which Wolf sets up an explicit, adversarial opposition of science/nonscience or science/antiscience—and in this case science's opposite happens to be literature. Science has usurped functions previously belonging to prose: newness, "the miraculous," curiosity, imagination. It has violated prose's identity boundaries and at the same time has questioned the integrity of identity, of the individual in general. Wolf's narrator admits that this notion of a human subject is a historical phenomenon that found its beginnings with the "bourgeois phase" [182], but far from using this history as a critical tool, as a means of distancing or of examining its composition from the author's (i.e., Wolf's) particular moment in history, defined by socialism, the narrator dramatizes the pathos of prose's plight, of "her" beleaguered state.

It is a coincidence of grammar that prose is a feminine noun in German ("die Prosa"); but it is not a coincidence that, beyond that given, Wolf explicitly figures this Other as feminine: as that which is written, that which is read, that which is the object of a "masculine" desire to write, to read. "She" is embodied, is victimized by the enemy represented by science. Her author as well as her reader can draw strength from her; she is the one in whom they can find themselves. She is even that which can save them from themselves. In fact, I would argue, it is the "Reader and the Writer" here who are doing violence to prose, forming her in their image in order that she reflect back to them what they desire to see: the "inviolable individual personality" [184]. Given this mammoth agenda and its attendant power politics, it is perhaps not surprising that Wolf conceals the site of (male?) power within the genre she is using—the essay—to defend that other, besieged (female?) genre—prose fiction.

A few years after "The Reader and the Writer," Wolf articulated her critique of science for the first time within a piece of prose fiction. "Self-Experiment: Appendix to a Report" (1974) is a series of reflections on social and philosophical issues of gender inequality that are framed by a futuristic narrative of a sex change experiment. My interest in this text is three-fold: first, the polarization of science and its Other; second, the figuring of that Other as Woman; third, the structuring of narrative authority and its connections to the essay form, even in a piece marked as "fiction."

In this tale of sex change, the masculine and the feminine are immediately circumscribed by and juxtaposed against the binary opposition of science/nonscience. Science appears in the form of "hard" science, the institution of science being embodied in the "Institute of Human Hormonetics" where the female protagonist works. Against this backdrop, Wolf is easily able to fill her characters with stereotypical qualities. The men in the text are at one with the institution they inhabit, with science, while the women who have sought a place there remain excluded, or rather partitioned—i.e., they must accept chauvinistic treatment at the hands of both their male colleagues and their male lovers, being called both inadequate women and inferior scientists. In the words of the protagonist's lover: "Women scientists all right, high female I.Q.'s by all means; but something that is simply not suitable for a woman is this inclination for the absolute" [117].

Thus, when the protagonist and first-person narrator, a leading scientist at the institute, becomes the first human test case for a new drug that can turn a woman into a man ("Peterine Masculinum 199"), she is critically situated both at the intersection of the sexes and at the intersection of the institution and gender. She is neither the one nor the other: "I never succeeded in feeling like a spy operating behind the opponents' front lines in the most perfect of all possible disguises. Instead, I started having difficulty using any of the forms of the personal pronoun 'I' " [121]. What I find interesting is the fact that this experience of multiplicity, of multiple identities, is not translated into a questioning of dualistic (Cartesian) gender identity. Rather than opening up a new space for the woman who is scientist, the narrator speaks a language that implies an originary female/feminine essence hidden behind cultural practices:

> If you look at it that way, Professor, you're right in your jocular remark that *Scientia*, science, though a woman, has a man's intellect. It cost me years of my life learning to submit to that way of thinking where the greatest virtues are non-involvement and impassivity. At present I'm having difficulty regaining access to all those buried regions inside me. [121-22]

The entire narrative consists of a reflective recounting of her experiences while she inhabits a man's body. Ultimately, she rejects that body and masculinity, having concluded that men are incapable of love, and chooses to return to her former female self.

Rather than examining the content of her/his experiences—these can by now be categorized with relative ease as fitting dominant Western notions of male/female gender differences—I would like to explore how these masculine and feminine identities or markings of the narrator are played off of one another in the structure of the narrative and just what they can tell us about the genderization of narrative itself. The polarization of gender identity plays itself out in the very form she chooses for her text. Indeed, she begins with a discussion of precisely this. The female scientist is ostensibly writing this "Appendix to a Report" out of the need for a different form in which to express her thoughts. We never get to read the report itself, the detailed, official account of the sex-change experiment. Instead, we have only the narrator's characterization of it as a text that is circumscribed by the demands of science and is thus as clearly gendered as is her response to it:

> Having had enough of pre-texts and restraining, I prefer to avail myself of straight-

forward language, a woman's prerogative that is far too infrequently used—an insight, by the way, from the time when I was a man, or more precisely, was in danger of becoming one. My experience, still piping-hot, clamors for expression. Happy to have words at my disposal again, I can't help playing with them and admiring their ambiguities, which however will not prevent me from declaring all the data you can extract from my report to be exact and correct and unambiguous. [113]

The simultaneous critique of science and of gender roles, brought here onto the level of narration, is an acknowledgement of the genderization of Western thought, virtually a mapping of Cartesian dualism, the mind/body split—and its consequences. Yet it is a critique that also implicitly accepts that Cartesian map, for the journey that is plotted out for woman in the future partakes equally of the dualism that created the disastrous mess to begin with. The "plot" of the appendix reminds us that the narrator also has mastery of, and participates in, the discourse she is criticizing. The narrator's dual personality does not lead her to engage in a dialectic between the two, resulting in a transformation of some kind in her own perceptions, nor does she acknowledge the irresolvable tension between the two parts of herself. Rather, she rejects one in favor of the other.

She is a scientist yet a woman, an outsider within. By positioning the narrator thus, by anchoring the critique from within, Wolf creates an incredibly powerful authorial voice—the narrator as author of the illicit appendix and of the official report itself. The narrator's authority has a dual location: she is a woman, is a scientist. She became a man. As a woman and scientist alone she had (presumably) nothing to say. Why did it take the experience of manhood to give her the insights that produced the "feminine" text? Becoming a man provides the ground for critique and the knowledge that results in his rejection. In the end, it is her dual experience, as man and woman (as female scientist?), that affords her total insight, makes it possible for her and her alone to see his—i.e., man's—flaw. (Does this merely illustrate her prowess as a scientist, that is, her power of observation?) S/he thus overcomes the blindness and separateness of both, only to reject the Other that is man for her. Indeed, while we never learn the female narrator's name, upon becoming male s/he gives him/herself the name "Anders" (which in German means "different, other"). In order to assert her own female subject position, i.e., to undertake her own process of becoming-subject, or de-objectification, it is as if she is forced to make man just as much an object as has historically been the case in reverse: man objectifying woman, science taming nature. Otherness moves from one pole to the other; woman becomes man, *her* Other. Just as science claimed universality of vision, so too does Wolf's narrator, blocking off the "opposition" by first occupying it. Thus, the model Wolf develops out of a story structured around the transgression of boundaries seems ironically more interested in undergirding a fixed identity and its rigid boundaries. The proclaimed "ambiguities" of her words belie the unambiguity of her position. Bilingual, bisexual, yet moving in no way toward valorization or celebration of that "bi-," of the multiple identities: they are merely a tool with which to affirm a singular identity.

Two more observations that can be made about the problematic structure of this critique help to underline its inner contradictions. The appendix is ultimately not a direct challenge to science or its discourse, i.e., to the official report, in at least two ways. First, it is structured as separate, as "the" alternative to scientific discourse. The "feminine" voice of the appendix never disrupts or disturbs the public report. The second point follows from this: the appendix remains ultimately a private text, an exchange between a man and a woman. While addressed to a man who indeed is not only her boss but also embodies Science itself, it is nevertheless no greater a challenge to the institution than an unpublished letter to the editor. In fact, it is only in the necessity of remaining secret that the narrator finds permission even to articulate her ideas: "The secrecy clauses binding us, which guarantee me the strictest discretion on the part of everyone with access to materials concerning our experiment, also set me at liberty to add these unsolicited notes to my personal report" [113]. "Liberty" here appears to be nothing more than the liberty of silence.

And there is yet another level to consider. This is not merely an anecdote being told to us, the readers. It is a text within a text: an appendix written by a fictional narrator within a short story written by Christa Wolf. Discourse within discourse. In essence, Wolf is having her narrator write an *essay*: that is, the appendix is an essay that is set in opposition to the report, to scientific discourse. Within this piece of prose fiction called "Self-Experiment," then, the essay, or essayistic text "is" or represents Woman, just as prose fiction itself was figured as Woman within "The Reader and the Writer," the essay written and narrated by Wolf. Genre is again gendered. And once again, it is most difficult to locate any space between the voice of Wolf and of her narrator. All clear distinctions between fiction and nonfiction evaporate on the level of narrative voice. In her essay, Wolf used the signature, the mark of nonfiction, to mask the constructedness of her narrative voice. In the short story, does Wolf use the mark of this genre, prose fiction, in order to mask her authorial voice? We are confronted here again with that hermetic seal that marks so much of her work and makes it so difficult to read against the grain of the texts.

In the years following "Self-Experiment," Wolf continued to explore the possibilities of an extended gendered critique of science, not with the literal figure of the woman scientist but with the (abstract) opposition of Woman and Science. This figure can be found at some level in virtually all of her subsequent texts as she moved—at least in the eyes of her Western readers—further and further along a path from Marxism to feminism. While there is indeed evidence of a paradigm shift in Wolf's work between the 1960s and the 1980s, that which remains constant, that which doesn't shift, is perhaps more interesting than that which does. An examination of the similarities, the points of convergence, in both the structure and the content of her later essays, can perhaps bring us closer to an understanding of a social, political, and cultural context quite different from that of the West (where feminism grew out of and/or replaced Marxism as a critical and political paradigm for many intellectuals). Given Wolf's different context, it is crucial to read the move differently. For her, it is less a rejection of her earlier positions than a continuation and extension of them.

Central to Wolf's idea of a socialist practice was the development of the notion of the artist, the writer, as instrument of social change. As early as the 1960s, her enemy is not the class enemy, but rather a way of thinking that undermines the end goal of true individual fulfillment. The enemy is called by many names, not the least of which is Science. This model remains present and central in Wolf's later work; the site occupied by the ideal author (or literature) is inhabited by an increasing number of different characters, but the structure remains the same, so that within this structure, the central positioning—the central authority?—of the author remains a constant, a symbol for the human subject.

In two biographical essays written in the late 1970s, we find Wolf juggling various "inhabitants" of this ongoing author paradigm as she performs her own reading of two women, both of whom were writers connected to German Romanticism: Karoline von Günderrode (1780-1806) and Bettine von Arnim (1785-1859). These commissioned essays—"The Shadow of a Dream: Karoline von Günderrode—a Sketch" (1978) and "Granted! But the Next Life Begins Today: A Letter about Bettine" (1979)—serve an informative historical function as well as an interpretive, politically and culturally framing one; yet they go far beyond their dual function as afterword or introduction.[10] Like Wolf's other essays, they are most definitely "essayistic," staging the presence of a very personal voice, the voice of the essayist. And, as we have seen, Wolf's narrative voice always takes great pains to establish a bond of identity with the character at hand (ideal author, woman scientist). However, as she encounters and tries to incorporate a new multiplicity of elements into her analytical structure, the author/narrator—socialist, Party member, public figure, woman— opens up fissures, moments of instability, even of vulnerability, particularly in the first of the two essays.

The ambiguity and ambivalence with which these problems cut through her texts can be illustrated with a few brief examples from the 1978 essay on Karoline von Günderrode. On the opening page of this lengthy piece, Wolf writes a peculiarly double-voiced narrative: "Before a person can write, he must live, *that is banal and holds for both sexes.* Women lived for a long time without writing; then they wrote—*if the expression is allowed*—with their lives and for their lives. They have been doing that until now, or are doing it now again" [*Dimension*, 55, my emphasis].[11] The seemingly straightforward assertion of these lines, namely that writing is and has been an extraordinarily difficult proposition for women in particular, is simultaneously retracted in her asides (marked by my italics), and it is in the retraction that we become aware of the narrator's presence. There is a curious dialectic of authorial presence/ absence at work here. For the narrator, who clearly wants to identify with Günderrode and sets out by defining her primarily as a writing woman, shrinks back from identification on that basis, as the apologetic rhetoric indicates. Wolf is exploring new territory with Günderrode and Arnim that apparently threatens the stability of her own narrative voice. How can the stable, sure,

central, knowing "I" of her earlier work deal with this new material, the dis-
affected, helpless, sometimes hopeless voices of women who, like Wolf herself,
were writers and social progressives?

There is a moment's hesitation as the author struggles with this clash of
gender and genre. Here the ideal of "subjective authenticity" is most transpar-
ently that, an ideal; if we look closely enough, the fault lines in the envisioned
co-mingling of author/narrator/character become visible. If Wolf were to draw
her connection to Günderrode and Arnim as a woman any more explicitly—
she thematizes them as women but not in connection to her "own" narrative
voice as a woman's—the authorial voice of the essay that Christa Wolf has developed would be threatened. The first person singular is notably absent from
the Günderrode essay: the reader must content herself with a "we" that is not
gender-identified but rather embeds itself within a larger social context (perhaps that of GDR intelligentsia, a modern-day elite that would bring us back to
the old European tradition of the essay form?) that encourages identification
with the Early Romantics in general:

> It cannot be an accident that we have begun to inquire about those who were writ-
> ten off, to challenge the judgment that was passed on them, to contest it and to
> render it void—fascinated by relationship and proximity, though mindful of the
> time and the events that lie between us and them . . . we look around, driven by the
> need that we can no longer deny to understand ourselves: our role in contemporary
> history, our hopes and their limits, our achievement and our failure, our possibili-
> ties and their restrictedness. And, if at all possible, the reasons for all of that. Look-
> ing backward . . . [we] stumble upon lines that touch us, dashed off in a generous,
> flowing, very legible woman's hand on green quarto stationery—green protects the
> writer's weak eyes—which we hold in our hand, not without being moved: "A pyg-
> mian age, a pygmian race is now at play, very good in its style." [56–57]

Ultimately, then, she does not invoke a specific woman so much as the Romantics as a group: "A small group of intellectuals—avantgarde without a hin-
terland" [58]. By finding and delineating a "we," the essay manages to tame its
subject and find its own equilibrium again. Rather than the material transforming the writing "I," the "I" transforms the material and its ambiguities, its
contradictions into a (newly coherent) narrative. Sense is made of it all. Fundamental to this "sense" is the humanist concept of "personality":

> To be known: the earnest desire of women who don't want to live through men, but
> through themselves. Its roots appear to be here, and it continues until today, and
> even now is more seldom fulfilled than unfulfilled, because the catchword "person-
> ality," with which the bourgeoisie took up its place, could never be redeemed by the
> majority of the producers. [75]

If there is a challenge raised here, it is not against a bourgeois ideology of Self,
simply against that ideal's exclusive application. And when Wolf's narrator is able
to link Marxist with feminist rhetoric and isolate the problem in terms of "self-
alienation" [68], one almost has the feeling that it is less historical sympathy or
political anger than personal affront. The blurring of fictional boundaries, the con-

fusion of author/narrator/subject matter is not necessarily a decentering one: as it is deployed in Wolf's texts, it comes around again to solidifying a central analytical, authorial, power position. Multivocality becomes control. Thus the narrative of Günderrode's and Arnim's particular alienation or objectification—as women, as political rebels, whatever—cannot and does not override but rather becomes subordinate to the "lamento" on the writer-as-outsider in German history: "The literature of the Germans as a battlefield—that would be another way of looking at it. Poets—and this is not a complaint—are predestined to be victims of others and themselves [*Opfern und Selbstopfern*]" [115].

It is certainly not unimportant to recall the specific circumstances in and under which Wolf herself is writing here. For an integrated member of GDR society, indeed, someone with a high degree of public and official regard, who nevertheless struggles to develop a critical voice within that context, narrative strategies are also clearly political strategies. To whom is she appealing with her "we" and "our"? Her fellow GDR citizens? Other voices of internal opposition? All her readers, everywhere? By employing a plural narrative voice, Wolf appears to be veiling the particularity of her own political situation with a universal(izing) notion of the writer. This is one of the most fascinating—and simultaneously difficult—contradictions I find within Wolf's work. She consistently foregrounds the individual human subject as a site of resistance in the face of totalitarianism, yet at the same time her ideal human subject itself partakes of morally totalizing strategies. Here again we see what is perhaps a reflection of Wolf's peculiar status within the GDR, as both insider and outsider. Seeking reform rather than revolution, she avoids the instability that a radical critique of GDR-style socialist humanism would cause; instead, she seeks to preserve the terms, (re)investing them with different values.

Another fascinating kind of contrary motion that we find here, particularly in the Bettine essay, concerns a simultaneous intensification of both the particular and the universal. The figures of the Writer and Woman and Socialism are conflated [*Dimension*, 127-28]. Abstract concepts that are positive for Wolf become gender-identified (such as socialism and Romanticism), and Woman herself becomes more and more synonymous with the notion of the ideal author. And just as women in particular are moving toward center stage as the embodiment of that ideal, just as certain abstract concepts are being personalized by the assignation of gender, the space occupied by the opposition—the enemy, so to speak—is expanding by leaps and bounds and is increasingly depersonalized, anonymous. That is, Science is now figured as the enemy of all of the above, as a monolithic negativity, the force which now confronts all that is good—not just "feminine" prose but all writing, women, humane principles as manifested in socialist and Romantic philosophy. In this particular incarnation of the general schema of Woman vs. Science that we have sketched thus far, Wolf picks up on and echoes a central moment in early Romanticism, namely the critique of instrumental reason, of an Enlightenment gone awry. But whereas the early Romantics saw themselves as ultimately connected to, implicated in, and even indebted to that which they were criticizing, Wolf presses the analogy into one of pure opposition, thereby preserving her own binary analytical structure.

Wolf's aesthetic response to the increasingly global nature of her critique is, as I indicated above, an increasing personalization of the split, an ever more intimate relationship with her material. As she becomes more comfortable with directly addressing women's issues, the hesitancy to identify, to mark herself as a woman begins to fade. We can see this in the Bettine essay in at least two ways. First, the narrative "I" returns, this time explicitly gendered. Second, it is joined by another implied "voice"—more properly an addressee, also figured as female. Perhaps the construction of a female reader for the text makes it first possible to construct a female narrator (or, in the doubled nature of things, to acknowledge that, behind the narrator, there is a female author writing). All this takes place within the context of a larger formal shift, namely to the form of the letter. Though the text itself is still heavily biographical, filled with factual information, at critical points Wolf's narrator, the writer of the "letter," steps forward and directly addresses her implied reader. These points of convergence, at which Bettine, narrator, and addressee are drawn into an intimate "dialogue," sometimes revolve around the political, sometimes around common female experience. The letter is used most consciously and explicitly as an echo of the epistolary novel to which Wolf is writing this as a companion essay. It is, as a form or genre in its own right, clearly seen as an alternative to the existing male-identified genres. Building upon the oppositional structure outlined above, Wolf now deploys the epistolary essay in order to draw all that has been marked as good into its clearly defined space, which for her is also the site of immediate experience, of an essence that has not yet been deformed.

This essay closes with a dramatic gesture as a contrast is drawn between this intimate image of women communicating through a letter and another, strangely abstract and foreboding voice. Echoing a particular exchange between Günderrode and Arnim in the latter's novel, in which Arnim has Günderrode speak of a universal voice that she must constantly resist, Wolf's narrator closes her letter by saying: "You know how, and about what, the universal voice speaks to us today" [154]. This cryptic statement is open-ended only in its vague abstractness. As a cipher for the ominous, the anonymous, it appears to encompass everything that is outside of that constructed female sphere of communication and preservation of values. Everything that has been criticized in the course of this essay—State, Man, Science, Technology—coalesces as a kind of totalitarian evil. In this sense, it in fact brings perfect closure to the essay.

Two years later, Wolf composed another epistolary essay in conjunction with her work on a novel about the myth of Cassandra.[12] Entitled "A Letter, About Unequivocal and Ambiguous Meaning, Definiteness and Indefiniteness; About Ancient Conditions and New View-Scopes, About Objectivity" (1981), this essay can be read both formally as an extension of the Bettine essay and philosophically as a revised version of "The Reader and the Writer" in which she updates her earlier aesthetic credo. Thirteen years after "The Reader and the Writer," Wolf's concerns are thoroughly gendered, and the authorial "I" is not the multi-layered one of the earlier piece. Instead, we find here a single narrative "I" that collapses the various levels of the earlier piece into a personal, consciously feminized voice. Thus, the locus of the authorial voice has shifted dramatically. Wolf's rhetorical strategies have clearly changed with her material. But has she "given up" any of that authorial power? If we keep in mind the development across time of her binary system of morality, of values, it would seem unlikely that her construction of an explicitly female author/narrator entails any such limitation.

"A Letter . . . About Objectivity," like the Bettine essay, is a stylized letter, that is, it imitates the letter, a form that is often associated with women historically and with the "feminine" aesthetically. Anne Herrmann has discussed Wolf's conscious insertion of the "feminine" letter into the "masculine" essay as creating "a tension between the two genres," emphasizing the historical private/public dichotomy between women's and men's writing practices [Herrmann, 41]. From the juxtaposition of the two genres, Herrmann draws the conclusion that the letter undermines the essay through its introduction of dialogue and the problematization of the position from which the subject speaks. This is clearly Wolf's intention, given the content of this essay, which attempts a full-scale critique of Western patriarchy and aesthetic norms from a feminist perspective. But to what extent does Wolf actually subvert, and to what extent does she support the kind of essayistic authority delineated above? What has changed, and what has stayed the same?

Herrmann writes that, historically, "Letter writing allowed a woman to create a network of relations maintained primarily on paper and to construct a subjectivity tailored to the expectations of the addressee. She gave pleasure by artificially composing a self that posed as artless, as the product of involuntary self-revelation" [37]. Thus, the tension that Herrmann describes between genres would generate the following pairs: masculine/feminine, essay/letter, public/private, artistic/artless. Ironically, however, in his attempt to define the essay genre, Graham Good recalls a different set of oppositions, noting that Montaigne saw the writing of essays "as artless rather than artistic" [Good, 13]. For all their differences, essay and letter would seem to exist on some kind of continuum, and the common attribute of "artlessness" is of particular importance if we consider the construction of narrative authority. And how do these dynamics shift further in the case of a letter that is not really a letter? Is it not possible that Wolf's fictional addressee — "Dear A." — is the means by which she can artificially compose a writing self that poses as artless; a different means in a different context, but ultimately the same goal as in "The Reader and the Writer"? The transparency of the signature that provides the essayist with such authority is still intact; and in fact, this "letter" functions by both doubling the signature, the mark of authenticity, and resting upon the already existing authority of the essay which remains, after all, the frame containing the letter here. As in "The Reader and the Writer," the construction of this kind of authority is imperative to Wolf's project, which is a somewhat dif-

ferent one by now but presented with the same moral urgency and an even
more global character. By using the letter form, Wolf not only makes a conscious gesture toward writing an alternative literary history that would include
women; she also develops a new rhetorical strategy for anchoring her authorial
voice in a new incarnation of "subjective authenticity."

The complicated and contradictory nature of this move becomes clearer
when we look at the content of "A Letter . . . About Objectivity." Wolf reads a
poem by Ingeborg Bachmann in which voice is the issue, and what Wolf finds
so fascinating—yet also irritating—about it is its ultimate indeterminacy:
"Whom is she addressing? Herself, addressed as 'you'? The woman whom she
later calls 'Love'? (Assuming that this 'Love' is a woman.) Do you have the
same experience with this poem that I do? The deeper I get into it, the closer to
its ground (which however I cannot feel underfoot), the more I am caught by
the puzzle [*die Irritation*—literally, the irritation] to which it bears witness, and
which it does not undertake to resolve . . . " [*Cassandra*, 275]. Wolf embraces
Bachmann's ambiguity and simultaneously resists incorporating it into her
own writing practice. "To be not allowed to be I, not allowed to be you, but 'it':
the object of others' purposes" [275]. This is the central point of Wolf's critique, one whose lines she draws from Greek mythology to Goethe to modern
science. And it is perhaps the singlemindedness of this focus that causes her to
render that critique of the objectification of women from what I would still call
a very male position, the authoritative position of the "masculine" essayist
posing as "feminine" letter-writer. She proclaims the need for aesthetic practices that would be predicated on an "I-Thou" relationship, yet relies herself on
the construction of a unified subject position that by definition precludes the
entrance of the Other. Wolf's text provides potential critical tools for uncover-
ing the politics of the essay; yet, ironically enough, this most "feminist" of her
work—her transformation of the essay into a letter—masks the underlying
structure upon which she and her authority depend.

NOTES

1. I am very grateful to Ruth-Ellen B. Joeres, Lisa Roetzel, Ginny Steinhagen, and
Arlene Teraoka for their helpful comments and incisive criticism of earlier drafts of this
article.
2. Graham Good writes:

> In so far as its utterances are not presented as fictional, the essay does imply a claim to count
> as knowledge. But this knowledge is not part of an organized whole. . . . The form emerges
> during the reorganization of knowledge in the late sixteenth and early seventeenth centuries,
> but it is not actually incorporated into the "new philosophy" of the seventeenth century (es-
> sentially what we now call "science"). We can see the essay as a commentary which has bro-
> ken free from its "text," and implicitly from "textuality" conceived as the unity and interde-
> pendence of all writing, to become self-contained and *sui generis*. [3]

3. See, for example, Herrmann, Kuhn [56-60, 186-90], and Sevin. Herrmann does address some specific issues of genre in her discussion of one particular essay. I have not, however, found any independent examination of narrative strategies in Wolf's essays.

4. Born in 1929, Wolf was 20 years old when the GDR was founded in 1949; 1989 saw both her sixtieth birthday and the "peaceful revolution" leading to unification of the two German states a year later.

5. One interesting manifestation of Wolf's dual identity is the fact that she was asked to write the preamble to a new constitution drafted by a "round table" group that existed during the brief experimental period before unification with the Federal Republic.

6. I am retaining the generic masculine that Wolf herself employs here. Interestingly, the English translation demonstrates the power of the "signature" in its pronominal transformations: "She decides to tell . . . foundation of her own experience."

7. It is interesting to note that the English translation of this essay stresses these identities all the more with its rendering of the title; in contrast, the original German ["Lesen und Schreiben"] emphasizes the process, literally "Reading and Writing."

8. The translation reads "learning to see for oneself." I have omitted the word "for," as this is a mistranslation of the German [*sich selbst sehen lernen*].

9. Though the German use of gendered [here: feminine] pronouns for inanimate objects makes no English "sense," I retain it here in order to emphasize my point about Wolf's genderization of "prose" on other levels, i.e. as body and as victim. The standard English translation quite properly reads: ". . . fights for *its* life . . . *it* has drunk the poison of self-abandonment" [my emphasis].

10. Both essays were written as accompanying pieces to new editions of their work: the essay on Günderrode appears in a collection of that writer's poetry and prose, the one on Arnim as an afterword to that writer's epistolary novel about Günderrode.

11. The translations from these two essays are my own.

12. Ostensibly a (feminist) retelling of the Trojan War, the novel *Cassandra* performs a global critique of postindustrial, nuclear, patriarchal civilization. Four related lectures that Wolf delivered in the West were published as essays in conjunction with the novel.

WORKS CITED

Good, Graham. *The Observing Self: Rediscovering the Essay.* London/New York: Routledge, 1988.

Herrmann, Anne. "The Epistolary Essay: A Letter." *The Dialogic and Difference: 'An/Other Woman' in Virginia Woolf and Christa Wolf.* New York: Columbia University Press, 1989. 32-61.

Kamuf, Peggy. *Signature Pieces: On the Institution of Authorship.* Ithaca: Cornell University Press, 1988.

Kuhn, Anna. *Christa Wolf's Utopian Vision: From Marxism to Feminism.* Cambridge/New York: Cambridge University Press, 1988.

Mowitt, John. "The Essay as Instance of the Social Character of Private Experience." *Prose Studies* 12 (1989): 274-84.

Sevin, Dieter. "The Plea for Artistic Freedom in Christa Wolf's 'Lesen und Schreiben' and *Nachdenken über Christa T.*: Essay and Fiction as Mutually Supportive Genre Forms." *Studies in GDR Culture and Society 2.* Ed. Margy Gerber. Washington, D.C.: University Press of America, 1982. 45-58.

Wolf, Christa. "A Letter, About Unequivocal and Ambiguous Meaning, Definiteness and Indefiniteness; About Ancient Conditions and New View-Scopes, About Objectivity." *Cassandra: A Novel and Four Essays*. Tr. Jan van Heurck. New York: Farrar, Straus, Giroux, 1984: 272-305.

_____. "Nun ja! Das nächste Leben geht aber heute an: Ein Brief über die Bettine" ["Granted! But The Next Life Begins Today: A Letter about Bettine"]. *Die Dimension des Autors*. Vol. II. Berlin/Weimar: Aufbau, 1986: 116-54.

_____. "Präambel" [Preamble], *Verfassungsentwurf für die DDR* [draft of new GDR constitution]. Arbeitsgruppe "Neue Verfassung der DDR" des Runden Tisches. Berlin: BasisDruck and Staatsverlag der DDR, April 1990.

_____. *The Quest for Christa T.*. Tr. Christopher Middleton. New York: Farrar, Straus, Giroux, 1970.

_____. "The Reader and the Writer." *The Reader and the Writer: Essays, Sketches, Memories*. Tr. Joan Becker. New York: International Publishers, 1977. 177-212.

_____. "Der Schatten eines Traumes: Karoline von Günderrode—ein Entwurf" ["The Shadow of a Dream: Karoline von Günderrode—a Sketch"]. *Die Dimension des Autors*. Vol. II. Berlin/Weimar: Aufbau, 1986: 55-115.

_____. "Self-Experiment: Appendix to a Report." Tr. Jeanette Clausen. *New German Critique* 13 (Winter 1978): 113-31.

CHAPTER SEVEN

Essay, Gender, and *Mestizaje*

Victoria Ocampo and Gabriela Mistral

AMY KAMINSKY

When Alfonso Reyes called the essay "this centaur of genres," he was, on the surface, referring to the form's irregularity, a cross between two species possible only in the imagination [quoted in Skirius, 10].[1] Yet Reyes's image is also unmistakably masculine—in its strength and power the centaur is always half man, half stallion, always bearded, often bellicose. On the other hand, the potentially transgressive nature of the essay, the otherwise unclassifiable, leftover prose form, suggests that it belongs in the camp of "the feminine," that elusive region of negation and difference. Or by resorting to still another gender stereotype we might say that, stolidly claiming its right to be literal and utilitarian, the essay is characterized by the purported practicality of the housewife and the down-to-earth straightforwardness attributed to the *campesina*, or peasant woman.

Clearly, there is too much meaning in the words naming gender difference for us to be able to gender genre. Claiming that the essay is a feminine genre is as meaningless as calling it masculine; the terms of gender are too fluid. It is not just that they carry different meanings in different times and places, but that even in a single time and place they bear so much meaning that their ostensible characteristics become a grab-bag from which we can pick and choose. It is easy to say the essay is masculine and call it hard, centaur-like, the product of a culturally authorized individual, or to say it is feminine and call it labile, practical, or the product of an idiosyncratic mind. To do either is to comply with traditional, most often stultifying, notions of masculinity and femininity. Rather than attempt to define the essay in the slippery terms of gender, it makes more sense for feminist criticism to name the women essayists—despite the fact that the category "woman" is contested—and see what their writing looks like. For however unstable "woman" might be, she is still a historical category recognizable to the neighbors, the grocer, and her publisher if she can find one. She has not been particularly visible to the authors of literary history, which makes it difficult to locate women in the official record of the essay in Latin America, despite the fact that journalism, which often meant essay writing, was probably the first manifestation of women's literature in at least one Latin American country, Argentina.[2] Moreover, recent research on women's journalism compiled by Janet Greenburg has unearthed 373 Latin American periodicals produced by and for women, the first dating from the seventeenth century. To say, then, that the Latin American essay is "masculine" is not to reveal some ultimate truth about the form itself but to point to the fact that those essayists who have made it into the canon are virtually all men. Antonio Urrello's recent and otherwise sophisticated study of the essay in Latin America is not unusual in containing no women at all.

Gabriela Mistral (Chile, 1889–1957) and Victoria Ocampo (Argentina, 1890–1979) are the women of their generation who have come closest to being taken seriously as essayists. Martin Stabb's study of the Latin American essay of ideas makes brief reference to both Mistral and Ocampo but refers to no other women; Mistral is the sole woman included in John Skirius's anthology of Latin American essayists; and David William Foster ignores Mistral but includes Ocampo as his token woman. Mistral and Ocampo are best known as icons of Latin American culture and letters, Mistral as an educator and Nobel laureate in poetry, and Ocampo as the founder and publisher of *Sur* (South), a long-lived and influential journal. Though they were contemporaries who were well acquainted with, and apparently fond of, each other, Mistral and Ocampo are rarely discussed together. To read them side-by-side is to juxtapose two women essayists whose similarities and differences suggest the tensions and contradictions within the essay form itself. To keep them isolated from each other, as so much criticism and literary history have, makes each one seem somehow monstrous in her singularity. This imposed isolation, conjoined with the critical neglect of their essays, serves, however unintentionally, to maintain the masculine hegemony of the genre.

Thus, the world of Latin American essay writing has been a man's world. Forceful, persuasive arguments from the pen of a woman are commonly read as shrill, and the very subjectivity that is, according to some critics, the hallmark of the essay is understood to be tempered in men's writing while in women's it is read as self-indulgence. This charge has frequently been made to discredit the essays of Victoria Ocampo. Gabriela Mistral, on the other hand, quite consciously chose to suppress personal and anecdotal references in her essays and to adopt a reassuringly neutral tone, avoiding censure. Ironically, like women essay writers within the region, the Latin American essay as a whole has been undervalued internationally, and even internally, because its concerns have not been the concerns of Europe.

In Latin America the essay is an instrumental genre primarily concerned with the identification and elaboration of national or regional identity—the construction of Latin America and its component nations. Writing about the nineteenth-century Spanish essay, Mary Lee Bretz argues that the form is primarily expository and persuasive and—unlike narrative—"always retains a direct and immediate connection with the author and the reader's world" [Bretz, 40].[3] As functional texts Latin American essays are meant to change minds and to change culture. In times of instability and ambiguity they seek to name reality. For that reason it is important that they be made available through inexpensive and quickly produced means. The book of essays intended as such—or the book-length essay—is rare in Latin America. Latin American essays are published in newspapers and magazines, or given as speeches, only sometimes to be later collected in edited editions.

The Latin American essay's traditional role as an instrument of nation-building has been seen as an unfortunately necessary prelude to dealing with "universal" topics. Latin American critics themselves have too easily accepted the fiction of a transcendent universality to which they wish their essayists would aspire. Alberto Zum Felde, for example, writes, "in comparison to the majority of essayistic production with an American theme—national or continental—the works with universal material—those that treat general problems of philosophical, esthetic, or sociological bent, are few" [quoted in Ferrer Aponte, 15].[4] Marie Solange Ferrer Aponte is less disapproving, but she too values the purported universal: "Few essayists reflect interests that transcend the American problematic in all its aspects. You have to know who you are before you can enter the intellectual community" [Ferrer Aponte, 15].[5]

The "parochialism" these critics lament is only a deficiency insofar as what is European is already coded as universal. Within this Eurocentric view, nevertheless, essays by Latin American women can only be received as the further particularization of an already scandalously private conversation. Such multiple marginalization makes these women's suppression in the official lists predictable. What is read as their excessive subjectivity or insularity, however, is really just a measure of the distance between the writing of the other (Latin American, woman) and the Eurocentric masculinist who occupies the space he himself calls normative. He, of course, can claim that his subjective stance is objective only because it coincides with his own definition of the universal. Yet this specious objectivity remains the sought-after prize. Ciriaco Morón Arroyo, for example, defines the essay as "the predisciplinary genre that treats the themes that now constitute the object of social science," asserting that "in the essay social realities are studied by individual observation while in science they are studied by means of statistics or other methods" [Morón Arroyo, 9].[6] Even so, he comes down, eventually, on the side of science, deauthorizing, in the process, the most subjective of writers—the national and gendered other.

But authority is crucial to the essayist, and, as Bretz points out, the essay's goal to move the reader to some sort of action or change of opinion results in a "discourse [that] invests a tremendous amount of energy into constructing its own authority" [Bretz, 45]. This authority, Bretz says, can be based on neither power, for the essayist, unlike the writer of a learned treatise, is not an expert, nor solidarity, since the essay is, in this definition, addressed to an audience that needs to be persuaded. Authority can, however, be based on social location.

The problem of authorization for the woman essayist is multiply vexed. Recently, feminists, Marxists, and deconstructionists have discredited the belief that a naturally occurring intelligence, unclouded by distracting issues, enables men of a certain class to write essays authoritatively. That belief was still current, however, when Mistral and Ocampo were writing; and we may well, even now, question how women, gerrymandered out of the district of objectivity, have managed to claim the authority to write. Bretz finds that in the essay "there is a constant movement of assertion and then denial of authority, of deference to the reader followed by the affirmation of authorial identity and will" [Bretz, 44]. The assertion/denial pattern is often covert, and, I would argue, the assertion mode particularly may occur extra-textually. Part of Ocampo and Mistral's assertion of authorial will in the essays under consideration consists in these writers' assumption that their readers know who they are. My presentation below of a considerable amount of biographical information is meant to convey that the "who they are" that helps authorize Mistral and Ocampo has to do with the very issues of *mestizaje*, the conflictual and generative mix of European and native, so critical to their writing.

Victoria Ocampo's Argentina and Gabriela Mistral's Chile belong to Latin America's southern cone, the part of the continent that is most Europeanized. This region has a smaller remaining indigenous population than the more northern Andean countries or Mexico and Central America, and fewer people of African descent than the Caribbean or Brazil. The particular relationships Chile and Argentina have with the rest of the continent and with Europe and the United States are nuanced differently from similar relationships in Mexico, for example, which is both in the immediate shadow of the United States and self-consciously *mestizo* in its identity. I will, nevertheless, argue that *mestizaje* is a useful metaphor for the essays of Mistral and Ocampo, and for the genre as a whole in Latin America.[7] Rather than the mythical, impossible mixture that is the centaur, the essay can be more profitably thought of in terms of the very present, localized *mestizo*—the American born of the contact in the struggle of, broadly speaking, two cultures, indigenous and Iberian. Though Ocampo wrote facing Europe and Mistral with an eye toward the indigenous world, each in her own way wrote to champion a syncretic America, composed of European and indigenous threads.

Victoria Ocampo was born in Buenos Aires in 1890 to one of the most powerful families of Argentina. As a young woman she made the grand tour of Europe required of her social class. Enthralled by the new art, music, and writing she encountered in Europe, Ocampo decided that the bridging of European and Spanish American culture would be her life's work. Her journal, *Sur*, had an immense impact on the development of Argentine high culture, and both she and it were part of a great controversy about the appropriate relationship between Argentine and European culture, in which issues of class, nationalism, and anti-colonialism came together. Ocampo found a personal authority grounded in her "good taste," which she attributed to the loosely constructed education she received as a daughter of the Argentine oligarchy. Her social status gave Ocampo the impression that she could affect the cultural reality of her country, and her class position provided her with the financial means and the sense of entitlement that made it seem inevitable to her that she do so.

Born Lucila Godoy Alcayaga in rural Chile in 1889, one year before Ocampo, Gabriela Mistral was raised in the town of Monte Grande in the Valley of Elqui. As a young teacher she won a national poetry contest for her trilogy, "Los sonetos de la muerte" (The death sonnets), launching her career as both a poet and an educator. The legend of the sensitive young poet grieving over the death of her beloved in these three poems stamped Mistral as the perpetual virgin poet-teacher who would dedicate her life to other people's children, her passion to God, and her energy to the wretched of the earth. Mistral's work for social justice was always expressed in terms of traditional gender expectations, though the life she led was hardly conventional. Mistral represented Chile in various international cultural organizations and served in ambassadorial posts or consul offices in Spain, France, Italy, Brazil, and Mexico. She taught in the United States and Puerto Rico and lived the last years of her life on Long Island, working for UNESCO. Like other Latin American émigrés, she earned a precarious living as a journalist, writing essays for magazines and newspapers. She published four books of poetry in her lifetime and left one posthumous volume.

Mistral, from a less privileged class than Ocampo, sought a different source of legitimacy for her writing. She assumed a moral or spiritual authority that would speak through her: the writer as conduit. Once Mistral became an internationally acclaimed poet, her authority as an essayist grew stronger, but she sought to avoid inserting herself into her prose. Ocampo, on the other hand, needed to be present in her texts since it was her very particular, idiosyncratic taste that authorized her to write. Unlike Ocampo, who was instrumental in institutionalizing her own and other people's writing, Mistral showed little interest in collecting and publishing her work. Their very different sources of authorization manifested themselves in different styles and modes and in distinct beliefs about what it meant to map the culture of a continent. The legends that surround these women set them up as opposites. Mistral: austere, shy, Indian-identified, old-fashioned, selfless; Ocampo: worldly, Europe-identified, modern, feminist, individualist. Women of the same generation, they had sharply opposing views on gender. Mistral was an essentialist; Ocampo tended toward a cultural constructionist view.

Mistral's and Ocampo's conflicting understanding of the place they wanted women to occupy in the world, and therefore their understanding of their own role as public figures and writers, decisively marked the way in which they entered the conversation about the nature of Latin American identity. Mistral was deeply affected by the class and race oppression she saw as the primary source of women's suffering. "Poemas de las madres" (Poems of mothers), a collection of prose meditations on pregnancy and motherhood, calls for a re-valuing of traditional feminine roles, a change in attitude toward motherhood and reproduction that would earn women the respect they deserved.[8] Mistral was able to

turn on its ear her extraordinarily conservative program for women as repro-
ducers and guardians of traditional values and utilize it for a radical political
agenda. In her 1931 essay, "Conversación sobre la tierra con las mujeres Portorriqueñas" (Conversation about the land with Puerto Rican women), she
maintains that because women are naturally connected to the land, it is they
who must raise the alarm and stop the foreign expropriation of Latin American
territory. This nationalistic argument cast in gender terms is a radical project
with a gender-conservative justification.

Unlike Mistral, Ocampo was a self-identified feminist who, in such essays
as "La trastienda de la historia" (The backroom of history), worked to change
the legal and social oppression of women by breaking down the notion of separate spheres for women and unmasking the injustice of prevailing laws, institutions, and assumptions that kept women from participating fully in society.[9]
Ocampo's milieu was urban rather than rural, her world-view cosmopolitan
rather than nationalistic. The criticism that she was too blithe about the dangers of incorporating European and North American values, though over-
stated, was not ill-founded.[10]

Mistral gained a platform from which to speak for and about indigenous
America by virtue of her stature in European America. Her success as a poet
was, almost from the outset, internationally determined, and her subsequent
participation in institutionalizing public education in Chile and Mexico led, in
turn, to an even wider international stage.[11] She was in a position to win the
Nobel Prize because her poetry, first nominated by Central Americans, was
available in Europe and promoted by the Swedish writer Ellen Key, who, like
Mistral, championed the cause of elevating the stature of traditional womanhood and giving motherhood its due.[12] Mistral lived most of her adult life as
an émigré, despite her passionate Americanism. Just as she lived a life she did
not affirm for other women, Mistral lived outside a Chile for which she felt
profound nostalgia.

Ocampo, on the other hand, travelled widely but always lived in Argentina.
Her Europhilia was firmly rooted in the South American metropolis. She challenged Latin American gender assumptions both in her life and her writing, using ideas that came from a myriad of sources and places, including Europe and
the United States. She brought the new ideas she found in the rest of the world
to Argentina, hosting a wide range of artists, writers, and thinkers. Ocampo
was aware that culture could be constructed, and she was going to be one of its
architects. The culture that she was building was striated, however, with elements that she may not have expected. To "elevate" culture in Latin America is,
by definition, to engage in a racially charged enterprise. In the 1920s and
1930s it suggested a rejection of the indigenous, the folkloric, the anthropo-
logically interesting, and an embracing of the European, the purely aesthetic,
the modern.[13] All the while, Ocampo insisted on her American identity and
championed a Latin American reality that had every right to claim and transform international culture but that could still claim its uniqueness through its
Indian ancestry.[14] Ocampo's Europeanism and Mistral's Indianism seem to be

opposite impulses, but structurally they are similar, since they are both about the consolidation of American identity, and each inevitably relies on the other for its fulfillment. They are manifestations of a *mestizo* America, and this consciousness of *mestizaje* not only informs the essays under discussion but also authorizes Ocampo and Mistral to speak.

Victoria Ocampo's "El último año de Pachacutec" (The last year of Pachacutec) is an outspoken demand for women's equality, but it also sets itself a subtextual task—the making of an authentic Latin American female self. The essay accomplishes this task by bringing together the European and indigenous strains in creating such an identity. In this one brief essay, written for the newspaper *La Nación* on the occasion of International Women's Year, Ocampo invokes both Friedrich Engels and Angela Davis, as well as two indigenous women from the period of Latin American conquest and colonization—Cortés' translator and mistress, Malinche, and her own Guaraní Indian great-grandmother Agueda.[15] In "Mujeres en la academia" (Women in the academy), Ocampo again invokes Agueda, in conjunction with Virginia Woolf and Gabriela Mistral: the Indian, the European and the *Mestiza*. This essay, which she wrote first as a speech for her induction into the Argentine Academy of Letters, has as its topic the making of the Latin American female writing subject. In it Ocampo claims that it was Gabriela Mistral's recognition of her as a quintessential American that justifies her admission into the Argentine Academy. Ocampo recalls how Mistral compared her to the ubiquitous *curro*, a spiny flowering shrub weed of the pampa, telling the Academy that that is "the only letter of recommendation [she wishes] to offer them" ["Mujeres," 21].

Mistral's America is indigenous in its impulse, but she is *mestiza* and necessarily constructs her Indian America from the outside. Here again Mistral effaces herself: she does not embody the America she champions. In contrast to Ocampo, who claims for herself all the physical concreteness and racial strains of America, Mistral absents herself as much as possible from her text. Mistral's companion essays on Indians, "El tipo del indio americano" (The American Indian type) and "Silueta de la india" (Silhouette of the Indian woman), are aesthetic constructions with political ends.

Most startling about "The American Indian Type," given Mistral's essentialist views on gender, is its *conscious* construction of race. Her intent in this essay is to counter the self-hate in *mestizos* that is the result of racism, based on the rejection of the Indian in society and the Indian in the self. She ascribes that racism to an aversion to the Indian "type"—the physical characteristics that are labeled ugly and that have a parallel in racial stereotypes that denigrate Indians, yet she comes perilously close to subscribing to racist stereotypes herself:

One of the reasons that dictate the Creole repugnance to confessing the Indian in our blood, one of the origins of our fear of saying, loyally, that we are *mestizos*, is so-called "Indian ugliness." It is held as an unassailable truth; it has been accepted as three and two are five. It goes together with other phrases engraved in stone: "Indians are lazy" and "Indians are bad." ["El tipo," 151][16]

After she points out that we neglect to teach our children that criteria for beauty are not universal, Mistral goes on to show that the idealized type that is the white race is based on a fiction created in Greece out of a composite. Mistral suggests the same sort of fiction be employed to design a beautiful Indian type, out of the best physical characteristics of the different indigenous groups: the body of what she calls the red-skinned Indian (here she conflates all the North American nations), the skull of the Maya, the eyes of the Quechua. She concedes that the nose and mouth are problematic—most Indian noses tend to be overly wide (too African?), but she comes up with the aquiline Mayan nose. Just as this begins to sound impossibly racist, Mistral swerves and begins to define these physical characteristics in terms of the social and cultural oppression of the Indians:

> The mouth, also, is too thick in some lower groups of the river basin, where the body is crushed by the heat or swelled in the primal mud; but just like the slender nose of the Arab, it may be found with lips as thin as a leaf of corn, a cut and cutting thinness that is most expressive of malicious humor and the grimace of pain. This Indian mouth tends to fall toward the sides with the disdain that marks these races, people who know they are as worthy as any other for their talents and virtues and who have been infinitely "humiliated and offended." The edges of those mouths fall with more melancholy than bitterness, and they rise abruptly in a mocking laugh, surprising those who believe the Indian is submerged in a sad animality. ["El tipo," 156].[17]

In this passage Mistral shifts the ground. Where first they were pasted together out of parts, Indians now acquire some agency. The thinness of their lips may "be cut" (passive), but it is also "cutting" (active). This facial feature is expressive of irony and pain, of disdain and melancholy. It is, finally, a surprise to those who would relegate Indians to a definition of ugliness that is a form of otherness, as well as to those who would merely pity them. In the end, Mistral rescues this essay from its apparent racism by compelling her reader to recognize the humanity of the Indian. This may not sound like a lot, and it may in fact seem paternalistic, but it functions as a step toward the recuperation of the Indian in the self of the *mestizo*, as well as an affirmation of an Indian perspective.[18] Mistral's love of the Indians is very problematic, yet it is real, derived from her experience as a teacher, her identification with the valley of Elqui, her respect for Indian cultures, but also from the white world's disdain—even as she repudiates it.

"Silhouette of the Indian woman" is one of Mistral's most frequently reprinted essays. In it, she reiterates that there is beauty in the Indian to which Western eyes are unaccustomed. The essay's terms are visual: silhouette, the line of the woman's shawl, the color of her skin and clothing. This is the Indian seen from a distance, as one of two corolla-shapes Mistral attributes to them, the open rose or the narrow jasmine. Mistral invites her reader to watch the Indian woman walk on and on, baby on her back, alongside her husband; she lauds the timelessness of this tableau, "the ancient woman, not emancipated from her child" ["Silueta," 100].[19] Mistral imagines the couple's silence:

"They walk on silently, through the landscape heavy with inwardness; they share a word from time to time, from which I glean its sweetness, not understanding its meaning" ["Silueta," 100–101].[20] But, far off as the observer is, how can she know they so rarely speak? And when she does hear, she can only judge the tone: she does not know their language and she cannot understand what they say. Mistral's portrait aestheticizes and romanticizes the Indian woman.

"Silhouette of the Indian woman" does little more than bring the Indian woman into the field of vision and make of her an object of beauty. Her visibility does not mean her audibility. Mistral silences her—through distance, through their mutually unintelligible languages. Mistral was truly concerned for the material well-being of the Indians and other distressed people, particularly women and children. She did things to make a difference, such as giving her poems to be published to raise funds for Spanish civil war orphans and insisting that after her death her remains be brought back to the Valley of Elqui, knowing her burial site would be a place of pilgrimage and would therefore bring outside money to the people there. She went to Mexico to help set up an educational system after the Mexican Revolution. She compiled a book of readings for women, *Lecturas para mujeres* (Readings for women), for a school in Mexico that was named for her and that was meant to educate women as mothers. And the same impulse that glorifies the land-bound, conservative, reproductively oriented woman is the springboard for Mistral's argument that it is the women who are best positioned to resist foreign encroachment on the land.

Mistral's argument concerning the beauty of the Indian is echoed in the formal beauty of her writing. There is no fissure anywhere in the text. The writer herself is pared down to an eye to see, an ear to overhear, and a pen to record. While Mistral's essays are carefully and tightly constructed, Ocampo's essays are loose, conversational, and associative. They invite conversation and speculation. "The last year of Pachacutec" is structured around the ideas of the historical oppression of indigenous women, by their own people as well as by the colonizers, and the oppression of contemporary women. The title refers to the story of the sister-wife of the Inca Pachacutec who in her consort's absence rules an empire, but who is made to lie prostrate at his feet in his presence. Ocampo locates herself in the essay, remembering a particular walk down a particular street in Madrid, with a particular friend. Her very personal recollections of that day recede as the friends enter a bookstore, and the book they discover on women of ancient America triggers a discussion of Malinche and memories of other books on women. But as Ocampo has made quite clear on other occasions, her reading experiences are every bit as personal as her interactions with people in the flesh. A passage from Engels on male dominance elicits a remark on pre-Columbian attitudes toward virginity. From there Ocampo moves to the subject of rape and a quote from Angela Davis. An oblique reference to great-grandmother Agueda ties reading together with family, the history of Malinche together with the ways in which women continue to suffer under male domination. None of these elements of the essay is overtly connected to any other; it is up to the reader to provide the transitions and do the editing. In texts like this, written first as essays, Ocampo invites the same personal interaction her speeches do.[21]

As in those of Ocampo's essays that start out as speeches, such as "Women in the academy," the "I" is easily read as the author.[22] Yet it is a constructed and partial "I" that only reveals itself selectively. The physical presence of the speaker may function to authorize or de-authorize: gender, race, class are all made visible by clothing, physiognomy, and demeanor; language, dialect, and accent are all audible. As speech is converted to written language, these visual and auditory social cues must be intentionally recreated.

One way Ocampo achieves "visibility" is by offering the reader a full picture of the self through an ongoing series of essays. The body of work, published over a period of time, or as a collection in book form, provides context and knowledge for reading each individual piece.[23] Ocampo was deliberate about creating herself as an essayist. Not only did she found a journal for which she wrote regularly, but she also made a point to publish her collected essays at regular intervals over a period of approximately fifty years. Mistral, in contrast, never seemed particularly to want to put anything into a book, but she was willing to allow others to do it for her. Nor did she hesitate to publish in more ephemeral—and more directly accessible—media.

It seems that there are almost as many definitions of essay as there are critics writing about the genre, though Latin Americanists tend to be hesitant about offering their own theory of the genre and rely heavily on others. Jorge Luis Gómez-Martínez uses an entire book to pile up definitions, trying to reconcile them, and Antonio Urello gives up on a single definition altogether. After genuflecting in the direction of Adorno, Pascal, Montaigne, Lukács, Ortega, and Alfonso Reyes, he concedes that "the definitions are . . . numerous, and they vary according to the source from which they come, having as almost the only prominent common denominator the variety of their points of view . . . " [Urrello, 7–9][24] John Skirius enumerates a series of the essay's characteristics and goals, gleaned from the writings of others [Skirius, 9–14].[25] A distillation of these attempts at definition yields a normative essay that is a written prose text expressing, primarily through exposition, a single author's ideas or reflections on any subject.

It would be easy for me to claim that, like these other theorists, I find the essay too wayward a genre to fit into any rigid definition. But it is as a feminist critic that I feel most uneasy about defining the essay's formal terrain. Staking claim to territory means establishing borders, which calls into play all the metaphors of marginalization that have, in the past, defined women out. Accustomed to questioning these boundaries, to seeing—seeking—what inhabits them, to de-centering rather than establishing the center, I resist what is an essay "proper." I am uncomfortable with a paring away that leaves me with a partial, fragmented text—the pure essay. For to define the essay proper means to discard what isn't essay—in this case Victoria Ocampo's open letters, which she does not separate out from the rest of her *Testimonios*, and Gabriela Mistral's prose poems, which she includes in her books of poetry and which her editors group with other prose.

While Mistral and Ocampo have written normative essays, to look only at them, or to pretend that their other nonfiction prose writing is of no account because it does not fit the strict criteria of "essay," is to undermine the feminist project of decentering, and to return to a formalist notion of genre that obscures much women's writing. Many of Ocampo's and Mistral's essays skirt the edges of the genre, entering the borderlands where essay overlaps with other literary forms.

Gloria Anzaldúa is a contemporary Chicana essayist whose notion of "borderlands" is helpful in understanding this indeterminate area of prose writing that is no longer normative essay but not yet narrative, life story, poetry, or journalism. Anzaldúa describes the border as a richly inhabited space, not simply a two-dimensional line that separates one sphere from another. Both demarcating and connecting two or more other spaces, the borderlands are, by definition, permeable and unfixed. Not incidentally, the borderlands, as Anzaldúa describes them, are the physical and metaphorical space occupied by the *mestiza*. The *mestiza* also contains the multiple and contradictory elements that characterize this space, and she is most at home within it. She combines aspects of European and indigenous cultures but within a single skin.

The borderlands essay that spills over into other genres encompasses Victoria Ocampo's letters, speeches, and reminiscences and Gabriela Mistral's prose poems. This idea of a borderlands essay allows the feminist critic to breathe more freely even while looking at those essays that most clearly fit the normative form. In the less restrictive context of the borderlands essay, the writer's normative essays are filled out, connected. In the osmotic border space where essay bleeds into poetry, fiction, oratory, or memoir, the writer can claim her voice and define it as she wishes.

Given the male claim on essay-writing, it is as borderland form that the essay is accessible to women. When Ocampo heard from Virginia Woolf that women must write so that a women's literary history could be made, she followed Woolf's directions and wrote: essays, ten volumes of them over a period of almost fifty years. Ocampo briefly tried her hand at playwriting, but the essay seemed to her more appropriate. For a woman who did not want to claim too much for her writing, the essay seemed a more direct, less pretentious form that still made personal statement and expression possible. Modest about very little else, Ocampo did not consider herself a literary artist.

The normative essay's troubling claim to authority and universality is connected to the tug between the center and the borderlands. The borderlands reveal that no single center can claim universality, nor is there a point from which to derive absolute authority. The border is between two places, both of which can claim centrality, albeit in different worlds. This notion of borderlands is most vivid in Anzaldúa, but there is other feminist work that evokes it. Sherry

Ortner locates woman in the border region between nature and culture, occupying space in both and, implicitly, making that place not just a line women
cross, but the multidimensional space they inhabit. Elaine Showalter's "wild
zone" in women's literary discourse is a similar frontier region. Similarly, Latin
America is not merely "marginal," one-dimensional, but rather both Western
and Southern, a quadrant that is filled. The critical factor that "woman" and
"Latin America" share is their non-normativity, the fact, if not the way, that
they call the norm into question.

The authority of the normative essayist and his essay derives, as I have
said, from a place of privilege that lends him automatic credibility. For that
reason I am troubled by the idea of essay *sui generis*, free of obligations.
As much as I am charmed by Ortega's definition of the essay as "science minus
the explicit proof" [Ortega, 23], which unmasks the dependence of objective
science on the merely subjective human, I note the way he deflects the authority
of science away from external methods of proof to the individual thinker,
a thinker who must then already have a means of authorizing himself.[26]
Ortega's seductive definition reinforces the idea of the independent text, of
masculine self-sufficiency which masks the massive system that supports it and
him. As Latin American women, Ocampo and Mistral had to find and create
their own means of support. Mistral, effacing herself, claims to speak for
the continent and on behalf of those who have no audible voice. Ocampo
cites sources and drops names. Each in her way lets us know where her obligations lie.

For Mistral, essay writing is a way to disengage from the emotional demands of poetry. This is very different from Ocampo, whose persona seems
always present. Ocampo writes, personally invested; Mistral withdraws. In a
letter she sent to Ocampo while she was living in New York, Mistral writes,
"My dearest: I've known this for a long time: it is restful and even healthy to
write absolutely objective things. Try to do this: rest your soul; it's almost an
act of cleansing, in any case, to exercise only the memory they call 'objective,'
merely objective" [quoted in Ocampo, "Gabriela," 75].[27] This statement of
resignation, for a poet whose work is spiritually and emotionally wrenching,
accounts for the cool tone of so many of Mistral's essays. Those she wrote for
the Costa Rican newspaper, *Repertorio Americano* (American repertory), collected by Mario Céspedes, are, for the most part, dispassionate, as are those
collected by Roque Estéban Scarpa and Alfonso Calderón. Mistral is a soul
turned inside out. Unprotected, she weaves her own protective text.

Even at her most personal, as in the memoir of her mother, there are few
idiosyncratic details in Gabriela Mistral's prose. While Ocampo writes personally, even confessionally, about her mother, Mistral writes hagiography.
Ocampo recalls a more socially, historically, and personally faceted relationship. Mistral offers a surface. Ocampo's class position, which helped shape her
personality, protects her. She is cared for by servants and family members. She
does not need to cover herself with text—she is, in a way, guileless, because
there is so little in her that is vulnerable. This is not to say that her anger at

women's oppression was not deeply and personally felt—but that at some level she knew that she was safe.

Ocampo's appropriation of an exotic indigenous past and Mistral's desire to make Latin Americans recognize the Indian in themselves are transformed a generation later and a continent away in Gloria Anzaldúa's work, where the other becomes the self. Ocampo seeking her Americanism through Agueda, Mistral admiring and protecting the Indian other, Anzaldúa claiming her Indian heritage, all point to the need to foreground indigenousness in order to claim American authenticity. On the part of these writers, that claim is, however, necessarily connected to the European part of their heritage. Without that, what is Indian would be self-evident, and the need to emphasize it would be superfluous. As *mestiza* writers, Mistral and Ocampo, and later Anzaldúa, need make the Indian visible, to bring to light what has been kept invisible. The *mestizo* essay is precisely that essay that acknowledges its hidden debts. It makes the indigenous and the feminine visible. Its contemporary incarnation in Anzaldúa also makes its sexuality visible.

Mestizaje's subtext is a transgressive sexuality that produced a people out of the often brutal sexual encounters between victors and vanquished. This historical reality was euphemized and mystified in the context of a sexually repressive culture. Sexuality was still very much a private issue when Ocampo and Mistral began writing. Ocampo included many details about her life in her essays, but she did not write about sex. It was no secret that Ocampo had a number of lovers, but she never wrote about these relationships as such in her essays, and even in her autobiography only referred to the men with whom she was involved by their initials. Sexuality was not a part of what she was developing as the appropriate place—and power—of women. Mistral channeled sexuality into motherhood in her writing. She tapped into a maternal strength for women that in fact was crippling, insofar as it relegated women entirely to functions deriving from motherhood. She did not want for other women what she had for herself—a public life and a creative one. The result is a mythology of Mistral as frustrated mother and broken-hearted sweetheart who never got over her beloved's suicide. Yet she raised a child she called her nephew and spent the last years of her life in a close relationship with another woman. A generation later, sexuality is an open issue for feminists, and Gloria Anzaldúa's lesbianism is central to her writing and theorizing. The borderlands she inhabits are not products only of the different class and race categories she inhabits. Nor are they limited to the actual geography of Aztlán, a territory that encompasses central and northern Mexico and much of the southwestern and western United States. They are also sexual.

The heterogeneous self is the *mestiza*, who builds on what has come before. The *mestiza* acknowledges not just the European father but also the Indian mother.[28] Acknowledgement is crucial here, because it is the Indian and mother who are otherwise lost. The idea of *mestizaje* includes the form and content of these women's essays as well as the identity of the essayists. Like the centaur, the *mestiza* writer embodies the idea of a powerful mixture, but unlike the classical Greek mythological creature, she is fully human and an American creation. *Mestizaje* is suggestive of the borderlands essay that defies rigid definition, requiring acknowledgement of its sources and grounding in material reality. It is, above all, American in its derivation and impulse.

This *mestizaje* is in constant negotiation. Ocampo may claim racial otherness through Agueda, but as a member of the oligarchy, raised by French and British nannies who taught her to read French before her native Spanish, and as the importer of French thought and literature (and also of European modernism in general), Ocampo was made European by a family that constructed itself. At the same time, Ocampo was immersed in the Argentine landscape. She was drawn to it and to the people she associated with it: the servants at the family estate. They were, for her, attached to the land in a feudal sense. Her inability to see them as free agents of their own lives is breathtaking in its naiveté, a racism unclouded by shame. She invests them with a primeval power, a power associated with food preparation, mystery, adulthood, and remembrance. She does not recall or reconstruct any unfairness here. Any oppression.

In Europe Ocampo is a sophisticated woman, fashionable; she moves in a circle of artists, musicians, and writers. It is when she writes of Virginia Woolf that she lets us see how at least that one Englishwoman invents her as an exotic. Ocampo writes in a loving, reverential, but also amused way of Woolf's imaginary Argentina, a luxuriant and mysterious New World that Ocampo embodies for the British writer. Many years later Ocampo recalls complying with this fabrication out of a desire to please the demanding Woolf, thus doubling the misappropriation ["Orlando," 80–81 and "Trastienda," 214–216].

Gabriela Mistral's international renown as a poet could have given her the same access to cosmopolitanism as Ocampo's class status gave her, but Mistral was aware, as Ocampo was not, of the irreconcilability of the claims and needs of the popular classes (particularly the Indians) with a blithely Euro-American identity that would integrate the Indian as exotic. So Ocampo sailed through life as a cosmopolite while Mistral suffered as an outsider. The invention of America in their essays is, ultimately, the invention of themselves as Americans: Ocampo, who traversed borders easily and for whom America had to be a part of Western civilization, and Mistral who, living beyond Chile's borders, immersed herself in the primal landscape and identified with its people.

NOTES

1. Reyes, a Mexican writer active in the early part of this century, wrote essays that

are widely considered to be outstanding examples of the genre. All translations from Spanish are mine.

2. Early newspaper writing by Argentinian women was often feminist. The history of feminist writing in magazines can be dated from the short-lived (Nov. 1830–Jan. 1831) magazine *La Aljaba*, whose separatist motto is breathtaking: "Nos libraremos de la injusticia de los demás hombres solamente cuando no existamos entre ellos" (We will be free of men's injustice only when we no longer live among them).

3. I thank Professor Bretz for making the manuscript available to me.

4. "Frente a la mayoría del la producción ensayística de temática americana — nacional o continental — las obras de materia universal — aquéllas que tratan de problemas generales de índole filosófica, estética o sociológica — son escasas."

5. "Son pocos los ensayistas que . . . reflejan unos intereses que trascienden la problemática americana en todos sus apsectos. . . . Hay que saber quién se es, para luego entrar en la comunidad intelectual occidental."

6. "el género predisciplinar en que se han tratado los temas que hoy constituyen el objeto de las ciencias sociales" "en el ensayo las realidades sociales se estudian desde la observación individual mientras en la ciencia se estudian por medio de la estadística u otros métodos."

7. *Mestizaje* is a Spanish word that refers to racial mixing, particularly between the native people of the Americas and the Iberian conquerors. Given the demographics of the Spanish conquest the *mestizo* (masculine form) or *mestiza* (feminine form) is most commonly the descendant of an indigenous woman and a European man.

8. The "Poemas de las madres" are among the few Mistral prose pieces that have been translated into English. Given the questions of racial consciousness that underlie this chapter, it is interesting to note that their translator was the Harlem Renaissance poet Langston Hughes. And given the theme of this volume, it is probably reasonable to mention that I (no doubt like many other New Yorkers) first knew of Hughes as an essayist, when as a child I faithfully read his regular column in the old *New York Post*.

9. This essay, and several others discussed in this chapter have been translated into English by Doris Meyer, who appends them to her biography of Ocampo. As a feminist Ocampo was concerned with women as social actors, but Ocampo did not, for many years, focus entirely on women. Her strategy was to incorporate her feminism into the other issues of concern to *Sur*, having to do with authorizing Latin America as a site of cultural sophistication and production. When feminism came around again in the 1970s, Ocampo wrote openly as a feminist.

10. Ocampo has been reviled by critics of Argentine culture for her determination to Europeanize Argentina, as if she were the only one to have engaged in this enterprise. Men who have done similarly, from Sarmiento to Borges and Cortázar, have been dealt with more gently. But women are supposed to attach to customs and traditions and to pass them on. A woman who refuses that charge, who looks outward, who is drawn to intellection, reason, artifice, is breaking the gender code that ostensibly maintains the societal balance of innovation and tradition.

11. Mistral's first book of poetry was published by a group of students and faculty at New York City's Columbia University. Her second was published in Argentina, but with Spain in mind — the proceeds would go to orphans of the Spanish Civil War. Victoria Ocampo financed and published this volume through the *Sur* publishing house.

12. I thank Cheri Register for pointing out that Key, a major feminist thinker and writer, is regularly omitted from histories of Swedish literature, no doubt in part because she was primarily an essayist.

13. Ocampo published the works of Woolf, Sartre, Caillois and wrote in praise of Stravinsky and Chanel.

14. It is typical of Ocampo that she did this by personalizing the issue, making a point of her own Indian ancestry once she discovered it. She claims this ancestry even though

her family kept the existence of its Indian foremother secret, and despite the fact that the life she enjoyed was the fruit of her European ancestors' conquest and colonization efforts. Yet there is a strong emotional pull toward this indigenous ancestor. Femininity also has a racial component, and Ocampo does not fail to draw the familiar analogy between race and gender when she discusses the oppression of women. Nor does she ignore the doubling of oppression when race and gender are joined rather than set up as rhetorical similars, as in her discussions of Malinche. It should not be surprising that Ocampo would claim a physical connection to the racial other, claim some racial otherness for herself in order to ratify her claim to dispossession.

15. The Spanish called Cortés' translator Doña Marina. Her Indian name was Malinali or Malintzin, and the Mexicans later came to call her la Malinche. Her role in the conquest of Mexico has been raised to the level of national myth.

16. "Una de las razones que dictan la repugnancia criolla a confesar el indio en nuestra sangre, uno de los orígenes de nuestro miedo de decirnos lealmente mestizos, es la llamada 'fealdad del indio'. Se la tiene como verdad sin vuelta, se la ha aceptado como tres y dos son cinco. Corre parejas con las otras frases en plomada: 'El indio es perezoso' y 'el indio es malo'." Here "creole" is a translation of "criolla," which means American of European descent—i.e., the Euro-American who does not have, or (Mistral suggests) will not recognize, any indigenous ancestry.

17. "La boca también anda demasiado espesa en algunos grupos inferiores de los bajíos, donde el cuerpo se aplasta con las atmósferas o se hincha en los barriales genésicos; pero al igual que la nariz prima del árabe, se la encuentra de labios delgados como la hoja del maíz, de una delgadez cortada y cortadora que es de las más expresivas para la gracia maliciosa y los rictus del dolor. Suele caer hacia los lados esta boca india con el desdén que viven esas razas que se saben dignas como cualquiera otra por talentos y virtudes y que han sido 'humilladas y ofendidas' infinitamente; caen los extremos de esas bocas con más melancolía que amargura, y se levantan bruscamente en la riso burlona, dando una sorpresa a los que creen al indio tumbado en una animalidad triste."

18. Onilda A. Jiménez points out that Mistral attributes certain aspects of style to geographical specificity and to race—and praises Indian sensibility by attributing it to canonical writers like Rubén Darío and Alfonso Reyes.

19. "Es la mujer antigua, no emancipada del hijo."

20. "Van silenciosos, por el paisaje lleno de recogimiento; cruzan de tarde en tarde una palabra, de la que recibo la dulzura, sin comprender el sentido."

21. Bretz, 23, points out, in fact, that the essay "consistently draws on spoken speech and foregrounds the complex interplay of speech and writing."

22. Ocampo's mentor, Virginia Woolf, provides a counterexample in *A Room of One's Own*, when she tells her audience that "I" is a convenience.

23. I thank Joanna O'Connell for suggesting this to me.

24. "Las definiciones son, pues, numerosas y varían según la fuente donde se originan teniendo casi como único denominador común prominente la variedad de sus puntos de vista, reflejando de esta manera la múltiple y personal composición de texto ensayístico."

25. Jorge Luis Gómez-Martínez, *Teroía del ensayo* (Ediciones Universidad de Salamanca, 1981). His book deals primarily with Spanish essay, but some of the theorists he discusses and cites are Latin Americanists.

26. ". . . el ensayo es la ciencia, menos la prueba explícita."

27. "Muy querida, hace mucho que sé esto: da un gran descanso y hasta salud escribir cosas absolutamente objectivas. Procura tú hacer esto: descansa el alma; es casi un higiene, en todo caso, hacer trabajar solamente la memoria que llaman 'objectiva', meramente objectiva."

28. This is Octavio Paz's model, from *The Labyrinth of Solitude*. It is overly simplified and conflates the feminine and the indigenous in troubling ways, but it has been widely accepted.

WORKS CITED

Anzaldúa, Gloria. *Borderlands/La frontera: The New Mestiza.* San Francisco: Spinsters/ Aunt Lute, 1987.

Bretz, Mary Lee. *Voices, Silences and Echoes: A Theory of the Essay and the Critical Reception of Naturalism in Spain.* London: Támesis, forthcoming.

Ferrer Aponte, Marie Solange. "Introducción." *Antología del ensayo español, hispanoamericano y puertorriqueño.* Ed. Juan Escalera Ortiz. Madrid: Playor, nd.

Foster, David William. *Para una lectura semiótica del ensayo latinoamericano.* Madrid: Porrúa Turanzas, 1983.

Gómez-Martínez, Jorge Luis. *Teoría del ensayo.* Salamanca: Ediciones Universidad de Salamanca, 1981.

Greenburg, Janet. "Toward a History of Women's Periodicals in Latin America: A Working Bibliography." *Women, Culture, and Politics in Latin America.* Ed. Seminar on Feminism and Culture in Latin America. Berkeley: University of California Press, 1990.

Jiménez, Onilda A. "La crítica literaria de un poeta: Gabriela Mistral." Proceedings of the *Hispanic Literatures 6th Annual Conference October 17–18, 1980, El escritor como crítico literario y El ensayo en la literatura hispánica.* Ed. Cruz Mendizábal. 310–11.

Meyer, Doris. *Victoria Ocampo: Against the Wind and the Tide.* New York: George Braziller, 1979.

Mistral, Gabriela. "Conversación sobre la tierra con las mujeres Portorriqueñas," *Gabriela anda por el mundo.* Ed. Roque Esteban Scarpa. Santiago de Chile: Editorial Andrés Bello, n.d. 149–56.

_____. *Croquis mexicanos.* Ed. Alfonso Calderón. Santiago: Editorial Nascimiento, 1979.

_____. *Elogio por las cosas de la tierra.* Ed. Roque Esteban Scarpa. Santiago: Editorial Andrés Bello, 1979.

_____. *Lecturas para mujeres.* Mexico: Editorial Porrúa, 1969.

_____. "Poemas de las madres." *Desolación.* New York: Instituto de las Españas en los Estados Unidos, 1922.

_____. "Silueta de la india." *Gabriela anda por el mundo.* Ed. Roque Esteban Scarba. Santiago: Editorial Andrés Bello, 1978.

_____. "El tipo del indio mexicano." *Gabriela Mistral en el "Repertorio Americano."* Ed. Mario Céspedes. San José: Editorial Universidad de Costa Rica, 1978.

Morón Arroyo, Ciriaco. "Ensayo y ciencias sociales." Proceedings of the *Hispanic Literatures 6th Annual Conference October 17–18, 1980, El escritor como crítico literario y El ensayo en la literatura hispánica.* Ed. Cruz Mendizábal. 6–22.

Ocampo, Victoria. "Gabriela Mistral en sus cartas." *Testimonios. Sexta Serie, 1957–1962.* Buenos Aires: Editorial Sur, 1963. 59–81.

_____. "Mujeres en la Academia." *Testimonios. Décima serie, 1975–1977.* Buenos Aires: Editorial Sur, 1977. 13–23.

_____. "La trastienda de la historia." *Testimonios. Novena Serie (1971–74).* Buenos Aires: Editorial Sur, 1975. 211–35.

_____. "El último año de Pachacutec." *Testimonios. Décima serie, 1975–1977.* Buenos Aires: Editorial Sur, 1977. 39–46.

_____. "Virginia Woolf, Orlando y Cía." *Testimonios. Segunda Serie.* Buenos Aires: Sur, 1941. 13–86.

Ortega y Gassett, José. *Meditaciones del Quijote 1924–1925.* Repr. Madrid: Espasa Calpe, 1964.

Ortner, Sherry. "Is Female to Male as Nature Is to Culture?" *Women, Culture and Society.* Stanford: Stanford University Press, 1974. 67–87.

Paz, Octavio. "Los hijos de la Malinche." *El laberinto de la soledad. Cuadernos Americanos*, 1950. Repr. Mexico: Fondo de Cultura Económica, 1959.

Showalter, Elaine. "Feminist Criticism in the Wilderness." *Critical Inquiry* 8 (Winter 1981). Repr. *The New Feminist Criticism: Essays on Women, Literature and Theory*. Ed. E. Showalter. New York: Pantheon, 1985. 243–70.

Skirius, John. *El ensayo hispanoamericano del siglo XX*. Mexico: Fondo de Cultura Económica, 1981.

Stabb, Martin. *In Quest of Identity: The Latin American Essay of Ideas*. Chapel Hill: University of North Carolina Press, 1967.

Urrello, Antonio. *Verosimiltud y estrategia textual en el ensayo hispanoamericano*. Mexico: Premia Editores, 1986.

Woolf, Virginia. *A Room of One's Own*. London: Hogarth Press, 1929.

CHAPTER EIGHT

A Voice of One's Own

Implications of Impersonality in the Essays of Virginia Woolf and Alice Walker

TUZYLINE JITA ALLAN

As spiritual leaders of two distinct, sometimes contentious camps within contemporary feminist discourse, Virginia Woolf and Alice Walker invite comparative scrutiny. Walker's growing esteem among African-American and Third-World feminist critics is rapidly approaching the venerable heights Woolf occupies in Anglo-American feminist circles.[1] Their appeal stems largely from the qualities that bind them: gender, an unyielding pacifism, a strong antipatriarchal, anticapitalist stance, powerful prowoman sympathies, and a serious commitment to literature and writing. However, the common ground on which these writers stand should not draw attention away from the world of difference that separates them along racial, cultural, and aesthetic lines.

Walker, the living member of this duo, has simultaneously acknowledged her ties to Woolf and demonstrated her difference from her. She recognizes, for example, Woolf's precursory role as the one "who has saved so many of us" [*Our Mothers' Gardens*, 14]. In all likelihood Walker is referring to Woolf's literary crusade against patriarchy as well as the textual influence she exerts on contemporary feminist writing. Many of her pronouncements on the female condition, for instance, serve as pre-texts to be mined for the appropriate word or statement. Her signature phrase "of one's own" is now common currency in feminist discourse, and Walker is one of its regular users.[2] But Walker also (re)writes/rights Woolf. An intertextual act of particular interest is her revision of an important section in Woolf's classic essay, *A Room of One's Own*.[3] Here she employs a narrative strategy Henry Louis Gates, Jr. describes as "the trope of the Talking Book," that is, "making the white written text speak with a black voice" [*The Signifying Monkey*, 131]. Walker inserts black womanhood in the spaces of Woolf's text to make room for her own voice. The reloaded text, then, is discharged bearing the double image of Woolf's "thwarted and hindered" but unenslaved female artist in sixteenth-century England *and* Walker's talented, brutally silenced black bondwoman in eighteenth-century America. What the black female voice communicates in this re-fashioned double-voiced discourse is that under patriarchal constitutional law not all women are created equal.

Walker's rewriting of Woolf "to make the [written] text speak" [Gates, *The Signifying Monkey*, 240] for the multiply oppressed and historically silenced black woman is a vivid example of the self-representational mode of her essays. Walker does not deny that the self is a complex entity, knowing full well how race, sex, and class (among other things) impinge on hers. She insists in the private space of the essay on voicing the self in all its multifaceted forms—not with a stammer but rather with the fluency of conviction. Hence, for all the respect she has for Woolf (a feeling that, according to Christine Froula, would have been reciprocated because "Walker ... is a woman writer ... Woolf might well have considered a hero" [156]), Walker easily rejects her predecessor's self-neutralizing aesthetic and voice-dropping narrative practice.

The essays I have selected for discussion underscore the difference in the writers' narrative deployment of personality and voice by the very nature of their thematic affinity. To draw attention to the authors' attitudes toward the writerly self, I will pair essays from Woolf's *The Common Reader: First Series* and Walker's *In Search of Our Mothers' Gardens* that resemble each other in subject matter and even attest to a closeness in the sensibilities of Walker and Woolf. My aim is to examine the relationship between the writers' different and shared realities of race, culture, and gender, and their engagement with the essayistic practice of self-revelation.

The essays that found their way into *The Common Reader* were written at the same time that Woolf was zealously searching for a new fictional form. Indeed, the strictures she leveled at the realist school of writers—Arnold Bennett, H. G. Wells, and John Galsworthy—were commensurate with her determination to be a standard-bearer for an alternative fiction. Topping the list of realist trappings to be discarded, in her view, was authorial presence. Not only was the world too much with those writers she called materialists, but their presence was felt in every page of their books, suffocating characters and readers alike. The new novel, she insisted, must free itself from dependence on external reality and the author "from the cramp and confinement of personality" ["How It Strikes a Contemporary," 302]. Woolf's own scrupulous performance in self-expulsion, which began in her fiction with *Jacob's Room* (1922), reached commendable heights in *Mrs. Dalloway* (1925) and *To the Lighthouse* (1927), and peaked in *The Waves* (1931) has earned her a seat of honor among modernism's (predominantly male) greats.[4] Some feminist critics, however, are not too thrilled about her disappearing act, seeing it as a pyrrhic victory for which her feminism was bartered. Such criticism has not spared even *A Room of One's Own* (1929) and *Three Guineas* (1939), two works of outright polemical intent. Elaine Showalter and Adrienne Rich, for instance, lament respectively the "denial of feeling" and "dogged tentativeness" of *A Room*, while Jane Marcus believes full-blown anger would certainly have enhanced, not damaged, Woolf's art in both essays.[5]

The fact is that Woolf did not regard the essay's method as significantly different from that of a good novel. She saw in the fragmentary, tentative, and open form of the essay the potential for "moments of revelation" [Hall, 82] not unlike those she expected from the modern novel. Woolf seemed more interested in what Adorno describes as the essay's "desire . . . to make the transitory eternal" [159] than in its reputation as an instrument of self-study. Very early in her essay-writing career, she acknowledged that "to write of one's self . . . is . . . a feat but seldom accomplished;" that "[c]onfronted with the terrible spectre of themselves, the bravest are inclined to run away or shade their eyes" ["The Decay of Essay-Writing," 26]. Happily, modern consciousness, she averred in a later essay, had come to the writer's rescue by merging the private "I" and the public "we" to produce an "expand[ed] . . . individuality" equipped with a "disinterested" voice ["The Modern Essay," 212-20]. This, in effect, is Woolf's version of T. S. Eliot's dissociated sensibility, the theoretical ideal that informs the *Common Reader* essays.

For Alice Walker, the modernist transmutation of the writerly self into an amorphous collective is antithetical to her role as a black woman writer. The first two terms of this designation (black woman) impinge on the third (writer). "Black woman" invokes a historical experience that Walker as writer simultaneously affirms and challenges. This dialectic receives significant play in her essays which, in addition to their autobiographical urgency, are an attempt to re-make black female subjectivity. Historian Bettina Aptheker uses the word "legacy" to describe the responsibility black women have "of determining self, scraping away the residue of centuries of racist/sexist encrustations and naming their matrilineage in authentic and exquisite detail" [4]. It is a legacy Walker steadfastly claims, one that explains the force of personality that permeates her essays.

Woolf's "Modern Fiction" and Walker's "Saving the Life That Is Your Own: The Importance of Models in the Artist's Life" offer a sterling example of the difference in the writers' narrative methods. Walker's title, I should first point out, carries signs of the uneasy bond between these two feminists that I alluded to earlier. Recasting Woolf's famous phrase "a room of one's own" as "the life that is your own," Walker is playing more than a word game. She is evoking the same spirit of ownership with which Woolf sought to imbue the female artist in *A Room of One's Own*. But by replacing "room" with "life" and annexing it to "saving," Walker adds a sense of urgency (indeed, emergency) that is associated in this essay with the state of black female creativity.

Further reverberations between Walker and Woolf occur at the thematic level. In both essays, the writers reflect on a subject of vital importance to the artist in general and to them in particular. Summed up in Walker's subtitle, it is a matter of literary ancestry. For Woolf, the new fiction called for the defiant act of self-disinheritance. Some literary fathers had to be disowned in order for her generation to achieve creative autonomy. Walker's concern also is about her generation's ability to write fiction in the face of white male hegemonic control and distortion of black life. She, too, wants to terminate one line of literary ancestry and begin another. Her desire, ultimately, like Woolf's, is to write what she regards as a readable book. It is clear, therefore, that both writers have a vested interest in their search for new beginnings.

Yet Woolf elects to eschew the personal. The spirit of defiance that underlies "Modern Fiction" is hampered by a conflicting desire to be civil. Woolf grants power of representation to a persona Phyllis Rose describes as "a woman, neither professional critic nor scholar, moderately informed, who is modestly, earnestly, trying to illuminate life through the reading of books" [42]. This is an individual with two strikes against her: gender and a lack of skill. In a self-protective move, then, she turns to something she knows well—the long-standing convention of appropriate female conduct. That means she will be modest and earnest when in fact she should be cocksure and irreverent. Woolf would later admit to playing this "Victorian game of manners" and wonder about its effect on her writing:

> But the Victorian manner is perhaps—I am not sure—a disadvantage in writing. When I re-read my old *Common Reader* articles I detect it there. I lay the blame for their suavity, their politeness, their sidelong approach, to my tea-table training. I see myself handing plates of buns to shy young men and asking them, not directly and simply about their poems and their novels, but whether they like cream as well as sugar. [*Moments of Being*, 129]

The Victorian manner permeates many of the essays in *The Common Reader*, but it is especially thick in "Modern Fiction" where Woolf tries to be polite over an issue that obsessed her. She firmly believed that her generation of writers would reach fertile creative grounds if it unburdened itself of any influence from Wells, Bennett, and Galsworthy. These writers were fact-mongers. They busied themselves with trivia and neglected the inner life. In short, they were unfit models for the modern writer whose gaze had turned inward. This, in a nutshell, is how Woolf really felt about the realists. They are strong feelings, and strong feelings are usually communicated by a voice which Stoehr defines as "the pervasive reflection, in written or spoken language, of an author's character . . . " [150]. However, opposed to authorial presence in writing and mindful of her Victorian manners, Woolf dilutes her criticism of Wells, Bennett, and Galsworthy by means of a scold-and-praise technique. All three writers, for example, "have excited so many hopes and disappointed them" at the same time. Their work is said to be "admirable and the reverse," and all in all we thank them "for having shown us what they might have done but have not done" [147].

The scold-and-praise method is also applied to the individual writers. Mr. Wells is disabled by a "fatal alloy in his genius," and Mr. Bennett, "perhaps the worst culprit of the three," is yet "by far the best workman." Finally, though we could never "find what we seek in [Galsworthy's] pages," still "profoundly . . . we respect [his] integrity and humanity" [147-8]. The pith of Woolf's criticism is in the word "materialists," but its definition neutralizes its censorious intent: "we mean by it that they write of unimportant things; that they spent immense skill and immense industry making the trivial and the transitory appear the true and the enduring" [148]. Clearly, Woolf is damning with not-so-faint praise.

Woolf must have felt most acutely the strain of being on this emotional seesaw in her commendation of Joyce as the modernist counterpoint to the materialist impulse:

> In contrast to those whom we have called materialists, Mr. Joyce is spiritual; he is concerned at all costs to reveal the flickerings of the innermost flame that flashes its messages through the brain, and in order to preserve it he disregards with complete courage whatever seems to him adventitious, whether it be probability, or coherence, or any other of these signposts which for generations have served to support the imagination of a reader when called upon to imagine what he can neither touch nor see. [151]

Woolf seems to overplay Joyce's worth in this passage, given her growing sense of him as an inferior rival. She knew, being among the first readers of *Ulysses* in *The Little Review*, that Joyce was onto her method, but she was also aware of his shortcomings—his "damned egotistical self" and the "underbred" character of *Ulysses*, for instance—and such knowledge gave her a psychological edge.[6] More to the point, the quoted passage, which I think captures the spirit of Woolf's own novelistic practice more so than Joyce's, is a fine illustration of Woolf's tea-serving metaphor. It is true that she drops hints of a problem with the Joycean method in this essay—the novel's "bright yet narrow room" and the author's self-interest [151]—but they are effective only as asides.

Woolf's rhetoric of self-concealment is most revealing in her use of the first-person plural pronoun "we." This may be a moot point because many a writer has sought a link with other humans or distance from the subject matter under the auspices of the pronoun "we." Indeed, Woolf seems to do precisely that. The essay's "we" is a community of "common readers" with whom she identifies. They are neither critics nor scholars but rather pleasure-seeking readers of literature. Woolf rescues these persons from the undeserved state of obscurity to which they had sunk in Samuel Johnson's *Life of Gray*, reinstates them to respectability, and aligns herself with them. Interest in the lives of the obscure is a Woolfian trait.[7] Her essays on little known authors offer proof not only of her eclectic reading but, more importantly, of the "fundamentally democratic" nature of the essay [Anderson, 303]. As Graham Good correctly points out, Woolf's "essayistic approach to criticism" made possible her recuperation of "the vast multiplicity of lesser viewpoints on existence" [125]. These include the opinions of her "common reader," whose unprofessional but sensible judgments about literature and life she allied with her own. Woolf's use of the communal "we," therefore, in true democratic form, "enfranchises both the reader and the writer" [Anderson, 303].

What is curious, however, is her total erasure of the "I," the uncontested marker of subjectivity. If Woolf's modernist mind rejected any notion of the essay as a self-exhibitionist tool and her feminist sensibilities recoiled from its authority-wielding tendency, she did not oppose, however, the more temperate view that it is "a *reciprocal* characterization"—of "object" and "maker" [Good, 22]. But, by expelling the "I" from the subject position in *The Common Reader* essays, Woolf shifts the creative balance in favor of characterization of the object, leaving the burden of proof of the maker's personality in the hands of language. As a modern essayist weaned on the formula of self-disinterest, Woolf believed that "the triumph of style" is the only triumph ["Modern Essay," 217].

The depersonalization campaign in "Modern Fiction" is further aided by rhetorical questions which are used to dwarf the importance of partisan commentary. A good example occurs where Woolf first declares the difference between two warring factions by stating what one might call their mottos—the modernist view of life as "a luminous halo, a semi-transparent envelope" and the realist version as "a series of gig lamps symmetrically arranged" [150]. Then, with the negative "not," she takes sides: fearing that she might have just been too transparent, Woolf dilutes her decidedly emphatic remarks in rhetorical indeterminacy. "Is it not the task of the novelist," she asks, "to convey this varying, this unknown and uncircumscribed spirit, whatever aberration or complexity it may display, with as little mixture of the alien and external as possible?" [150]. By offering what is easily the gist of her argument as opinion, rather than dogma ["The Modern Essay," 212], Woolf directs the reader's gaze toward the subject and away from herself.

The omnipresent first-person pronoun "I" is the most salient feature of Walker's narrative repertoire and a marker of her radically different rhetorical style. In "Saving the Life That Is Your Own," Walker, like Woolf in "Modern Fiction," is thinking about a literary line of descent. But while Woolf is like a rebellious child ready to strike at cloying parents, Walker feels orphaned. Her forebears were invalidated by the same intellectual history that imbued Woolf's with significance. The black self, as Gates has so cogently outlined, was held hostage to a curious Enlightenment reformulation of the Cartesian principle: I write, therefore I am. In his words, New-world "blacks could not achieve any true presence by speaking, since their 'African'-informed English seems to have only underscored their status as *sui generis*. . . . If blacks were to signify as full members of the Western human community, they would have to do so in their writings" [*Figures in Black*, 6]. The need to prove a reasoning black self, according to Gates, underlies the African-American literary enterprise.

For Walker, then, inheritor of a history designed to strip blacks of presence, the essay, defined by Good as "an act of personal witness . . . at once the *inscription* of a self and the *description* of an object" [23], is a necessary site for the aggressive recovery of self and race. In particular, hers is the pressing task of recuperating excised black female creativity and linking it with her own, an act that, for her, is doubly life-saving. Such a project defies anonymity, and in "Saving the Life That Is Your Own," Walker as writer is as much subject as she is medium. The essay begins with Van Gogh as a classic example of the artist atrophying from a lack of models. His suicide, Walker implies, is the enactment of the death of the unnourished soul. Using Van Gogh's tragedy as a framing device—an example of her fondness for what she calls "the larger perspective"—Walker goes on to narrate her own search for models. She is inspired by Kate Chopin and Flannery O'Connor, white women writers who violated certain sanctities and created new ways of seeing. But for "air and water" she turns to Zora Neale Hurston, only to learn that this black woman writer and her book belong to an endangered, indeed almost extinct, species—"most of them out of print, abandoned, discredited, maligned, nearly lost" [9].

With another of her characteristic narrative devices, the anecdote—that great leveler of distance between writer and reader—Walker enters the heart of the essay's matter. This section opens with the following sentence: "But the incident that started my search began several years ago. I sat down at my desk one day, in a room of my own, with key and lock, and began preparations for a story about voodoo, a subject that had always fascinated me" [9]. Here is another instance of Walker's double take on Woolf: the inscription of sameness and difference. Woolf's imagined ideal woman writer has materialized (in Walker), fully equipped with the requisites for creative production. But her subject matter may not be one Woolf had envisioned. Walker's fascination with the *craft* of voodoo fundamentally sets her apart from her British, upper-middle-class predecessor, whose equally strong spiritual sense did not go beyond Romantic organicism.[8] It is my view that Walker's rewriting (and re-visioning) of Woolf, in this and other instances, lacks any satirical intent. I see it instead as an attempt to foreground the significant fact of difference among women, in spite of the rallying force of their gender sameness.

Walker's voodoo anecdote is about the archeology of model-making. Her mother's storytelling gift would most certainly have given her *griot* status in Africa—as transmitter of the tribe's legends. But in the New World where the written word occupies a higher order than the spoken, her art takes the form of a private transaction between mother and daughter. Walker, as medium, transmutes her mother's stories into written art. But the creative act does not occur in a vacuum; it is assisted by the hand of tradition, what Woolf describes as "many years of thinking in common, of thinking by the body of the people, so that the experience of the mass is behind the single voice" [*A Room*, 69]. At this critical crossroads where tradition meets the individual talent, Walker, in the middle of a creative act, suddenly feels abandoned. The path to a black female tradition is bare and, fearing for her own safety in a world that seems to blot out her kind, she panics:

> . . . where are the *black* collectors of folklore? Where is the *black* anthropologist?
> Where is the *black* person who took the time to travel the back roads of the South
> and collect the information I need: how to cure heart trouble, treat dropsy, hex
> somebody to death, lock bowels, cause joints to swell, eyes to fall out and so on.
> Where was this black person? [11]

Regaining composure, Walker decides to dig past the hard, impervious layers of white male "voices of authority" [11]. Finally, she strikes gold: "the
name of Zora Neale Hurston" tucked away in a "*footnote*" [11]. The essay
marks this discovery with a dramatic shift in tone—from anxiety to
jubilation—and in the confirmation ritual that follows, Walker's celebratory
rhetoric reaches the intensity level of the black sermon:

> Zora Hurston, who went to Barnard to learn how to study what she really
> wanted to learn: the ways of her own people, and what ancient rituals, customs,
> and beliefs had made them unique.
> Zora, of the sandy-colored hair and daredevil eyes, a girl who escaped poverty
> and parental neglect by hard work and a sharp eye for the main chance.
> Zora, who left the South only to return to look at it again. Who went to root
> doctors from Florida to Louisiana and said, "Here I am. I want to learn your
> trade."
> Zora, who had collected all the black folklore I could ever use.
> *That Zora.* [12]

This passage, with its incantatory rhythm and breathless repetition, sym-
bolically enacts Zora's rebirthing, renaming, and reassignment to her proper
role as model. Walker is writer-as-witness, testifying on behalf of a black
woman whom history rendered anonymous. Rescuing Zora from the dung
heap of neglect and scorn, she relocates her in the clean, airy spaces of her discourse where blood ties are renewed. The result is a literary troika, what
Walker calls "the happy relatedness of Zora, my mother, and me" [12]. Bask-
ing in her newly-found security, Walker is able to achieve artistic success in the
"Revenge of Hannah Kemhuff."[9] Thus, to a room, a desk, and privacy Walker
has added the life-saving presence of a literary ancestor.

Another pair of essays, Woolf's " 'Jane Eyre' and 'Wuthering Heights' "
and Walker's "Beyond the Peacock: The Reconstruction of Flannery O'Connor," show the two writers once again meeting on a thematic common ground
through different discursive routes. The spotlight in both essays is the woman
writer, her ability to write and the inevitable link between that ability and her
material circumstance. For Woolf, there is a definite correlation between the
creative imagination and material condition. Imaginative "webs," she writes in
A Room of One's Own, "are not spun in midair by incorporeal creatures, but
are the work of suffering human beings, and are attached to grossly material
things, like health and money and the houses we live in" [43-4]. Given wom-
en's material deprivation, then, their small creative output and its generally inferior quality, according to Woolf, are logical outcomes. Walker, characteristically, adds race as a crucial fourth term to Woolf's thinking about the
alignment of gender, poverty, and creativity. "What did it mean for a black
woman to be an artist in our grandmothers' time?" she asks. Her reply, with its
compelling suggestion of the unique burden of black femalehood, is vintage
Walker: "It is a question with an answer cruel enough to stop the blood" [*Our
Mothers' Gardens*, 233]. But it is apparent that Woolf and Walker do not read

the same signs from women's social (con)text. Where the former sees paralysis, the latter imagines possibility.

In " 'Jane Eyre' and 'Wuthering Heights' " Woolf takes on a subject as close to her heart as the modernism/realism split discussed in "Modern Fiction." It is the equally obsessive topic of the quality of women's creative imagination. In fact, the two essays are in some ways related because Woolf found realists and women equally guilty of the failure to escape from fact. Both scored low marks on her modernist litmus test, the only difference being that while the entire school of realists flunked, sometimes a woman or two made the mark. But these offenders do not receive the same punishment. In "Modern Fiction" the realists get a slap on the wrist compared to the reprimand Charlotte Brontë receives in this essay. Woolf's dissatisfaction with the author of *Jane Eyre* for allowing what Jane Marcus refers to as "the large, ugly 'I' " ["No More Horses," 276] to disfigure her writing seeps through the anger-proof mask of her dignified persona. It is quite visible in a passage that Woolf herself might consider, if not declamatory, somewhat heavy-handed. For writing the self, Charlotte Brontë is made to look like a fumbling amateur next to the skilled and seasoned, albeit equally self-centered, Thomas Hardy:

> Of this power, of this speculative curiosity, Charlotte Brontë has no trace. She does not attempt to solve the problems of human life; she is even unaware that such problems exist; all her force, and it is the more tremendous for being constricted, goes into the assertion, "I love," "I hate," "I suffer." [157]

As a rule, Woolf detested authorial presence in writing, but she was especially opposed to female presence because she feared its potential to validate the stereotype of the autobiographically-prone and therefore unserious woman writer. A letter to Ethel Smyth reveals the degree of Woolf's sensitivity to this issue and its effect on her own aesthetic practice:

> I didnt write 'A room' without considerable feeling even you will admit; I'm not cool on the subject. And I forced myself to keep my own figure fictitious; legendary. If I had said, Look here am I uneducated, because my brothers used all the family funds which is the fact—Well theyd have said; she has an axe to grind; and no one would have taken me seriously, though I agree I should have had many more of the wrong kind of reader; who will read you and go away and rejoice in the personalities, not because they are lively and easy reading; but because they prove once more how vain, how personal, so they will say, rubbing their hands with glee, women always are; I can hear them as I write. [*Letters*, V. 194-95]

Such confessional release is common in Woolf's letters, which Catherine Stimpson has described as "a psychological and rhetorical middle space between what she wrote for herself and what she produced for a general audience" [168], in other words, the link between her diaries and her art. The information relayed in the quoted passage is instructive on two levels. First, it points to the deep anger Woolf felt as a gendered subject. Second, it suggests that her self-denying aesthetic has its origins in a self-protective impulse: she resented and resisted the stigma of the carping female.[10] Strangely, however, what may have begun for Woolf as a face-saving tactic would be transformed literally within the universe of patriarchal discourse she sought to inhabit into the loss of her female face. "[T]he rhetoric of *universal*," to borrow Deborah Pope's useful terminology, permits only the "*nonfemale*" [Pope, 27]. Unfortunately, one might add, Woolf had a fatal attraction to this rhetoric. The self-excising aesthetic she developed as a result had a wasting effect on her, both physically and emotionally. Yet she could not bring herself to appreciate women like Charlotte Brontë whose self-affirming discourse offered a wholesome alternative to the crippling hidden agenda of universalism.

In " 'Jane Eyre' and 'Wuthering Heights' " Woolf scolds Charlotte Brontë for unashamedly writing the self and applauds Emily Brontë for her disembodying capacity—that "rarest of all [female] powers" [161]. Incidentally, while Woolf's critique of the fact-driven realists gains strength incrementally— from the mild tone of "Modern Fiction" to the "greater boldness" of "Mr. Bennett and Mrs. Brown," for instance—she is consistently disparaging of Charlotte Brontë for the twin offenses of writing the self and writing in anger. What is downplayed in this essay is the root cause of Charlotte Brontë's anger—the combined oppressive force of gender and material reality. Woolf's insistence that there be no "agree[ment]" between the "life within" and "the life outside" ["Montaigne," 59] leads her away from such detail or any detail from her own life of material advantage that might have helped to give perspective to her reading of Charlotte Brontë as a failed artist.

In "Beyond the Peacock: The Construction of Flannery O'Connor," Walker offers her own thoughts on the juncture of female creativity and material circumstance. Indeed, it is an uncannily specific illustration of Woolf's idea that literary production is "the work of suffering human beings [which is] attached to grossly material things, like health and money and the houses we live in" [*A Room*, 43-4]. But once again Walker problematizes Woolf's theoretics on "the woman question" by adding "the race factor." The "reconstruction" of (white) Flannery O'Connor by (black) Alice Walker is also a configuration of racial difference within gender sameness. The essay tells the story of two women fitted differently in patriarchy's mantle and, as a result, made to stand on unequal social grounds. Their houses, situated "within minutes of each other on the same Eatonton-to-Milledgeville road" [42], embody the racially differentiated worlds they inhabit in spite of their shared gender. But Walker and O'Connor share more than the same sex; they are writers who create artifacts from the hard facts of life. How the creative minds of these writers are shaped by their material conditions or, put simply, the view (of the world) each sees from her (socially allocated) room is the central theme of the essay.

Walker employs a quasi-fictional technique to recount a real life experience. The plot records the narrator's journey back into her past in search of clues to explain (and relieve) her angst-filled present. The crisis of the moment is occasioned simultaneously by shame and loss. In college Walker had "read [O'Connor's] books endlessly, scarcely conscious of the differences between her racial and economic background and my own," until she learned of other women writers she "had not been allowed to know" [42] because they were black. Consequently, she cast O'Connor aside and read every black woman writer she could find. As a subscriber to canonistic pluralism, she "missed" O'Connor, yet she could readmit her only on new terms that required a "reconstruction" of her and of their relationship.

Characters and dialogue are two other fictional devices Walker utilizes in her narrative method. Walker as narrator speaks for herself and for O'Connor, while Walker's mother plays the important secondary role of interlocutor. As Walker's traveling companion, she is the other voice in the essay's flavorful dialogue which she sprinkles with folksy humor and homespun wisdom. She is also a skilled interrogator. Her questions provoke answers that are important pieces in the re-modeling job being done on O'Connor. A good example is the exchange that follows Walker's critical synopsis of "Everything that Rises Must Converge." To her mother's pointed question "What did the black woman do after she knocked the white woman down and walked away?" Walker offers the richly suggestive answer, "O'Connor chose not to say and that is why, although this is a good story, it is, to me, only half a story. *You* might know the other half . . . " [51].

The cornerstone in Walker's reconstruction project seems to me to lie right here. It is the piece that completes the complex make-over of O'Connor that occurs in the essay's middle section. Walker's recital of O'Connor's artistic virtues—her vision of fallen but redeemable humankind; her demythologization of southern genteel culture; her unorthodox religiosity and, above all, the force and beauty of her language—rises to a crescendo of praise that constitutes a fitting tribute from a devotee. But this image is suddenly overlaid, indeed, nearly erased, by another—the picture of two houses: Andalusia, O'Connor's well-kept, guarded, unoccupied "large white house at the top of a hill with a view of a lake" [57], and the rotting remains of the "sharefarmer shack" [44] that was once home to the young Walker and her large family. The impact of the second image hurls Walker from the seductive imaginary realms of fiction down to earth where the unimagined reality of racial difference vitiates her gender, artistic, and southern ties with O'Connor. The epiphanic moment calls for candor and Walker does not hold back: "Her house becomes—in an instant—the symbol of my own disinheritance and for that instant I hate her guts. All that she has meant to me is diminished, though her diminishment within me is against my will" [51].

This moment vanishes as quickly as it came and is replaced once more by the imperishable idea of O'Connor as artist. Walker decides that O'Connor's legacy as creator of supreme fictions out of a disabling environment and from the prison-house of a disabled body is more important than their shared heritage of racial segregation. Yet for all her readiness to be comforted by the vernacular wisdom contained in the expression "Take what you can use and let the rest rot" [59], Walker's reconstruction of O'Connor produces not a copy of the original text she read unself-consciously as a college student but rather a palimpsest with a subtext that speaks to what Walker sees as O'Connor's unwillingness to complete the black woman's story in "Everything that Rises Must Converge." According to the tale of two houses which the essay narrates, Walker is right to think that it is her (nonliterate) artist-mother, not O'Connor, who is properly situated for access to the view that will round up the black woman—that is, move her from caricature to full humanity. The idea of positionality as it affects perspective is an important narrative construct that undergirds Walker's reconception of O'Connor. With books providing only a partial view, Walker needed to move closer (literally) to O'Connor to get the full picture of a woman who was like her but much more unlike her. It is this kind of intersubjectivity that is missing in " 'Jane Eyre' and 'Wuthering Heights',", where Woolf's objective pose does not allow for any mention of the obvious class difference that set her apart from and shaped her view of the women who are the subject of her essay.

Walker's essay, "If the Present Looks Like the Past, What Does the Future Look Like?" could easily be retitled "How It Strikes a Contemporary," the last essay in the first volume of Woolf's *The Common Reader*, because in both, the writers take stock of the present in light of an overdetermined past and an uncertain but hopeful future. Also, for both, literature is the clearest articulation of the shaping forces of history. But the essays' synonymy of outlook is not sustained at the narrative level where Walker's obsessional self-writing habit stands in bold opposition to Woolf's penchant for authorial disguise.

"How It Strikes a Contemporary" is Woolf's effort to evaluate the modernist literary enterprise in which she was a key player. There is a discernible firmness in the tone and timbre of this essay compared to the conciliatory mood of "Modern Fiction," written four years earlier on a related subject. Such observation lends support to Alex Zwerdling's argument that Woolf's voice grew bolder with time and maturity.[11] In this essay, *Ulysses* is still offered as a paradox—"a memorable catastrophe—immense in daring, terrific in disaster" [235]—but the terms of negation are weightier. And the description of Lawrence as having "moments of greatness, but hours of something very different" [235], is a masterful deployment of understatement that is wounding. She also has a few stern words for her era. She calls it "barren and exhausted," "lean," and the repository of "enormous rubbish heaps." Woolf seems to have lost some of her tea-table manners, but, if that is the case, then it is a cruel irony that she should gain in voice and personality as she advocates the very loss of these attributes.

Personality is the demon Woolf seeks to exorcise in this essay. The possessed modern writer, she argues, is caught in its grip and is unable, therefore, to "generalise" ["How It Strikes a Contemporary," 239] or to move toward the universal. Woolf's tool for loosening the stranglehold of personality on her generation is hyperbole. She exaggerates the failures of her age by juxtaposing them with the (equally exaggerated) successes of the past. Her generation's "fragments" are made to look like childish doodles next to the crafted "masterpieces" of her predecessors just as their "endeavour" falls shamefully short of their "genius." All this is to shock her peers into disengagement from self.

But the hard line has the makings of a pose because what Woolf is holding back and finally manages to let out is her fascination with the "new art from the fragments and sensations of the present" [Bradbury, 7]. The moment, transient, yet ripe with meaning and sensation, is, for Woolf, the unique feature of modernist art and the hallmark of her own fiction. Its eruption in this essay attests to the attraction it held for her and betrays the pose in her rhetoric of opposition:

> Meanwhile it is one of the first fine days of spring. Life is not altogether lacking in colour. The telephone, which interrupts the most serious conversations and cuts short the most weighty observations, has a romance of its own. And the random talk of people who have no chance of immortality and thus can speak their minds out has a setting, often, of lights, streets, houses, human beings, beautiful or grotesque, which will weave itself into the moment forever. ["How It Strikes a Contemporary," 235-36]

Woolf envisioned modern life as fleeting, fragmentary, and chaotic, the result of the change in the perception of reality that occurred around December 1910 ["Mr. Bennett and Mrs. Brown," 320]. Proof of the modern writer's caliber is in her/his ability to capture and hold the new reality in a timeless capsule. That she abhors the overemphasis on self (what she sometimes conflated with the male ego) by writers like Joyce is irrefutable. However, that she condemns modern literature's fragmentary character—the very thing that excited her—gives a strong impression that she is throwing her voice in the wrong direction. Woolf's voice may have grown louder in this essay, but one hears a good deal of double-talk.

"If the Present Looks Like the Past, What Does the Future Look Like?" gives Walker an opportunity to comment, as Woolf does, on a subject that collates past and present times for a reasonable determination of the future. What strikes (and appalls) Walker, however, is not the obsession with self by a historically overdetermined group of people but rather the denial of self by persons already terribly underdetermined. "Colorism," defined by Walker as "the prejudicial or preferential treatment of same-race people based solely on their color" [290], is, in her mind, the scourge of black Americans, a veritable sign of their double (or triple) conquest in light of its kinship with "colonialism, sexism and racism" [291]. Indeed, as she sees it, colorism as black-on-black racism and sexism is the final and most dangerous stage in the historical campaign to deny blackness and invalidate black female identity. But her goal here is to reveal blacks' complicity with this effort. With colorism, Walker argues, blacks practice a divide-and-conquer maneuver that will hasten the demise of blackness through the annihilation of "the black black woman" [291]. Characteristically affirming of both blackness and femaleness, Walker therefore takes aim at the perpetrators of colorism, in life and in literature.

Her multiple target—"light-skinned black women," "black black women," near-white black men, and black-skinned men—calls for a discursive ventriloquism, a rhetorical strategy akin to Mae Henderson's concept of "speaking in tongues" [22]. According to Henderson, "intimacy with the discourse of the other(s) [enables] black women writers [to] weave into their work competing and complementary discourses — discourses that seek both to adjudicate competing claims and witness common concerns" [23]. Walker uses "we" in this essay to refer to the African-American community of which she is a part to facilitate the expression of shared concerns. But unlike Woolf, she does not lock up the "I" in a communalistic "we." Instead, she grants it a free-agency status so that it can speak with and against (as well as blend with and stand apart from) the group.

Walker stakes out her own racial grounds unequivocally in the opening letter to a light-skinned "sister." "I myself, halfway between light and dark — a definite brown — must align myself with black black women" ["Present Looks Like Past," 291]. It is a vantage point that invigorates her subsequent reading of the disturbing signs of self-denial inscribed in black social and written texts. In both, the black female body, as a repository of otherness, is the site selected for dis-identification. Walker seems to link the appropriation of black femininity by the marketers of a bleached blackness to the social status of the black woman as a double "other." She is an easier prey compared to the black male, whose racial "otherness" is compensated in patriarchal society by his gendered "first-ness." To underline the principle of female exploitation embedded in colorism, Walker finds it necessary to revise W. E. B. DuBois' famous statement on race relations. Calling it "a true statement" but "a man's vision" [310], Walker renders it from a contemporary black female perspective: " . . . the problem of the twenty-first century will still be the problem of the color line, not only 'the relation of the darker to the lighter races of men [sic] in Asia and Africa, in America and the islands of the sea,' but the relations between the darker and lighter people of the same races and of the women who represent both dark and light within each race" [211]. Walker's agreement with and dissent from DuBois — a venerable figure in black racial politics — exemplify a discursive technique that accommodates other voices but leaves sufficient room for her own.

This technique embodies Walker's womanist vision of putting black female audacity to work for change. *In Search of Our Mothers' Gardens* is the book in Walker's canon that inaugurates womanism as a theoretical construct for determining difference between black and white feminists. A womanist is a "black feminist or feminist of color" who is distinguished from her white counterpart mainly by her "audacious . . . behavior" and nonseparatist political stance [xi]. Both attributes imply a critique of white feminist selective preoccupation with sexual oppression to the exclusion of other equally invidious forms of oppression such as race and class. The womanist's readiness to confront all, not just some, of patriarchy's "lies and secrets" (to borrow from Adrienne Rich's title) testifies, in Walker's view, to her unflinching boldness.

In the wake of poststructuralist destabilization of identity, Walker's womanist assumptions have remained relatively underexplored by both black and white feminists who are afraid of being caught in an essentialist trap. Essentialism, however, needs to be critically examined so that it does not become like the prescriptive modernism of Woolf's day and it is not another gag on the female voice (see Fuss, xi). I have argued elsewhere the merits and limitations of womanism as a critical tool.[12] In this context, however, two points deserve mention. The first is that the narrative posture Walker adopts in her essays clearly benefits from womanist "willful[ness]" [xi]. Walker does not hesitate "to tell it like it is," no matter who is listening.[13] Second, I submit that the current recall by some feminist critics of the personal voice lost in the labyrinth of master discourses for over a decade is a sign that womanism can be made to serve all feminists.[14]

"There's no doubt in my mind that I have found out how to begin (at 40) to say something in my own voice; and that interests me so that I feel I can go ahead without praise" [*A Writer's Diary*, 46]. Thus wrote Woolf in 1922 as she reflected on the public response to *Jacob's Room*, her newly published modernist experiment in fiction. This statement of self-affirmation takes on a tinge of irony, however, when one realizes that, in Woolf's aesthetics, a gain in voice generally implies the loss of authorial presence. Woolf's commitment to write off the self earned her tremendous success in the novel, but it ran into some difficulty in the essay, the meeting place for the self and the world. The *Common Reader* essays I discussed in this paper show Woolf's reluctance to unveil herself even in the hospitable quarters of the essay, a sign that she held, in Epstein's words, "too pure, too constricted a conception of the essayist" [407].

Walker takes a different position. She would support Epstein's definition of the essay as "a pair of baggy pants into which nearly anyone and anything can fit" [400] because it conjures up an image of a democratic, antibourgeois vehicle of expression that will accommodate her essayistic project of unabashed self-recreation; though, as a womanist, she may very well challenge the pants metaphor.

NOTES

1. *Women's Studies* 4, no. 2/3 (1977) and the *Bulletin of the New York Public Library* 80 (Winter 1977) began the groundswell of feminist interest in Woolf that has gone unabated. Walker's essay "In Search of Our Mothers' Gardens: The Creativity of Black Women in the South," in which she enunciated the unique qualities of black female creativity, laid the foundation for both a burgeoning black feminist criticism and the critique of white feminist exclusionary theoretical and critical practices (*Ms.*, May 1974, 64-70, 105). Walker's concept of womanism, introduced in 1983 with the publication of her volume of essays *In Search of Our Mothers' Gardens*, allies Third-World feminist aspirations with those of African-American feminists.

2. Examples of titles alone include Walker's "One Child of One's Own: A Meaningful Digression Within the Work(s)" in *In Search of Our Mothers' Gardens*, Elaine Showalter's *A Literature of Their Own* (New Jersey: Princeton University Press, 1977), Susan

Squier's "A Track of Our Own: Typescript Drafts of *The Years*" in *Virginia Woolf: A Feminist Slant* (Lincoln: University of Nebraska Press, 1983).

3. See "In Search of Our Mothers' Gardens" in Walker, *In Search of Our Mothers' Gardens*, 235-40, esp. 235-37.

4. In Malcolm Bradbury's *The Modern World: Ten Great Writers*, for example, Woolf is the only woman writer.

5. Elaine Showalter, "Virginia Woolf and a Flight into Androgyny" in *A Literature of Their Own*, 263-97; Adrienne Rich, "When We Dead Awaken: Writing as Re-Vision" in *On Lies, Secrets and Silence: Selected Prose, 1966-1978* (New York: Norton, 1979), 37; Jane Marcus, "Art and Anger," *Feminist Studies* 4 (1978):94.

6. See Woolf's *A Writer's Diary*, 22 and *The Diary of Virginia Woolf*, vol. 2 (London: Hogarth, 1977), 199.

7. A July 20, 1925 entry in *A Writer's Diary* shows Woolf contemplating *Lives of the Obscure*, "which is to tell the whole history of England in one obscure life after another" [79]. She ended up writing essays, instead of a book, on the subject. "Outlines" and "Lives of the Obscure" in *The First Common Reader* contain some examples of these unknown lives.

8. In *Mrs. Dalloway* Clarissa speculates on the relocation of the spirit after death in the persons and places one associated with in life [231-32] and in *To the Lighthouse*, Mrs. Ramsay's spirit continues to inhabit the people and places she knew.

9. See Walker's *In Love and Trouble* (New York: Harcourt Brace Jovanovich, 1973), 60-80.

10. See "Women and Fiction" in *Granite and Rainbow* (New York: Harcourt Brace Jovanovich, 1958), 79-80. Here Woolf's paradigm of the failed artist is the complaining racial, sexual, and class "Other."

11. Alex Zwerdling, in *Virginia Woolf and the Real World* (Berkeley: University of California Press, 1986), also states that *Three Guineas* is "a book Woolf could not have written before her mid-fifties" [33].

12. Tuzyline Jita Allan, "*Womanist and Feminist Aesthetics: A Comparative Study*," dissertation, State University of New York at Stony Brook, 1990.

13. Elizabeth Fox-Genovese also uses this vernacular expression in her essay with respect to Zora Neale Hurston. See "My Statue, My Self: Autobiographical Writings of Afro-American Women" in *The Private Self: Theory and Practice of Women's Autobiographical Writings*, ed. Shari Benstock (Chapel Hill: University of North Carolina Press, 1988), 64.

14. See, for example, Jane Tompkins's "Me and My Shadow," *New Literary History* 19 (Autumn 1987): 170, and Barbara Christian's "The Race for Theory," *Feminist Studies* 14 (1988): 67-69.

WORKS CITED

Adorno, Theodor. "The Essay as Form." Trans. Bob Hullott-Kentor. *New German Critique* 32 (1984): 151-71.

Anderson, Chris. "Hearsay Evidence and Second Class Citizenship." *College English* 50 (1988): 300-308.

Aptheker, Bettina. *Woman's Legacy: Essays on Race, Sex, and Class in American History*. Amherst: University of Massachusetts Press, 1982.

Bradbury, Malcolm. *The Modern World: Ten Great Writers*. New York: Penguin Books, 1988.

Epstein, Joseph. "Piece Work: Writing the Essay." *Plausible Prejudices: Essays on American Writing.* New York: Norton, 1985. 397-411.

Froula, Christine. "The Daughter's Seduction: Sexual Violence and Literary History." *Feminist Theory in Practice and Process.* Ed. Micheline R. Malson, Jean F. O'Barr, Sarah Westphal-Wihl, and Mary Wyer. Chicago: University of Chicago Press, 1989.

Fuss, Diana. *Essentially Speaking: Feminism, Nature and Difference.* New York: Routledge, 1989.

Gates, Jr., Henry Louis. *Figures in Black.* New York: Oxford University Press, 1987.

_____. *The Signifying Monkey.* New York: Oxford University Press, 1988.

Good, Graham. *The Observing Self: Rediscovering the Essay.* London: Routledge, 1988.

Hall, Michael L. "The Emergence of the Essay and the Idea of Discovery." *Essays on the Essay: Redefining the Genre.* Ed. Alexander J. Butrym. Athens: University of Georgia Press, 1989. 73-91.

Henderson, Mae Gwendolyn. "Speaking in Tongues: Dialogics, Dialectics and the Black Woman Writer's Literary Tradition." *Changing Our Own Words: Essays on Criticism, Theory and Writing by Black Women.* Ed. Cheryl A. Wall. New Brunswick: Rutgers University Press, 1989. 16-37.

Marcus, Jane. " 'No More Horses': Virginia Woolf on Art and Propaganda." *Women's Studies* 4 (1977): 265-90.

Pope, Deborah. "Notes toward a Supreme Fiction: The Work of Feminist Criticism." *Women and a New Academy: Gender and Cultural Contexts.* Ed. Jean F. O'Barr. Wisconsin: University of Wisconsin Press, 1989. 22-37.

Rose, Phyllis. *Woman of Letters: A Life of Virginia Woolf.* New York: Oxford University Press, 1978.

Stimpson, Catherine. "The Female Sociograph: The Theater of Virginia Woolf's Letters." *The Female Autograph.* Ed. Domna C. Stanton. Chicago: University of Chicago Press, 1987. 168-79.

Stoehr, Taylor. "Tone and Voice." *College English* 30 (1968): 150-61.

Walker, Alice. *In Search of Our Mothers' Gardens.* New York: Harcourt Brace Jovanovich, 1983.

Woolf, Virginia. "The Decay of Essay-Writing." *The Essays of Virginia Woolf.* Ed. Andrew McNeillie. Vol. I. New York: Harcourt Brace Jovanovich, 1986. 24-27.

_____. *The Letters of Virginia Woolf.* Ed. Nigel Nicolson with Joanne Trautmann. 6 vols. London: Hogarth, 1975-80.

_____. "The Modern Essay." *The Common Reader: First Series.* Ed. Andrew McNeillie. New York: Harcourt Brace Jovanovich, 1984. 211-22.

_____. *Moments of Being.* Ed. Jeanne Schulkind. New York: Harcourt Brace Jovanovich, 1976.

_____. "Montaigne." *The Common Reader: First Series.* Ed. Andrew McNeille. New York: Harcourt Brace Jovanovich, 1984. 58-68.

_____. "Mr. Bennett and Mrs. Brown." *Collected Essays.* Ed. Leonard Woolf. 4 vols. London: Hogarth, 1966, 1967. 319-37.

_____. *A Room of One's Own.* New York: Harcourt Brace Jovanovich, 1929.

_____. *A Writer's Diary.* New York: Harcourt Brace Jovanovich, 1953.

Women's Essays as
Political Intervention

CHAPTER NINE

The Passionate Essay

Radical Feminist Essayists

RUTH-ELLEN BOETCHER JOERES

> Radical feminist and lesbian theory is passionate.
>
> Carol Anne Douglas,
> *Love and Politics*

At its inception, the essay was an elitist genre that directed itself to a particular exclusive audience.[1] Even if Montaigne and Bacon were rebelling in some way by presenting a new form and by filling that form with unusual thoughts and ideas, they remained gentlemen, aristocrats whose years of experience had given them the wisdom and insight that they were in a privileged position to share. Their audiences were hardly mobs or even a vast middle-class reading public, which did not yet exist, but rather the educated, literate upper classes, the empowered, the European, the mostly male. And if their successors were born into somewhat less hierarchical times—if Addison and Steele and Charles Lamb and Herman Grimm were faced with a reading audience that included increasing numbers of women, for example—the class consciousness certainly remained, despite the fact that everybody now wanted to be bourgeois instead of aristocratic.[2] The essay has been through a variety of changes, but historically, at least, it has almost always been a tool of the privileged classes. For one thing, it has almost always implied leisure: those who wrote essays as well as those who read them had to be in a position of ease. Montaigne, after all, retreated from the world of public service and wrote his essays at his country estate. The whole matter of self-reflection, the usual activity of the essay, is not generally undertaken in the midst of great and distracting external activity.

As to what was transmitted through the essay: it was hardly a challenge to the status quo. The form itself might have been viewed as unusual; the content might well have been seen as antischolastic, as more flexible and tolerant than the treatises and discourses that preceded it. But essentially, what Montaigne wrote showed his readers how he was living in the world as he perceived it, and what Bacon wrote resembled above all a "how-to" manual. Learning to adjust to the world does not necessarily involve a radical challenging of that world: it takes for granted that the world is as it is, and that we, the individuals living in it, must use that fact as our point of departure, as that which will frame all of our responses.

But what happens when a radical writer selects an elitist form like the essay and, as Marlis Gerhardt says, fills the old wineskin with new wine? [Gerhardt, 343]. Is there a tension created between the historical weight of the essay as it was and the essay now (at least metaphorically now: I am not claiming that radical essays are only a thing of the present moment)? Are the history and tradition of the essay thereby repudiated in the process of its becoming a tool for social and political change? And what if the tradition that is challenged is the patriarchal tradition? What if the radical essayists are women, radical feminists? If the essayist has always been understood to be a man (and that is common), and if the essay itself is feminine (for it is always described as a subjective, flexible, yet materially-based, as opposed to abstract, form, that is, as possessing characteristics that have often been aligned with the feminine), what happens when the essay is appropriated by women, and most particularly by radical feminist women whose goal is to challenge the patriarchal system, indeed to send it into a state of upheaval and revision? It is obviously a mighty step in another direction if the "feminine" essay, which is produced by the male essayist, now becomes the feminist essay in the hands of a radical woman writer who sees herself and her writing as active, opinionated, revolutionary.

Obviously, difficulties exist in a discussion of this nature. As far as I know, the radical feminists who are included in my article have not made overt statements concerning their selection of the essay form nor any acknowledgment of the form. But given the tradition of the essay, I think we can assume that the essay's history accompanies the selection of the form: in other words, like writers in general, radical feminists may well be cognizant of the implications of the form they choose in which to transmit their messages. Furthermore, a radical feminist might well select the essay, despite its traditional elitist history, because it can look very much like the political tract whose purpose is to argue for change, or like the speech that is by nature a tool of communication. The choice may also be a matter of prudence and expedience: what other genre is there that allows the flexibility of the essay? At the same time, the specific history of who has written essays, who has read them, and the ways in which essays have been analyzed, criticized, and perceived, provides a framework in which essays can be understood and read, and possibly written.

On the other hand, despite the essay's elitist history, it has also been considered a boundary form, that is, a genre that does not comfortably fit into the traditional classical lyric-epic-dramatic pattern. One need only examine the theoretical and methodological treatments of the essay to sense the defensiveness with which most scholars of the genre approach the form, the immense difficulties they encounter even when they are trying to define it. Its elusiveness, but more important its fringe nature, might well make the essay appeal to those who are themselves on the fringe. Shaping one's radical arguments within a form that is itself off center, somewhere on the boundary of the traditional ideas about genre, provides a certain advantage. Thus, in addition to challenging standard perceptions of the essay as a presentation of the collected wisdom of white European and American men, the radical feminist might well not only appropriate and revise the form to her own liking but at the same time feel an affinity with a genre that even today is still being explored and continuously redefined by those who cannot fit it comfortably into any standard traditional generic framework.[3]

There is also the paradoxical and problematic matter of appropriating a form that exudes authority, a form like the bourgeois essay, in order to assume an authority that marginal groups do not have. The mere choice of the essay, with the heavy weight of male importance and exclusivity historically connected with it, may well place the radical feminist in a world in which she is by definition neither welcome nor appropriate. As a means of public self-identification, the essay is particularly helpful to those who know they need to mark themselves, yet the use of such a form can also be read as accepting an entire series of unfortunate assumptions that have to do with the privileging of such middle-class values as the unified self and the supreme power of the intellect. Contradictions obviously arise when it comes to thinking about the male essayist, the female essayist, and the "female" essay, the elitism as well as the boundary nature of the essay, and the matter of who is writing and who is reading it.

My focus on the radical feminist essay has to do with what happens to a discussion of the genre when its use by groups far from those most traditionally connected with it is examined. Since the history of the essay is one heavily tied to a male tradition, and since nonradical women who have chosen to use the form tend to reflect standard perceptions of the essay, what it should contain, and how it is structured, it strikes me as particularly useful to investigate the other end of the spectrum: those whose use of the essay immediately challenges our usual understanding of the form. I could have chosen male essayists of color, for example, who obviously have their own perspective on literary forms that were not created with them in mind. But I share the view of many feminists that gender is the "original" and in that way the most decisive factor in the determining of self-perception as well as the perception of others; it is the point of departure that is of course in constant tension with race and class.[4] And by selecting radical feminists, those whose commitment to feminism is most pronounced, I have chosen those who will by definition represent a gender-specific position far afield from that of the male essayist who shaped and furthered the essay but who nevertheless have used the form frequently, vociferously, passionately, to communicate their ideas.

As Carol Anne Douglas states in *Love and Politics: Radical Feminist and Lesbian Theories*, defining the radical feminist is not an easy task. The essayists whom I will discuss also indicate a range that may well make one wonder why they have been thrown together for this purpose: they are German as well as American, they are women of color, they are white, they are lesbian, they are heterosexual, they share certain political assumptions but their radicality varies considerably. I see value in Douglas's positing two major groups of radical and lesbian feminists, although I am not absolutely convinced that these groups are more characteristic of radicals than of any other feminists (or indeed that the division into only two groups clarifies the matter). Douglas's groups resemble in a way what I elsewhere have labeled the optimistic and the pessimistic feminists [Joeres, 137–38], that is, those who focus exclusively on women and those who see equality with men as the predominant goal. Douglas adds nuances of meaning to her descriptions: for her, pessimistic feminists by my definition are the "classic" radical feminists, whose politics claim that "basically men and women are more similar than they are different, and that men used the differences that exist in reproduction to oppress women and define them as inferior" [Douglas, 11]. In contrast, those whom I call the optimists are labeled "the focus on women" group by Douglas. This group

> holds that there are greater differences between women and men than the classical radical feminist position maintains. Some even suggest that men are inherently more violent than women. Women's reproductive capacity is not a burden in itself. . . . Women can gain more from being with one another than with men. Women are not more limited than men and do not need to learn from them. . . . Some of these women believe that the goal should be creating societies separate from men, or perhaps ruling them—in a gentle, matriarchal way. The appropriate tactic is building separate, independent women's communities, not confrontation with men. [Douglas, 12]

If these positions can be claimed by radical feminists, then those whose essays I shall examine indeed can be defined as such. At the same time, by broadening my sample to include non-American women, I am deliberately introducing another variable, namely that of nationality, which should at least make clear that "American" cannot and should not be an unmarked category. The feminist beliefs held by these women fit under the rubric of radical-feminist; the issues, the particular emphases, the contexts in which they write their essays are, however, not the same. My purpose remains an attempt to answer the question: what occurs when a gender-specific group of like-minded individuals, whose shared goals challenge much of what the essay traditionally represents, uses the essay as an instrument to achieve those goals?

> Forms: the forms of hierarchy, of institutions, of habits, the ways things are done; the forms of language, gesture, art, of thought, and, equally, of emotion. What we say to one another being often what it is predictable that we will say; what I will say, if you say that: Dialogue. [Griffin, "The Way of All Ideology," 641]

Susan Griffin writes book chapters that resemble essays. Even her "academic" publications—including the above, excerpted from an article that appeared in *Signs*—seem more like essays than articles, with their clear focus on the subjective, their open-endedness, their monologic/dialogic mixture. Thus I have chosen to have her illustrate the first assertion I want to make: that *the whole issue of form, whether overtly or only obliquely referred to, does indeed*

*play a role in the selection, use, and adaptation of the essay by radical femi-
nists.* The form itself becomes an obvious statement, pressing itself insistently
forward into the reader's consciousness, occasionally varying enough from the
expected to call attention to itself as different.

Griffin's observation is a more overt commentary on form than one finds in
most radical-feminist essays. It also offers contradictions, the ambivalence that
feminism has traditionally felt toward matters of form (if form implies schools,
canons, separations, hierarchies), as well as the sense that form is also the essential component of language, art, emotion, and gesture, all matters with
which we are constantly involved. Form itself can produce skepticism, particularly for the feminists among us who translate the concept into categorization, schematization, ordering, rigidity—who see form as that applied from
without, generally upon those of us who are marginal, powerless, and without
authority—generally by the white, middle-class patriarchy that rules us (but
occasionally even by other women, indeed other feminists, who cannot incorporate us easily into their perception of the world). Form is control; form is
limitation. Form is someone else's rules and qualifications. Equally important,
form suggests levels of quality and acceptance: compliance and imitation will
bring success and approval, whereas breaking the rules (changing the forms)
will simply lead to greater marginalization and non-belonging. A use of form
also smacks of institutionalization: that is, if we select an already-established
and accepted form in which to express our thoughts, we might well be simply
co-opted, our radicalism dulled at the edges, by allowing ourselves to be included in a scheme of things in whose formation we had no part.

At the same time, form is inevitable, the omnipresent and necessary framing
for our thoughts and actions. In its most broadly understood sense—form as
definition—form will give us parameters within which to present our ideas;
form will empower us, will allow us to establish our own definitions, to present
our own thoughts. Form, if deliberately selected and shaped by us, will allow
us to be heard.

A radical feminist approaching the issue of form as she deliberates how she
wants to present her ideas might feel some hesitation at the idea of selecting a
form as loaded with tradition, with maleness, with whiteness and middle-class
gentlemanliness as the essay. If she is convinced that it is the appropriate vehicle, however, then it seems to follow that she will want the form to represent
her and not its history. As a feminist, she perforce thinks and acts in political
fashion: *form* for her might well become *forum*, a means by which she can
communicate her form-breaking ideas. In any case, her radical feminism will
clash with the traditional historical expectations of the essay, its acknowledgment of the status quo, its efforts to explain life within that apparently absolute
and unchangeable site. It will no doubt also challenge the inevitable aesthetic
rules that are always connected with the essay, which may well be "nonfictional" but which also echo the belletristic, the formulations of ideas and messages in what is viewed as an aesthetically appropriate way.

Susan Griffin also mentions another aspect of form in the *Signs* excerpt, namely dialogue. A radical feminist, thinking politically, needs above all to communicate, not only to express her ideas and thoughts, but also to stimulate a resonance to them, to create a response, and by so doing, to open the way to dialogue and ultimately to action. Even in its most traditional interpretation, the essay stimulates and emphasizes communication: one need only recall such essays as Montaigne's "On the education of children," or virtually any of Bacon's essays, which overtly or covertly address themselves to others, sharing advice, wisdom, and ideas. Nevertheless, if the essay has a specific political purpose, and the essays of radical feminists will by definition be of this variety, the communication will go beyond the one-sided offering of information and advice and at least imply the need for a response; the essay must at least signify dialogue although it is itself a monologue.

Given the utterly confusing state of essay definition, it is hard to imagine how one might define the typical essay. At the same time, if we select certain male models both early (Montaigne, Bacon) and more recent (Emerson, E. B. White), or even female models that are not radical-feminist (Agnes Repplier, Virginia Woolf), we see general formal characteristics that tend to be present in all or most of them: brevity, an expressed authorial subjectivity, a tendency toward nonfictional representation. Although it is not only radical feminists who depart from these and other characteristic elements, it is nevertheless remarkable how often they do digress from the expected essay form. In a piece on Emily Dickinson, for example, Adrienne Rich challenges not only the standard form of the academic article but the expected form of the essay as well [Rich, 157-83]. By ultimately allowing Dickinson to take over as the principal voice, breaking down the barriers between subject and author, revising even the idea of subjectivity by giving narrative voice to both her own subjectivity and that of Dickinson, Rich ruptures our expectations of a scholarly article by turning it into something resembling an essay. At the same time, on several levels she also challenges the form of the traditional essay, going, for example, far beyond the common habit of essayists to provide quotations: whereas Montaigne explains his use of quotations by self-consciously commenting "I only quote others to make myself more explicit" [Montaigne, 52], Rich, a poet, uses quotations from Dickinson's poetry to illustrate her own arguments, specifically in the matter of Dickinson's love for women but also in allowing the quotations from Dickinson to take over her own words. The quotation becomes the authority, thus lessening the role of the authoritative essayist Rich and putting her in a position behind her subject Dickinson.

This challenge to form, to definition and to the expected, will leap out at the reader on many levels, among them form itself. Adrienne Rich calls our attention to the way in which she treats content—her radical re-reading of Dickinson, her "meeting" with Dickinson as a lesbian sensing another lesbian—but most specifically in revising the form to illustrate the content she is presenting. Thus the initial expectation of a reader approaching Rich's piece, that she is about to be presented with an academic treatment of Emily Dickinson's poetry, is countered by a subjective essay. And the sense that this subjective essay will be traditional is also countered by a text that undermines the standard perception of the essay by focusing far more on an other than on the self, by overrunning the essayist's text with the words of her subject.

The fact that Adrienne Rich's essay on Emily Dickinson was initially a lecture gives her essay a sense of initiated dialogue, of communication, that also removes it from the interiorized self-examination practice of many traditional essays and connects it with the material conditions present in the production of her essay. A remarkable number of essays by radical feminists indeed have their origins in speeches, talks, comments, and despite the inevitable revisions that occur between speech and essay, the impression of speaking-to, communicating-with, stimulating response remains paramount.[5] In a speech, words are written with a visible audience in mind, with the idea of communication made concrete, tangible, central, thereby certainly affecting the message, tone, and form of the speech itself. Whatever the effect of the mode of speaking that is implied and embedded in many radical-feminist essays, an obvious sense of connection with an audience will on occasion be recognizable even on the level of syntax.[6]

In the matter of syntactic internal form, Audre Lorde's intriguing movement among personal pronouns in her "Poetry is Not a Luxury" can be seen as a clear effort to create connections, dialogic and otherwise, between the essayist and her readers/listeners. From the outset, there is a presence of what could be viewed as a collective "we": no single individual, instead a group despite the single authorship. This "we" is not immediately gendered—the first two paragraphs use what amounts to a metaphorically "female" language by employing images of birth—but as of the third paragraph, references become more specific: "For each of us as women . . . " [Lorde, 36]. Now the "we" has become a defined group of women, as opposed to the "white fathers" mentioned several paragraphs later. But another distinction emerges, namely the differentiation between an overt living in the so-called "european mode" and "our own ancient, non-european consciousness of living" [37]. The interjection of race by means of nationality indicates something other than an exclusively white, genderless world; it indeed begins to feel as if the white world she refers to is male, and the other world is female—and non-white. In essence, and no matter how indirect, these references all point to the fact that the normative "we" is no longer in place.

Most interesting, however, is the obvious importance for Lorde of the subjective inclusiveness for the group to whom she is talking and to which she claims to belong. Here it involves the use of what feel like syntactically odd, yet strategically appropriate devices, as the following examples show: "I believe that women carry within ourselves the possibility for fusion of these two approaches so necessary for survival . . . " [37]; and "Women see ourselves diminished or softened by the falsely benign accusations of childishness, of non-universality, of changeability, of sensuality" [38]. The necessity of designating gender, in this case, the nonpersonal noun "women," but then to include herself ("ourselves"), may be grammatically awkward but is absolutely essential as an inclusive device connecting those spoken to with the speaker herself. When race is again specified ("The Black mother within each of us . . . " [38]), Lorde has once again created a group that in all probability also implies inclusivity, for if the Black mother is the poet—and if poetry is the essential part of our lives—then we are all a part of this picture. By complicating the subject through both differentiating and generalizing, Lorde forces us as readers/listeners to think about the matter of the subject and by no means to assume that anything like a universal neutral subject exists. Aside from the fact that the essayist marks herself as to gender and race, Lorde gives a strong sense that both the topic (the necessity of poetry in our lives) and the author/readers are ever more inclusive: "as women, as human . . . " [38] indeed implies that the human race is her audience. This obviously deliberate playing with pronouns and designators creates a back-and-forth between speaking/writing essayist and her public that requires response.

The same sense of dialogue can be found in many of the essays of June Jordan, whose use of several voices creates a dialogue even within the essays themselves. In the case of her report on a trip to Nicaragua in 1984, Jordan marks herself from the outset as an African-American woman, also as an "I." By the second paragraph, she has also used a "you," thus setting up a dialogue. Within the essay itself, however, there are at least three voices at work: the reporting voice who provides the facts of the trip; the commenting "I" who relates these facts to the level of personal experience; and the "I" who presents the insights gained from the trip. Facts are superseded by lived memory; lived memory is ultimately replaced by a clarion political call for action. The individual becomes the all-inclusive, extending beyond the world of personal experience, extending beyond even Nicaragua, to what it is we—readers of all sorts—can do. For Jordan, the essay has become gender- and race-specific, but also June Jordan-specific: above all, we see how she, an African-American woman, has reacted to Nicaragua, how she connects that experience to her own identity, and ultimately how she connects that to the identity of other African-Americans of both sexes. The essay is both personalized and politicized, internally including a variety of voices in discussion with each other and externally attracting an ever larger group of voices whom Jordan wishes to influence and stimulate to action. Here the essay has become a polemic whose principal goal is to incite.

The specific markings of both gender and race found in June Jordan's, Audre Lorde's, and Adrienne Rich's essays lead me to a second observation about the essay in the hands of radical feminists: *a radical feminist using the essay form will not only overtly address an audience; as a woman, as a member of a marked gender (and possibly of a marked race), she will spend considerable time marking her self and her point of departure.* As to whether this observation can be exclusively applied to the essay—or indeed to radical feminists—I suspect not. Nondominant groups in general are convinced of the need to identify themselves in their writing in ways that dominant groups do not, no matter what textual form they are using. But the essays of radical feminists stress self-marking and identifications, in part because of their inherently political messages, messages that more often than not have to do with the particular social, gender, racial, historical location of the author, who speaks on the authority of a particular subjectivity. Whereas Montaigne also spoke of the text being himself, however, that self could and did remain unmarked in any specific fashion. Montaigne did not have to specify himself: he represented the empowered in the matter of gender, race, and class. The same could be said for E. B. White, or Charles Lamb, or Alexander Smith: as white men in a Western world, they assumed a dominant position and by not needing to define it, paradoxically gave that position even more power and substance.

The process of overt self-identification and self-labeling is certainly strategic as well as informative. If the essays of radical feminists wish to speak to a particular reading public, it behooves them to establish connections with that public. A radical essayist has, in a sense, a dual purpose to self-labeling/marking: on the one hand, she will need to establish her own particular point of view (and if she is a radical feminist, she will believe that that point of view emerges in large part from her gender and probably from her race and class as well) and to assume the authority that that point of view gives to her. On the other hand, however, as someone engaged in the business of change, she will want to reach and connect with an audience who may well resemble her, or if not, who will need to understand her self-marking point of departure in order to grasp her message.

In her autobiographical essay, "Identity: Skin Blood Heart," Minnie Bruce Pratt provides a series of markings, ever more differentiated, in her search for self-definition. The form of the essay itself is noticeably different: this is neither an autobiography nor an autobiographical novel, but an essay that can also serve as autobiography. The focus of the piece, however, is essentially a lengthy and ever more intricate and differentiated marking of a self as the point of departure, the means, and the goal. Although it is marked structurally by a strong sense of dialogue, with overt addresses to the reader, frequent references to an audience she knows is there, with the periodic use of "you" and a number of directed comments in addition to the more straightforward narrative sections, the essay focuses in every possible way on the self and on a depiction of that self in the process of becoming. Here the narrative "I" is identical to the authorial "I." Pratt is in search of an authentic identity, and she tries to eliminate anything bordering on fictionalization: she is indeed author, narrator, and subject (in both senses of the word) of her essay.

Pratt's search for self must be not only overt but also exact; it is essential to her that she find the appropriate markings, that she place herself in some credible context. Therefore, much of her essay details a powerfully personal calling of things into question: the reactionary views of her father; the use of the term "home," which in America (and elsewhere) has such conservative, conserving overtones; the institution of marriage. Even the community to which she had moved after she left the reactionary southern world of her upbringing and young adulthood is suspect, namely the early feminist community of NOW, the attempts at consciousness-raising, etc., for in these places she also concealed a part of herself, her lesbianism.[7]

The markings are many. Some are assumed, then discarded; others emerge, and even at the end no clear sense of an attained or absolute authority exists, only partial answers, and the impression that the attempts to mark will continue (the last sentence ends: ". . . I continue the struggle with myself and the world I was born in" [Pratt, 57]). The programmatic title itself reflects the efforts at marking and illustrates evidence of the process and struggle accompanying self-identification. *Skin* represents the privilege of whiteness but also Pratt's effort ". . . to be at the edge between my fear and outside, on the edge of my skin, asking what new thing will I hear, will I see, will I let myself feel, beyond the fear" [18]. There is also a sense that staying in one's skin is "to be caught within the narrow circle of self . . . not just a fearful thing, it is a *lonely* thing" [18]. Skin is both a separating and a determining element: it isolates, but it also can lead to social condemnation.

The idea of *blood* emerges as Pratt begins to investigate her own past; this "blood" of kinship is also the blood of violence: "I had set out to make a new home with other women, only to find that the very ground I was building on was the grave of the people my kin had killed, and that my foundation, my birth culture, was mortared with blood" [35]. Like skin, blood has multiple and contradictory meanings: it implies connection but limitation and exclusion as well, since it limits the number of connections we can have: "It took me so long because so much in my culture is based on the principle that we are *not* all connected to each other, that folk who seem different should be excluded, or killed, and their living culture treated as dead objects" [40]. Even on the level of *heart* Pratt expresses ambivalence. Heart is the hardest to put into question, for "[w]e don't want to lose the love of the first people who knew us; we don't want to be standing outside the circle of home, with nowhere to go" [48]. In the process of self-identification, Pratt fears the loss of both family and friends, yet here too she calls any attempt at facileness into question:

> But if we are from families and a culture that enforced, either overtly or subtly, separation by skin and blood, I believe we need to look seriously at what limitations we have placed in this "new world" on who we feel "close to," who we feel "comfortable with," who we feel "safe" with. [49]

—in other words, on those whose relationship to us can best be described as loving, as related to "heart."

Pratt's efforts to define and describe herself provide a strong, perhaps an exaggerated example of the need for self-marking that I find characteristic of essays by radical feminists. The complexity that emerges in the tension between a desire for acceptance and the awareness that difference is not always easy to broach or subject to understanding is an additional part of the picture. On a less exaggerated, but equally noticeable, level are the markings of Audre Lorde evident in her complex treatment of "I" and "we" in the essay mentioned above, or of Adrienne Rich, who will almost always remind or inform her audiences that she is a lesbian. In all such cases, the markings become a point of departure, a rationale, a defense: a response to an outside world that, at least in its majority, will not resemble the author.

Even in cases literally more foreign to the American essay reader, for example, in the essays of the German feminist writer Christine Thürmer-Rohr, who tends more to mark politics and gender than social class or race, the same effort at self-labelling becomes apparent. Thürmer-Rohr's autobiographical essay about her father, a soldier whose death in World War Two led to his virtual sanctification on the part of the family, is a good example. Her mother in particular raised her daughters to glorify and certainly never to question their father's activities or his motives or in this case, the many letters that he had written to his children, which they were led to believe contained poignant and loving messages rather than telling evidence of Nazi ideology. Thürmer-Rohr's essay is an attempt to come to grips with these ambivalent messages, with the trickeries of memory, the duty of loyalty to one's parents, the obvious love she continues to feel for her long dead father, by also acknowledging and marking her own position as a female child in a time of political confusion and chaos.

The way in which the process of learning occurs focuses on what amounts to a gender-specific analysis of the letters of her father, most particularly in terms of the messages that she and her sisters, representative of those females left behind (always females—males left behind would be weaklings or traitors), received as to their role and the manner in which they were expected to think and act. Although specific markings abound—markings that have to do with a time and a place as well as a gender and a nationality—the analytical level of the essay tries to draw other meanings from the specifics of this case and ultimately posits a general critique of the patriarchy, specifically those elements that focus on violence. This is, however, no simplistic generalization about men and war, for it is precisely the mix of what Thürmer-Rohr calls "male war interests and loving feelings,"[8] the combining of traditional male and female realms, that is most chilling: "The normal, dangerous aspect of our letters is the *inseparability* of love and lie" [75]. It is, Thürmer-Rohr says, "seductive to want to extrapolate [from the letters] the so-called objective content, the so-called political function and to separate them from 'private' feelings . . . " [75], but it is precisely that mixture that she stresses. The gender critique that takes place is thus particularly focused on the need to mark both genders, to see each in an insidiously prescribed role and to follow through to its logical conclusion where those roles will lead and indeed led.

Marking means differentiation, particularization, the attempt to be precise. This does not rule out generalized statements; marking remains simply the effort that must be made to determine the point of departure, while at the same time setting things up for establishing connections with others. The necessity of marking a self is another instance of the specificity that undermines the universalizing messages of the traditional essay, which does not need markings, thereby simply implying that we are all like Montaigne, Bacon, Emerson, or White because they represent the unmarked, the empowered. In Montaigne's hands, the essay was meant to present Truth through example; we the readers were meant to extrapolate wisdom from Montaigne's portrait of himself. Yet in order to do so, readers who do not resemble him in gender, class, or race, must—as they must so often do when they read most texts—translate his universals into their own lives.

Without equivocation, *the radical-feminist essay is political*. But in terms of the traditional perception of the essay, the radical-feminist essay presents already an unusual revision of a form that has not been overtly political, at least in the hands of those who are considered the standard essayists. A radical-feminist essay will by definition be polemic, persuasive, will take on overtly ideological overtones that separate it from the location a traditional essay occupies. The radical-feminist essay seeks not only to identify and place its author, it reaches out with that information to find response and to goad into response. The radical use of the essay (by radicals of either sex) may well have to do with the raising of questions that go beyond the essay's content itself and the insights of the essayist and are absorbed by the readers, who may produce further questions and insights that will potentially lead to action. The necessity of defining difference will be stressed as well as the genuine need for change: the essay as polemic, the essay as personal statement from a position of difference, the essay as political argument, perhaps using the authority of the personal to bring about change in the political, the essay as literally and figuratively open-ended, not only in the sense of connecting to readers who are expected to react, but in leaving open the way to further thoughts and actions. Minnie Bruce Pratt, for example, who is by no means telling the world to be as she is, but who, by focusing on the complexities and the problems of identity, the terrible false assumptions that are connected with it, the danger of the uncritical acceptance of concepts like Home, shows us, the readers, our delusions and the necessity of change and preciseness for all of us.

The politics of the radical-feminist essay are not always overt. Susan Griffin's essays in *Women and Nature* reveal above all, through the subtleties of language and syntax, an often indirect, yet never absent, voice. In the essay entitled "Land," for example, Griffin employs no "I" in her essay; at the same time, she does not act like Bacon, who also uses no "I," by presenting an array of firm and generalizable conclusions. With Griffin there is a strong sense of story, a method that may well lull the reader into expecting a narrative that will demand little of her except attention to the text. But the political contribution of this essay emerges in Griffin's particularly subversive use of language: almost every sentence in the text can be read in two ways, the "obvious" literal one as well as the gendered way. An utterance as simple as "He is conqueror" [*Women and Nature*, 48] speaks overtly of the male explorer who first discovers, then exploits the land. But in Griffin's women-focused scheme, the land is also feminine, and it is the exploitation of the feminine that is also implied.

Griffin's voice is apparent in these dual meanings but even more overtly in the parentheses that appear in the latter part of her text and that are already prefigured in her title, with its bracketed subtitle "(Her Changing Face)." Here is a subversive presence, secondary, marginal—indeed, quite literally bracketed out—but all the more insistent because it calls the reader's attention to a series of facts and observations that contrast with what is related outside the parentheses (in the outside, more superficial and obvious world?). The narrative subtext catches our attention because it provides a counter-narrative. In the section called "Guide," for instance, examples like the following abound:

> She knew her skill and she knew it well. She could speak more than one language. She spoke their language, and she spoke her own, which they could not speak. (The father, it was recorded, frequently disposed of his infant daughters in marriage to grown men, for the use of their sons.) She had learned all the customs of their people and of her own people, which they did not know. (The compensation, it was written, given in such cases consisted of horses or mules delivered to the father.) [50]

Griffin's insistently political voice is in evidence throughout. In addition to tying the identity of land to women, to the feminine (which is done by using the gendered "she"), she makes other significant connections, such as providing a list of damaging elements that represent danger to women as well as to land/nature:

> Phosphoric acid, nitrogen fertilizers, ammonium sulfate, white phosphate, potash, iron sulfate, nitrate of soda, superphosphate, calcium cyanamide, calcium oxide, calcium magnesium, zinc sulfate, phenobarbital, amphetamine, magnesium, estrogen, copper sulfate, meprobamate, thalidomide, benzethonium chloride, Valium, hexachlorophene, diethylstilbestrol. [53]

The poetic tone of the whole is also deceptive. Poetry is indeed not a luxury. The sense of story might not only cause us to take the whole less seriously but perhaps to conclude as well that this is "simply" a protest against the way "man" has treated land, an ecological message. But it is not. It takes another level of reading to realize that another protest is included: a completely gendered and radical-feminist protest that offers a passionate political statement about the oppression of women. In Griffin's piece, the essay has in essence been deconstructed; the expected "I" has been removed and reconstructed in a certain and definite sense of political protest with a variety of meanings and an unstated but nevertheless powerful call to action.

Almost as ostensibly "unpolitical" are the so-called glosses of the radical lesbian-feminist German linguist Luise Pusch. Here context and message remain equally important: Pusch, an academic who appears to have been systematically cut out of the German university system because of her strongly stated radical-feminist and lesbian beliefs and her insistence on propounding feminist linguistics as a valid area of scholarly inquiry, has chosen the public forum of glosses for her essays, which are published in newspapers in Germany and Switzerland. The gloss is brief, personal, open-ended, focusing on recurring everyday topics that she has read or heard about, usually in the media; it has, in other words, the standard characteristics of the essay. Like Susan Griffin, Luise Pusch seems to work on at least two levels of meaning, one linguistic-theoretical, the other overtly political. A gloss entitled "Stilleben" [still life], for example, is ostensibly about the strange linguistic basis of certain words, both German and English: she illustrates her discussion with the English adjective "still," which means silent, not moving, conceivably dead (as in "stillbirth" and "stillborn"), and is indeed translated into German with compound words including the word for death. The word ultimately is connected to the German verb *stillen* (to nurse a baby), a memory of a Katharine Hepburn retrospective, specifically a film of Hepburn portraying Clara Schumann, whose performance in a recital depicted in the film is cut short when one of her many children, a baby, needs nursing. Pusch's ironic comment on the nursing scene in which Hepburn's back is to the audience is coupled with her angry paraphrase of St. Paul that women are obviously not only supposed to be silent in the community but also in concert halls and just about everywhere else that borders on the public realm. These scattered, almost cryptic comments are only ostensibly about linguistics; their political content is equally obvious. A final observation concerns the French word for still life, *nature morte*, "dead nature," reminding us that still lifes indeed portray objects, dead things, often decoratively arranged. Within the scope of a few paragraphs, the political importance of linguistic concepts is made clear: words are a source of immense power that can and will influence the way we perceive the world [Pusch, 223-24].

Political messages within essays clash with the form only insofar as these messages counter the perception of essays as nonideological, timeless, and capable of presenting universal truths, often in the form of exemplars. As E. B. White tells us about the summer around 1904 when his father rented a cabin in Maine, a practice White himself then continued as long as his children were young, he effortlessly moves from that archetypal experience of father and son to making himself the father and adding his own son. The message that things change but really stay the same gets translated into the idea that fathers and sons will essentially experience similar emotions, indeed that even events will repeat themselves, no matter what the generation, that things are ultimately timeless and non-political [White, 198-203]. But radical feminists, in contrast, will counter such a perception by using the essay to show politics in everything from the mistreatment of the land to the use of language to an old Katharine Hepburn film to the uneasinesses of a white female southern upbringing. The essay provides the appropriate vehicle for such assertions, whether the form is adapted into the brevity of a witty gloss by Luise Pusch or into the story-telling of a Susan Griffin piece or into the autobiographical form employed by Minnie Bruce Pratt.

Radical feminists do not seek only to express themselves politically in the essay; *they also bring other voices into play by virtue of their consistently marked personal identity as well as their concern with multiple viewpoints and perspectives.* Individual essays (like the previously-mentioned essay of June Jordan) can, in fact present several voices, the differentiated shadings of one complex individual. The frequent academic-feminist practice of publishing anthologies, with the purpose of presenting a variety of viewpoints, is echoed in the radical purpose of collective anthologies that seek to represent populations that otherwise remain unheard: *This Bridge Called My Back*, for example, consists almost entirely of essays by radical women of color (marked as such in the subtitle), who use the essay as a tool to present different and rarely heard voices in America (although "America" itself remains unmarked, unremarked-upon, taken for granted as a sort of norm). A particularly vivid example is Audre Lorde's "An Open Letter to Mary Daly," written in response to Lorde's receipt of Mary Daly's *Gyn/Ecology*. Here, the letter, overt, by definition communicative, becomes an essay commenting on the important intersection of race, gender, sexuality, and radicality, a deliberate attempt to force an acknowledgment by Daly of what Lorde represents. For Lorde is not only "an african-american woman in white patriarchy," a "non-european woman," she is also one of the "women-identified-women" [An Open letter to Mary Daly," 95] who is particularly outraged by a radical white feminist ignoring her or misusing her words. Even within radical feminism divisions and differences exist: by focusing on those differences, Audre Lorde uses the forum of her essay/open letter to present her self, her voice, as a contrast: "But to imply . . . that all women suffer the same oppression simply because we are women, is to lose sight of the many varied tools of patriarchy. It is to ignore how those tools are used by women without awareness against each other" [95].

In *Passionate Politics*, a collection of essays tracing her development as a radical lesbian-feminist against the background of the second wave of feminism, Charlotte Bunch makes an overt effort to offer the particular voice of a lesbian activist-scholar whose concerns center on the importance of global feminist activity. Even within an essay with the academic title of "Lesbian-Feminist Theory," her voice is obvious and present, and this "scholarly" discussion of theory becomes instead theory in practice: a series of observations that counter the purely "objective" academic discussion we might have expected with prescriptive messages on how we as feminists need to proceed. Like Audre Lorde in "Poetry is Not a Luxury," Bunch uses similar inclusive/exclusive/marking devices that call attention to a subjective, present voice: "Tactics will vary widely according to circumstances, but lesbians must ground ourselves in lesbian-feminist theory" [Bunch, 202]. In a way, Bunch's approach is an appropriation, not only of the form but of the academic nature of her topic: the reader sees "theory" and expects an academic treatment but discovers instead an essay that marks its author as a particular and defined voice, that talks about experience, presents strong political statements, deals very much with the practical facts of the world in which we live, and seems, in other words, to blend praxis with theory and to single out and stress the former. Theory itself is being reinterpreted and reconceptualized. The use of the essay form simply adds to that difference: here the essay begins to resemble an article, but its form is in constant tension with its content.

Bunch's use of the essay as a form that can subvert typical academic style leads me to a particularly vital example of what can happen when a radical feminist performs her academic role in subversive fashion by her use of the essay as opposed to the standard form of an academic article. When the radical lesbian-feminist philosopher Marilyn Frye comments in the preface to *The Politics of Reality* that her essays are "written at least as much for the ear as for the eye, perhaps more so; I hope they will be read aloud, both in and out of academic settings" [Frye, viii], she signals the importance of communication on oral as well as written levels. Her volume represents for me the ultimate radical response to whatever has been asserted about the essay in the past. Everything I have discussed thus far can be found in Frye's essays: the personal, the political, the explicit radical-feminist focus, the acknowledgment of many voices, all clothed in this ostensibly elitist, bourgeois form. As a radical feminist, Frye seems to be showing us the way to what might be our most important contribution as feminists to academic debates, the use of a form that is by no means typically academic, a form that combines both Movement and Theory, that focuses on dialogue, communication, accessibility.

A good example is the volume's final piece, "To Be and Be Seen: The Politics of Reality." In many ways it resembles what we might recognize as a typical essay: brevity, explicit personal focus, use of quotations to illustrate the argument, application of experience as a guiding authority. The essay nevertheless focuses on a topic with academic overtones, namely the problematic nature of definition, particularly if we confine ourselves to the usual standard authorities of definition, namely the OED, Webster's, and other dictionaries. Frye's essay veers away from the usual and expected academic framework because of her own stated and engaged involvement: in this effort to define the concept "lesbian," she writes "I say, 'I am a lesbian . . . ' " [155]. It is not just the presence of the "I," which is currently not foreign to much academic writing; it is far more the placing of that "I" within the very substance of the topic. Frye is not only attempting to define, or at least to deal with the problematics of defining, the concept of lesbianism from the standpoint of a feminist scholar: she is trying to define herself. As she moves through the stages of her argument, she therefore involves herself continuously and explicitly, and the reader gains the impression that if she fails in her defining, the result will be drastic and critical for her.

If one can generalize about the essay as form in any way, it is this involvement of the "I" that is often paramount—even Montaigne introduced his essays by commenting "I am myself the substance of my book" [Montaigne, "To the Reader"]. Frye is doing precisely what an essayist tends to do: implicating herself not only as a self-identified narrator, but also and more importantly as the participating observer who is more participant than observer.

> Lesbian.
> One of the people of the Isle of Lesbos.
> It is bizarre that when I try to name myself and explain myself, my native tongue provides me with a word that is so foreign, so false, so hopelessly inappropriate. Why am I referred to by a term which means *one of the people of Lesbos*?
> The use of the word "lesbian" to name us is a quadrifold evasion, a laminated euphemism. To name us, one goes by way of a reference to the island of Lesbos,

which in turn is an indirect reference to the poet Sappho (who used to live there, they say), which in turn is itself an indirect reference to what fragments of her poetry have survived a few millenia of patriarchy, and this in turn (if we have not lost you by now) is a prophylactic avoidance of direct mention of the sort of creature who would write such poems or to whom such poems would be written . . . assuming you happen to know what is in those poems written in a dialect of Greek over two thousand five hundred years ago on some small island somewhere in the wine dark Aegean Sea.

This is a truly remarkable feat of silence. [160]

Here the "I" retains its prominent originating and central location, connecting overtly with the audience she is addressing, not just as the informed scholar but also as a figure as much the subject of this essay as Minnie Bruce Pratt is of her "Identity: Skin Blood Heart." Emphasizing the dialogic function of the essay, Frye pulls her readers into the peculiar arguments she mocks and makes them see the absurdities. Like Luise Pusch, she often works on basic linguistic levels, deconstructing the fatuous words of others, making her readers see as well as hear what is clearly wrong. She couples her linguistic and cultural discussion of the meaning of "lesbian" with obvious political statements, thereby illustrating how intertwined theory and practice really are. In her work, the essay becomes, at one and the same time, political, personal, and analytical. When she says in her preface that she wants her essays read inside as well as outside the academy, she sets up a program that is at the core of radical feminism, namely the need to communicate across any barriers, real or perceived. And to do so, Frye has selected the form that can be a forum, that can indeed lend itself best to her purpose of sharing her self and acknowledging the others with whom she is determined to connect.

In a talk/presentation that she gave at the West Coast Women's Music Festival in 1981 (and then turned into an essay for *Home Girls*), Bernice Johnson Reagon speaks/writes of the little barred rooms that we have set up for the sole (and not necessarily negative) purpose of exclusion:

Now every once in awhile there is a need for people to try to clean out corners and bar the doors and check everybody who comes in the door, and check what they carry in and say "Humph, inside this place the only thing we are going to deal with is X or Y or Z." And so only the X's or Y's or Z's get to come in. That place can then become a nurturing place or a very destructive place. Most of the time when people do that, they do it because of the heat of trying to live in this society where being an X or Y or Z is very difficult, to say the least. The people running the society call the shots as if they're still living in one of those little villages, where they kill the ones they don't like or put them in the forest to die. . . . When somebody else is running a society like that, and you are the one who would be put out to die, it gets too hard to stay out in that society all the time. And that's when you find a place, and you try to bar the door and check all the people who come in. You come together to see what you can do about shouldering up all of your energies so that you and your kind can survive. [Reagon, 357-58]

That little barred room is then further described by Reagon as a nurturing space that can only ultimately be used as a point of departure for action outside the room: "It is not a womb no more. And you can't feel comfortable no more. And what happens at that point has to do with trying to do too much in it. You don't do no coalition building in a womb. . . . Coalition work has to be done in the streets" [359].

The image of the little barred room is reminiscent of the form of the essay which, for all its implied openness, is nevertheless traditionally preserved as a closed-off space, unique unto itself, perhaps even self-sufficient in an egotistical sort of way. Traditionally, the essay has been a meeting-place for writing and reading minds who did not need to define themselves: who knew they were an elite, who knew they were in power, and who retreated from the busyness of their normal powerful worlds to reminisce, to ponder, to reconfirm their position in a world that effectively was very much of their making. Much like the eighteenth-century aristocrats who dressed up as country folk, who slummed and wrote rustic verse before shedding their play clothes and returning fully to the privilege of their real world, white male essayists have pretended a sort of rebellion but always from an undenied position of power. For them, the essay might purport to be a dangerous trip into themselves, but the point of departure and return has never been in doubt. These canonic essayists represent an unmarked voice—perhaps aristocratic, perhaps solidly middle-class, whatever is dominant at the time in which they are writing. They too have a little barred room, their protestations to Universal Democracy notwithstanding.

How do the radical feminists differ in their approach to the essay? For them, I suspect that Bernice Reagon's image of the barred room that is both a refuge and potentially a trap runs the risk of being absolutely appropriate—as if Virginia Woolf's "Room of One's Own," once provided, had suddenly been seen as the limiting space it ultimately is. Like other separatist movements, radical feminists tend to need a retreat for sustenance, but for them, the essay is transformed into a place to start establishing and asserting themselves, identifying themselves, engaging in a dialogue with others, although always from that safe position of the monologic word. Like the room, however, the essay cannot and must not remain a shut-off space for them, a place to play with aesthetic ideas and to forget the rest of the world. If radical-feminist essayists have anything in common, it is their shared passion, their desire, their need, indeed the absolute imperative they feel to communicate and to use their words as a stepping-off point to action. Unlike the essays of Bacon and Montaigne or even of E. B. White, their essays tend to reach out with questions, not necessarily to give answers. They are unabashedly political in the broadest sense of the word; their essays are removed from any neutral or subjective realm where danger of an impossible universalization exists. They dwell on difference, between themselves and the patriarchy, among themselves. On occasion, radical-feminist essayists even mark the essay form with their difference, transforming the expected into something else, transforming a letter or an academic article or a speech into an essay.

As to what particularly distinguishes their essays from the essays of other radicals or of those men who do not fit the norm, it is likely that the difference lies in the content, in the new wine. But in the tension that arises between the perception of the essay as one thing and its very different presentation by radical feminists as another, we can see a characteristic that goes beyond content, that involves the reader at a level expected of her when she reads these passionate essays, that by their very implementation represent a challenge, a change, a re-vision. Like so much else that has changed since the advent of the second wave of feminism, we cannot imagine that the essay will ever go back again to what it once was. In her effort to get her listeners/readers to act, to leave their barred rooms, Bernice Reagon has summed it up: "There is not going to be the space to continue as we are or as we were. . . . It must become necessary for all of us to feel that this is our world. And that we are here to stay and that anything that is here is ours to take and to use in our image. And watch that 'our'—make it as big as you can—it ain't got nothing to do with that barred room. The 'our' must include everybody you have to include in order for you to survive" [Reagon, 363, 365]. In the hands of radical feminists, essays have become more than barred rooms: they provide space, but also opportunity; retreat, but also connection; sustenance, but also relation; individual identification, but also the bridge to community, to re-evaluation, to the imperative need for change.

NOTES

1. I am most grateful to Elizabeth Mittman and Marilyn Frye for their helpful comments on an earlier draft of this article.

2. Herman Grimm (1828–1901) is probably the most famous of the male nineteenth-century German essayists; indeed, he is generally viewed as the first important German essayist. His first book of essays was published in 1859; in it he mentions Emerson (rather than Montaigne or Bacon) as his principal source of inspiration.

3. Among recent studies of the essay, I would suggest Gerhardt and, despite the fact that they have virtually nothing to do with gender (with the exception of an essay or two in Butrym), the following: Bensmaïa, Réda, *The Barthes Effect: The Essay as Reflective Text* (Minneapolis: University of Minnesota Press, 1987); Alexander J. Butrym, ed., *Essays on the Essay: Redefining the Genre* (Athens: University of Georgia Press, 1989); Good, Graham, *The Observing Self: Rediscovering the Essay* (London: Routledge, 1988).

4. See Douglas, 15: "Many, but not all radical feminists believe that the oppression of women by men is the 'primary' human oppression in that it occurred first historically; is the first oppression that an individual human being learns about and participates in; and is the most widespread oppression, occurring in virtually every human society and placing nearly every human being in an oppressed or oppressing sex class."

5. A particularly interesting case study of the intimate relationship between speech and essay can be made by examining Virginia Woolf's essay "Professions for Women" as well as the speech delivered in 1931 on which the essay is based. Despite the noticeable

differences between the two texts, the emphasis on dialogue is essential to and obvious in both. "Professions for Women" is reprinted in *Women and Writing*, ed. Michèle Barrett (New York: Harcourt Brace Jovanovich, 1979), 57–63; the speech can be found in *The Pargiters*, ed. Mitchell Leaska (New York: New York Public Library & Readex Books, 1977), xxvii–xviv.

6. I would like particularly to thank Maria Lugones, who triggered this thought, albeit in another context, during a discussion of how the feminist educational process should differ from traditional educational practice by emphasizing verbal and communicative rather than written communication. I also appreciate a comment on this section sent to me by Marilyn Frye: "The audience is *essential*—we [radical feminist essayists] are 'hearing each other into speech'—collectively making meaning. Without that audience we literally could not compose the sentences and paragraphs."

7. A very useful article on this essay (that, however, has nothing to do with its form) is Biddy Martin and Chandra Talpade Mohanty, "Feminist Politics: What's Home Got to Do with It?" in *Feminist Studies Critical Studies*, ed. Teresa de Lauretis (Bloomington: Indiana University Press, 1986). 191–212.

8. [Thürmer-Rohr, 75]. The translations from Thürmer-Rohr are my own. During the writing of this article, a translation of Thürmer-Rohr's book has appeared: *Vagabonding: Feminist Theory Cut Loose*, trans. Lise Weil (Boston: Beacon Press, 1991).

WORKS CITED

Bunch, Charlotte. "Lesbian-Feminist Theory." In *Passionate Politics: Feminist Theory in Action, Essays. 1968-1986*. New York: St. Martin's Press, 1987. 196-202.

Douglas, Carol Anne. *Love and Politics. Radical Feminist and Lesbian Theories*. San Francisco: ism press, inc., 1990.

Frye, Marilyn. "To Be and Be Seen: The Politics of Reality." In *The Politics of Reality: Essays in Feminist Theory*. Freedom, Calif.: Crossing Press, 1983. 152-74.

Gerhardt, Marlis, ed. *Deutsche Essays von Frauen des 20. Jahrhunderts*. Frankfurt: Suhrkamp Verlag, 1987.

Griffin, Susan. "Land (Her Changing Face)." In *Woman and Nature. The Roaring inside Her*. New York: Harper & Row, 1978. 47-55.

Griffin, Susan. "The Way of All Ideology." *Signs* 7 (Spring 1982): 641-60.

Joeres, Ruth-Ellen B. " 'That girl is an entirely different character!' Yes, but is she a feminist? Observations on Sophie von La Roche's *Geschichte des Fräuleins von Sternheim*." In *German Women in the Eighteenth and Nineteenth Centuries. A Social and Literary History*. Ed. Ruth-Ellen B. Joeres and Mary Jo Maynes. Bloomington: Indiana University Press, 1986. 137-56.

Jordan, June. "Nicaragua: Why I Had to Go There, January, 1984." In *On Call: Political Essays*. Boston: South End Press, 1985. 65-75.

Lorde, Audre. "An Open Letter to Mary Daly." In *This Bridge Called My Back: Writings by Radical Women of Color*. Ed. Cherríe Moraga and Gloria Anzaldúa. New York: Kitchen Table: Women of Color Press, 1981. 94-97.

Lorde, Audre. "Poetry is Not a Luxury." In *Sister Outsider: Essays and Speeches*. Trumansburg, NY: Crossing Press, 1984. 36-39.

Montaigne, Michel de. "On the education of children." In *Essays*. New York: Penguin, 1958. 49-86.

Pratt, Minnie Bruce. "Identity: Skin Blood Heart." In *Yours in Struggle: Three Feminist*

Perspectives on Anti-Semitism and Racism. Ed. Elly Bulkin, Minnie Bruce Pratt, and Barbara Smith. Ithaca: Firebrand Books, 1984. 9-63.

Pusch, Luise. "Stilleben." In *Alle Menschen werden Schwestern: Feministische Sprachkritik.* Frankfurt: Suhrkamp Verlag, 1990. 223-24.

Reagon, Bernice Johnson. "Coalition Politics: Turning the Century." In *Home Girls: A Black Feminist Anthology.* Ed. Barbara Smith. New York: Kitchen Table: Women of Color Press, 1983. 356-68.

Rich, Adrienne. "Vesuvius at Home: The Power of Emily Dickinson." In *On Lies, Secrets, and Silence: Selected Prose 1966-1978.* New York: Norton, 1979. 157-83.

Thürmer-Rohr, Christina. "Liebe und Lüge: 'Meine geliebten Kinderchen.'" In *Vagabundinnen: Feministische Essays.* Berlin: Orlanda Frauenverlag, 1987. 57-75.

White, E. B. "Once More to the Lake." In *One Man's Meat.* New York: Harper & Row, 1982. 198-203.

CHAPTER TEN

Latin American
Women Essayists

"Intruders and Usurpers"

LOURDES ROJAS AND NANCY SAPORTA STERNBACH

Do Latin American women's essays represent the history of Latin American feminism?[1] Does a study of nineteenth- and twentieth-century Latin American women's essays ineluctably lead us to the evolution of Latin American feminist thought? However attractive, tempting, and provocative this association may be, there are also dangers in making too facile a connection between these women's essays and the history of feminism. In the first place, Latin America is a vast continent comprising more than twenty Spanish-speaking countries alone, not to mention Brazil, or the English- and French-speaking Caribbean, each with a discrete history and a differing array of political and economic systems and conditions. Any attempt at formulating the history of Latin American feminism is necessarily delineated by these differences in ethnicity, race, language, geography, and political climate.

These limitations notwithstanding, a clearly defined picture of Latin American feminist thought emerges with an analysis of these texts as the foundation of a feminist discourse in Latin America.[2] By using examples of women's essays from the last two centuries, we will discuss the dynamics of the essay as a genre, the gendered perspective of the writers, as well as the particular historical and political institutions and circumstances that influenced their thought. What concern us here are the relationships posed and created by the intersection of gender and genre when they are examined in conjunction with the history of feminism in Latin America.

Fundamental to our discussion are the etymology and translation of the word "essay" in Spanish. *Ensayo* derives from the infinitive *ensayar*, which means "to try, to attempt, or to rehearse." We may argue that the absence of a literary tradition for women essayists made those who took up the pen in the nineteenth century new to the genre, as if they were rehearsing, in the literal sense of the word, in their attempts to enter a field traditionally dominated by men as well as initiating their performance as essay writers. When women entered the social and political debates of their times through their essays, they began rehearsing their new voices within the political and social discourses of their time, simultaneously introducing gender issues as part of the broader social and political preoccupation of the emerging Latin American nations. The extent to which these two contexts combined to create a more fertile arena for women's voices or actually hindered the development of a tradition of women's essays on the continent is one of our major concerns in studying these essays.

LATIN AMERICAN WOMEN WRITERS

In recent years, even readers with a minimal knowledge of Latin America have suddenly become aware of, if not interested in, Latin American women writers as a result of the myriad of anthologies, critical works, and translations published throughout the eighties. Finally, critics, theorists, translators, and readers began to adjust the paradigms that had previously defined the Latin American canon.[3] Certainly the immense popularity and marketability of an Isabel Allende have made a general reading public aware of the fact that, indeed, such a thing as a Latin American woman writer exists. The very presence of writers such as Allende underscores the existence of a Latin American tradition of women of letters from which she emanates and to which she is heir.

Since pre-Colonial times, there have been women writers in Latin America, who, like women everywhere who chose the pen, often faced hostility and ridicule by their choice of profession.[4] Nevertheless, Latin American literary history offers many examples of women who continually broke the mold and transgressed the boundaries of decorum in order to be writers. Some, however, de-emphasized themselves as writers in order to be just that, as was the case with the Argentine essayist and educator Rosa Guerra, who felt the need to assure her reading public that her reasons for writing were not "a desire for a literary reputation" which would only bring "criticism and ridicule" [Guerra, n.p], but rather to bring about social change through her writing. Equally transgressive was Clorinda Matto de Turner's directorship of a major Peruvian newspaper in 1883 [Berg, 121-24]. The reaction of many of their male counterparts could be summed up in the statement by a certain Argentine periodical which deemed that women could be writers only when they had lost "their teeth, hair, and all hope" [*sus dientes, sus cabellos y sus ilusiones*] [*El Mosquito*, 1877]. Thus, in Latin America, too, the profession of writing was male-identified; women who stepped out of their female role to become writers were considered traitors to their sex and treated as such, or were deemed masculine, "bearded" [*barbudo*], or "a lot of man" [*mucho hombre*]. The celebrated case of the Cuban writer Gertrudis Gómez de Avellaneda, who was denied entry into the Royal Academy of the Spanish Language because of her sex, is a telling example. She commented in her series of essays called *La mujer* [Woman] (1860):

the literary and artistic world has been disputed as exclusively masculine every inch of the way, and even today the woman who enters it are looked upon as intruders and usurpers, and consequently treated as not worthy of their trust, judging by the way they are distanced from the *bearded* academies. Let's have a look at that adjective, my dear readers [feminine], because it has occurred to my pen to mention those illustrious corporations of literate people whose first and most important title is that they *have beards*.[5]

Yet, in an apparent paradox, at the same time that women were proscribed from being writers, especially of serious literature, certain genres were considered to be "feminine"—and none more so than poetry. A quick survey of any, and almost every, anthology of Latin American literature cites the same four women poets as examples of Latin America's "letras femeninas": Juana de Ibarbouru, Delmira Agustini, Gabriela Mistral, and Alfonsina Storni [Miller, *Women*, 11-17].[6] By reducing women's literary space to one genre—poetry— male critics encased women within a predominantly lyric tradition that exalted sentiment above reason, romantic love above politics, and affairs of the heart above affairs of the state, a categorization that would virtually exclude them from being essayists. As long as women poets were content to stay within this tradition alone, they also appeared to conform to and duplicate the role that their society had assigned them. Their poetry was allowed to create a space that did not appear to transgress the already defined boundaries of women's subjectivity. However, not only did they transgress those boundaries, they served as literary foremothers to contemporary women writers who show a "belligerent intention to tear up the garments of patriarchal power" [Guerra Cunningham, 10].

THE ESSAY IN LATIN AMERICA

The gender/genre identification was not confined to lyrical poetry: it crossed over into all literary genres. If poetry was identified as a feminine endeavor, men seemed to appropriate the novel, especially during the Boom era.[7] Since then, Latin American feminist scholarship has demonstrated the male exclusivity of the Boom in spite of the fact that women indeed wrote novels during this period.[8] Yet in spite of the associations of women with poetry and men with novels, no genre in Latin America has ever been so severely and rigidly assigned to one gender as the essay. More than any other, the essay has been defined by the gender of its known writers. In this manner, when Latin American literary critics speak of the essay, they are, in fact, only discussing male production.

Despite the paucity of studies dedicated to the essay as a genre, most critics still accord it a high degree of importance, for within Latin American literary history its initiation coincided with the political independence of the continent. Thus, the exclusion of women is all the more notable. In the project of nation-building before them, Latin Americans ostensibly called for women's participation [Sommer, *Fictions*]; in reality, however, women's place as angel of the house had changed little from the European model. Moreover, many nineteenth-century writers also held political positions in addition to their writing careers, so that writing on philosophical or political subjects was a natural consequence — if, of course, the writer was a man. One need not be a literary historian of nineteenth-century Latin America in order to invoke the names of Andrés Bello, Domingo Faustino Sarmiento, Eugenio María de Hostos, and José Martí, a small sample of the men who combined the theories of their essays with their political activism. But no such canon exists for women essayists.

At the same time, this little-studied genre in Latin American literary criticism is also one of the most popularized forms of writing in both the nineteenth and twentieth centuries.[9] Latin American writers, women and men alike, have generally viewed the essay as the most appropriate discourse for social and political reform. Where they differed was in the subject and articulation of that very discourse. Furthermore, because the men already owned the public space, their discourse had no need to appropriate it in the way the women's did, as we shall see. Several factors contributed to Latin American women's exclusion from the essay. First of all, like their European counterparts, Latin American intellectuals considered the essay a philosophical treatise of social and political engagement that required a conflation of both philosophy and imagination as essential to its discourse. Thus understood, there was no reason why women could not participate. Nevertheless, the perception that the essay emerged from paternal roots and sired only male offspring effectively marginalized women's discourse. Also like Europeans, Latin Americans naturally traced this masculine lineage back to Montaigne, whom they too considered the "father of the essay." If the origins of the essay are rooted in a patrilineal tradition, and one had to be a man to inherit them, women could not claim a legacy to this heritage. Yet even women bold and brave enough to ignore those injunctions would find themselves ill-prepared for the task at hand, for the essay writer was assumed to be a combination of scientist and philosopher. At a place and time when women had barely gained access to formal education, Latin American women essayists would hardly have considered themselves either scientists or philosophers, in spite of their desire to become either or both.

Just as some of the definitions of the essay excluded women, one definition in particular could be used to their advantage: the quality of being able to "poeticize in prose the full range of the writer's intelligence and imagination" [poetizar en prosa el ejercicio pleno de la inteligencia y la fantasía del escritor] [Anderson Imbert, 5]. Because women's intellectual capacity was ignored, or at best questioned, in order for the essayists to exercise the full range of their intelligence in argumentative, rational discourse required by the essays, the assumption that followed was that the writer had to be a man. However, it also permitted women to choose for themselves those topics that would best illustrate the full range of their intelligence and imagination. Thus, while women were relegated to a continuity of exclusion, on the one hand, they were also freed to create their own program. That is, by not having to conform to a constricting set of rules, they could forge a path for themselves to *ensayar* (rehearse) another way of thinking.

When the intellectual Carlos Ripoll published in 1966 one of the most important anthologies of the Latin American essay, *Conciencia intelectual de América* [Intellectual consciousness of America], it should not surprise us that he not only did not include any women, he never saw the need to mention one.[10] In fact, to date, no literary critic has ever systematically studied Latin American women's essays. While it is true that the male essay is the least studied of all genres in the Latin American canon, or perhaps at times "forgotten," women's essays are virtually unknown. If ever there was a genre defined by men, in their roles as producers, readers and interpreters, the Latin American essay is precisely that, or what Sidonie Smith, in reference to autobiography, has called a "male generic contract" [14].

Ripoll suggested by means of his title and his exclusion of women that intellectual consciousness or the stirrings of political activism were the sole domain of men. The example he provided in the following passage, one that is rife with male symbols and male agency in history, leaves little place for a woman's voice, no place for a woman's imagination: "The Latin American essayist has to become an anxiety-ridden Diogenes who scrutinizes the Indian, questions the *conquistador*, tries history, does an autopsy of the tyrant, converts his heroes into oracles, or who lights the face of his spirit to find the roots of his culture [14]."[11]

We must concur with Ripoll that the male essayists' primary task was to find the roots of their culture, to forge a national identity, and to consolidate the newly emerging nation states. But the same goals do not apply to Latin American women essayists. Rather than focusing exclusively on questions of national identity, as did so many of their male counterparts, women essayists of the nineteenth century expanded their vision of Latin American society by including their concerns about women, children, and other oppressed groups across the social spectrum. This proved to be a valuable legacy for twentieth-century women essayists.

POINTS OF DEPARTURE:
MAPPING THE DIFFERENCES

Throughout the nineteenth century, Latin American writers saw their literature as a vehicle of social reform. Its purpose was utilitarian: it was meant to contribute to the social well-being of the newly emerging nations. At the beginning of the century, the wars of independence and the consequent vying for power known as *caudillismo* occupied center stage.[12] Later on, the focus moved to more specific social issues central to establishing a Latin American identity, such as the condition of the indigenous population, the continuation of slavery in many countries, prostitution, corruption of the government and the church, the peasants and land reform, and the legacy of colonialism. Consonant with their role as writers, male essayists contributed to the political and social debates of their day. Turn-of-the-century essayists, while not abandoning the political concerns of their predecessors and comfortable now in their role as essayists, began to publish a series of works scrutinizing and defining their Latin American identity. Instead of measuring themselves against Spain, from whom they were finally free, Latin Americans now faced the challenge and threat of the new North American imperialism.

While confronting the same historical and political developments as male writers, women essayists designed a unique path. Throughout the nineteenth century, they also felt the need to support the ideals of national independence and political autonomy while at the same time lending their optic to woman-oriented topics in particular. Rather than privileging one of these options over the other, many women essayists found a way to incorporate both alternatives into their discussion by demonstrating the interconnection of all forms of oppression in the emerging Latin American nations. Predictably, gender oppression ran high on their agenda. These essayists also became voices of denunciation of social inequality and demanded accountability from lawmakers. In Argentina the oppression endured by the population at large under the Rosas dictatorship (1852) was equated with the oppression of women. Its fall signalled the end of the censorship that had silenced women's voices up until that time.[13] The Dominican Ercilia Pepín, for example, related feminist reforms to the need to contribute to the "progress of the nation," even at a time when it was impossible to implement any kind of revolutionary framework. From each part of the continent, the snippets that appeared with the regularity of clockwork, and which we now call essays, affirmed Latin American women essayists as pioneers in the literature of protest. It is each of these little pieces, each stitched in a different country, with different threads, that we suggest comprised the pieces of a "continental" patchwork quilt.

The emergence, existence, and continuity of an alternate canon that coexisted, sometimes coincided with, but frequently departed from the established tradition of the male canon, is evident from our examination of Latin American women's essays. While women were indirectly maintaining a dialogue with the traditional canon as essayists, they also developed their own network through a commonality of patterns that allowed, fostered, supported, and validated them as women writers in general and women essayists in particular, regardless of their country of origin. These commonalities were shared in the nineteenth century by the popular press, and in the twentieth both in the popular press and in lectures that were later published and circulated, often at the women's own expense.

One of the single most important components of this alternate canon is an appropriation of the public arena via the essay. Latin American women invaded the public sphere by converting the intimate, personal, and anecdotal, those topics usually reserved for women's salons, into valid forms of literary discourse through the essay. A typical trajectory would be as follows: a luminary figure such as Clorinda Matto de Turner or Alfonsina Storni would be invited to give a talk at the Ateneo de Buenos Aires, for example. After declaring herself unworthy of the praise she had just received, a tactic employed to mitigate her radical message, she would then go on to deliver an important speech on women's rights. That speech, in turn, would be printed as a pamphlet and sold for twenty centavos. Many years later, this same speech might be printed as a book. In this manner, a woman's word is transformed into a woman's text and passed around from woman to woman, thus assuring a wider readership than a single audience at the salon or the Ateneo could accommodate.

FORMS OF THE ESSAY

Where can we find these Latin American women's essays? Even for dedicated scholars looking for them, it is not an easy task. Like so many other forms of women's writing, the actual essays themselves are fragmented, lost, or literally decaying. Our own research led us to five distinct sources of women's essays: (1) the published salon talks mentioned above; (2) working papers from academic sources; (3) medical or scientific reports written by women doctors active in the struggle for women's rights; (4) travel journals which analyzed and compared women's situations in distinct countries; (5) and most frequently those found in the periodical press. Given the enormous production of periodicals in which women's essays appear, and the alternative feminist press which has proliferated all over Latin America in the last decade and shares many qualities with its nineteenth-century forebears, our analysis will concentrate on this form of the essay.

The same frustrations and fragmentation attendant to writing and publishing the original essays are duplicated when the feminist critic attempts to retrieve them.[14] Having been published often at a woman's own expense in a newspaper she herself founded and singlehandedly financed and edited [Manso, 1], it was not unusual for a nineteenth-century essay to end abruptly with the words "to be continued."[15] The reader, especially the late twentieth-century reader, is lucky to find that essay in another paper, with a different name, perhaps a week, or even a month later. When, in fact, the essays can be retrieved from the "depósito" (cellar), the inevitable signs of age, neglect, and rot are invariably present.

Precisely because the essays were not known, points the women made in them were often lost to the community. This is obviously the case with the Puerto Rican Eugenio de Hostos's famous essay, "La educación científica de la mujer" [Women's scientific education], which feminists have readily acclaimed as an example of Hostos's progressive thought [7-66]. However, the essay, in fact, reiterates many ideas already expounded by women in these journals as much as twenty years earlier. Yet because the Hostos essay has been anthologized and thus made accessible, it appears to be the first one that deals with the important subject of women, education, and science.

In their time, these works appeared all over the continent in newspapers, small magazines, journals, or as leaflets (*folletos*) published by small or alternative presses. Limited distribution and geographical obstacles hindered what could have been a widespread readership and consequently, most of these essays remained fragmented. Only rarely were they compiled into books during a writer's lifetime. However, the fragmentation that characterized women's essays, an extension of the fragmentation that has always been a component of women's lives (especially Latin American women), was not always a disadvantage.[16] Conscious of their limitations of time, space, and funds, women essayists found ways to adapt their writing to those constraints. By organizing the essay in self-contained, short units that could be interrupted without losing concentration, they created a final product that, viewed from the vantage point of our late twentieth-century perspective, resembled a great patchwork quilt in which the sum of the parts was greater than the whole.

While fragmentation became a common stylistic device in Latin American women's essays, metonymy was the favored rhetorical figure. In their deployment of metonymy, Latin American women essayists subverted the metaphor so favored by male essayists. While a metaphor addresses adjectival changes, metonymy proposes a substantial transformation in the essence of the noun itself. Thus, metonymy functioned as a vehicle through which women essayists presented a radically different way of conceptualizing the world around them. For instance, in many Latin American women's essays the readers were presented with the metonymy of the individual female citizen as a compendium [*compendio*] of society. This perspective on Latin American society dramatized the importance of the concrete (each individual woman) in relation to the abstract (the entity called society), thus forcing the readers of those essays to establish the necessary connections between the particular situation of women and that of Latin American society as a whole. This position is best illustrated by the demands for education that raged throughout the nineteenth century.

Instead of demanding women's right to education as a constitutive element of the democratic societies Latin Americans were trying to form, women essayists told their readers, male and female, that educated mothers made better citizens, and better citizens helped to civilize their countries—a task for all. Gómez de Avellaneda [124], for example writes: "In countries where women are honored, you'll find civilization, progress, public life. In countries where women are not, there is nothing grand; servitude, barbarism, and moral ruin are the inevitable fate that they found themselves condemned to . . ." [124].[17]

The use of the metonymical figure of the good citizen had far-reaching implications, for it manifested itself in the expression of women's political, legal, and professional participation, which included everything from the right to vote, to representation in political office, to programs and ministries and organizations dedicated to women within each country. In Perú or Bolivia, that participation might include organization of *campesinas* to address social problems of women as members of that group, while in Uruguay or Argentina it could encompass women shoe factory workers, or in the Caribbean it would entail women sugar cane workers. In their writing, though, women's demands remained focused: arguing and fighting for changes in laws, especially those that would protect women, children, and the elderly [Hernández, 112].

Metonymy also proved useful in the paradigm of educational reform in order to address issues of larger concern, as became obvious in Ercilia Pepín's writing. Although she began as a follower of Hostos's pedagogical principles, Pepín became disenchanted with the Puerto Rican educator's weaknesses in understanding the causes of social problems. In her own essays, she offers an analysis of education and defends women's equality and the right to participate in all aspects of the sociopolitical debates of her day. Thus, education serves as a springboard that would enable women, in Pepín's words, to contribute as much as men to "the great task of universal progress" and "to rebuild the nation with their labor in the pure sanctuary of the home" [Pepín, 36].

While Latin American women used metonymy as a literary device to substitute the part for the whole, they also used the genre—as did their male counterparts—as an explicit tool of political intervention. Yet women's essays participated in the political arena with a clearly distinct voice, creating an alternate canon that we have identified as a transgressive discourse [discurso contestatario][18] that best characterizes women's essays in both centuries. We may witness this transgressive discourse in Perú, when the group Evolución Femenina [Feminine Evolution] initiated a letter- and essay-writing campaign to various newspapers in Lima between 1914 and 1922 focusing on women's participation in "Sociedades de Beneficiencia Pública" (charity organizations). Using the charity organizations as their first target for reform, Peruvian women essayists proposed radical changes in the Peruvian Civil Code. In a letter addressed to the Peruvian Congress and later published as an essay in El Comercio, María J. Alvarado Rivera, founder and president of Evolución Femenina, argued for a vindication of women's and children's rights. Like her Dominican contemporaries, Alvarado Rivera saw the importance of woman's contribution to society beginning with her task of educator of her children. Drawing from examples from other societies where women had obtained better civil and legal rights, Alvarado Rivera's essays espoused a situation which would enable women to enjoy "in its fullness, the social dignity and the legal rights inherent to a human being" [2].

SUBJECTIVITY

If Latin American male essayists such as Alfonso Reyes, Octavio Paz, Borges, and Carlos Fuentes followed Anderson Imbert's ideas about the essay as a place where "logic starts to sing" [5], or saw the essay as a confluence of the poetic and philosophic, they still only considered their essays secondary to their fiction or poetry. The fact that they cultivated these other genres implies that they viewed their first occupation to be writers: their essays, while still occupying an eminent position in their oeuvre, were only ancillary to their fiction and/or poetry.

Women's essays, on the other hand, seem to follow a different program. In the first place, no single "I" appeared in the initial essays. But before we can examine the role of this "I," we need to spend a moment discussing how it is commonly used in Spanish expository prose. Most critics, for example, unless they are extremely famous, actually speak in the first-person plural, even when the subject is clearly singular. As a literary convention, it seems less pedantic to temper the strong first-person singular with a plural, and thus we often see the "nosotros" [we] form, even when it refers only to one speaker. However, this "nosotros" is a world apart from the feminine "nosotras" we encounter in the first essays by women.[19] For here, they did so as speakers for a group and their "nosotras" not only included themselves as a collective but also their readers, whom they knew to be highly literate [Masiello, 528]. They were acutely aware from the beginning that their readers were other women, the audiences that they sought, who, although literate, were not initially or necessarily drawn to the essay for its political or even aesthetic importance. Rather, they read the essays as a discourse that involved, engaged, addressed, and even "interpellated" them [Belsey, 45]. Consistently, and in spite of social situations that might evoke other responses, the woman's voice in their essays was one of sarcasm, wit, irony, and humor. The Mexican writer Rosario Castellanos, who cultivated every genre, illustrated this point:

> The new world which we must inhabit and which we will leave to the generations that follow us, will require the effort and collaboration of everyone. And among those everyone are women, who possess a potential for energy that sociologists are counting on, and they know the score, as they plan our development. And we certainly wouldn't want to embarrass them [*Mujer*, 41-42].[20]

The journal or newspaper was one of the quickest ways to reach a readership. Their language, too, instead of the alienating pedantic tone that is sometimes associated with the essay, adopted an invitational format. In this manner, what might have been rejected as a mere topic of gossip in a woman's salon now has been charged with the authority of the printed page. We can discover a pattern in the essays as well that is similar to women's talk or gossip, which is itself often ridiculed for not following a linear, chronological description.

The essayists themselves made continual reference to their readers as "nuestras lectoras" [Acosta de Samper, 1]. Thus, we may affirm that the "we" of women's essays was shaped by the dialogic nature of their writings. With respect to this dialogic nature, the readers also knew that the writers were women. With that in mind, the case of Amanda Labarca Hubertson, the Chilean educator and feminist, author of many books of essays, and the first woman to hold a *cátedra* (endowed academic chair) in Latin America, takes a bold discursive step (yet only at the culmination of her long career) which deserves special mention. In her essays, she has the "audacity" to refer to herself using the form of "I" rather than the common, perhaps less modest "we" that essay writers normally appropriated. When the nineteenth-century essayists spoke in the feminine "nosotras," they truly were a collective. As we can see with Labarca, moving from the "we" to the more personal "I" also indicates, as Patricia Pinto Villarroel has pointed out, a transgression, but also a subject who is sure of herself [58]. This "I" to which Labarca refers is obviously gender-specific. There is no doubt, as with the plural "nosotras," that the subject is a woman, even if it is not automatically built into the language as it is in the plural.

In examining the use of the collective "we" or the plural "I" as the voice of the narrator in recent women's testimonial literature, Lillian Manzor-Coats points out how this collective subject allows the reader to challenge the "function and the textual presence of authority" [15]. According to Manzor-Coats, the "we" in testimonial accounts (such as Alicia Partnoy's *The Little School: Tales of Disappearance and Survival in Argentina*) gives voice to other silenced voices, thus allowing them to participate in the rewriting of Latin American history. If, in the twentieth century, Latin American history is rewritten when one person speaks for a group (of the disappeared, for example), in the nineteenth century, that one voice could participate in the actual *writing* of it since all those nations were constructing themselves in those years.

Yet the power of this feminine "I" did not emanate from the authority of the narrative voice (usually associated with males) or from the position of observer and critical viewer of that reality. Rather, what we observe here is an unfolding of the subject into an "I" whose final formulation not only considered, but also depended on the participation of the Other, that is to say, the reader. Therefore, women's essays, unlike men's, whose legitimation rested upon the authorial stance of the narrative persona and who often addressed readers in the imperative, were looking for their own legitimation outside the text. Women's essays reflected an open text in which the "I" was only one of many possible voices for reflection. The essay, thus, becomes a fluid text and the subject becomes polyvocal.

As open texts women's essays tend not to be those in which problems are solved; rather, they are spaces in which the problem is put forth as a question: wouldn't society be better if women were educated? Wouldn't democracy be better served if women had equal rights and access to privileges? Dominican feminist Camila Henríquez Ureña employed such a strategy in defense of her Instituto de Señoritas, a school of higher education for women, rhetorically questioning whether women would have a hand in shaping the destiny of their nation via an awareness of self through education [Demorizi Rodríguez, 10]. Almost one hundred years later, Magaly Pineda, also Dominican, inherits this format in stressing the need for women to raise a Latin American feminist consciousness based on Latin American tactics, alliances, and goals. In proposing "the realization of a utopia," Pineda has explored new avenues again by questioning the way to create a new society [Pineda, "Feminismo," 17].

Inasmuch as the style in these and other women's essays was dialogic, the tone, too, avoided categorical conclusions that are sometimes associated with the genre. In so doing, women's essays redefined the genre. Instead of conforming to the authoritarian text of their male counterparts, women's essays took as a stance the feminist motto of the personal as the political.

The decision that prompted the first essayists to facilitate the accessibility of their essays to their readers was not merely stylistic. Since the ultimate purpose of the essay itself was not the glorification of the author (the "I"), but rather a transformation of society, and by implication, women's roles in it, a sense of urgency always prevailed in these writings. In the interstices of the texts, the reader perceives the desire to change the world.[21] Therefore, the writers of these texts had to ascertain that they were indeed read. No medium would lend itself better to the diffusion of ideas more economically and swiftly than the periodical press. While their male counterparts were concerned with the poetics of the essay, the women instead chose a language that evoked this sense of urgency through a directness of style and a concise prose that would create an impact on its readers.[22]

Throughout the nineteenth century and well into the twentieth, these middle-class women who wrote essays shared a continental press, informing their readers of activities in their own countries, Europe, the United States, and wherever else their readers might travel. One example is Soledad Acosta de Samper, whose travel journals were published in Colombian newspapers [Ordóñez] or Clorinda Matto de Turner's impressions about her travels through South America. In the latter part of the twentieth century, without completely withdrawing from the benefits of the periodical press and due to increasing interest in the market, women have found another viable means of publishing their essays through university presses. A third alternative, especially for the feminist voice, is the "prensa alternativa" (alternate press) that has cropped up in virtually every country with a feminist movement and co-existed side-by-side with the leftist alternative press. In fact, many Latin American feminists began their political education with their activism in leftist organizations [Sternbach, Navarro, Chuchryk and Alvarez]. With the new Latin American feminisms of the eighties, more open dialogues and discussion and more platforms for ideological debates exist. Not only have these dialogues created a space in which women could air their views and express their discontent, they have also been instrumental in the establishment of a feminist subjectivity where the voice of feminist protest continues.

Although most nineteenth-century essayists (as well as writers of other genres in Latin America) and most of their twentieth-century counterparts enjoyed a comfortable middle- or upper-middle class background, their concerns in the essays transcended class. Many used their class privilege and status to serve a dual function: on the one hand, they could investigate and denounce the situation of women in the lower classes, and on the other, they adopted a critical position vis-a-vis their own class, unmasking the privilege ascribed to them and their counterparts. Because of the privilege of middle-class status, they were able to become the speakers or voices of those who did not share their position, while at the same time they developed a critical consciousness of their class and the women who accepted it unquestioningly. Though Victoria Ocampo is probably the foremost example, Rosario Castellanos's "¿Existe una cultura femenina?" [Is there a feminine culture?] and Gabriela Mistral's *Lecturas para mujeres* [Readings for women] also illustrate these points.[23]

Latin American women essayists have developed this class consciousness in a voice that takes the point of view of the oppressed, whether they were other women, the indigenous, blacks, or prostitutes. In this manner these essayists reject the pretense of impartial observers of social malaise usually associated with the scientific (male) essay. Though examples abound in many essays, it suffices to point out Rosario Castellanos's simultaneous discussion of women's rights and the plight of Indians [*Oficio de tinieblas*], Clorinda Matto de Turner's *discurso contestatario* in reference to the Indians' difficult situation in Perú [*Aves sin nido*], and Magaly Pineda's vindication of black women in the Dominican Republic [*Mujeres*].

Their compassionate, rather than detached, position on social ills would, in our view, makes them more attractive to their readers. This tone of compassion or sympathy has also helped to break down divisional barriers between the essay and other literary genres, and the sentimentality that is normally associated with poetry. Women essayists have become adept at "threading" their sentiment and subjectivity with the factual, objective observations normally associated with the genre. In so doing, these women are establishing at least the possibility of connecting two apparently different genres while proposing new definitions for each of them.

The privileging of spirit over matter has long been identified as a defining cultural trait of Latin Americans from Enrique Rodó's *Ariel* to Roberto Fernández Retamar's *Calibán*. Increasingly conscious of the overwhelming technical superiority of industrialized nations and their expansionist ideas, Latin American essayists in the nineteenth and twentieth centuries have raised Rodó's banner and adopted this sense of spiritual superiority, not only as a weapon against developed nations, but equally important, as a characteristic of Latin Americans, who with José Vasconcelos's pronouncement could now consider themselves the "cosmic race" or the race of the future. While women essayists have identified to a certain degree with this mechanism of survival and self-definition, they have also subverted it to their own devices. Rather than becoming entangled in the men's discussions, they have used the same arguments to parallel women's position in patriarchal society. Gómez de Avellaneda's *La mujer*, for example, defended woman's superior moral caliber as a valid reason for her right to active participation in society. Thus we can see how the essay in women's hands has become a more effective tool for social reform. In fact, its didactic intention is paramount to its purpose.

FEMINISM AND THE ESSAY

As with other genres written by women, the scope of women's essays has been considered to be only women's concerns, although in reality women who write essays are concerned vitally with the betterment of their societies. However, they have always approached this improvement through the condition of women, which has gained them the label of being too specific. Nearly everywhere, women who have fought for women's rights in their essays related those rights to the contribution of a better, more democratic society. Thus, women essayists have maintained an interchangeable bipolarity of activists and writers throughout both centuries. For many women, essay writing has been only the first step in their feminist activism. Many of the essayists studied here chose professions of either teachers or writers. We cannot underscore enough the significance of women's literacy to the development and evolution of the essay. Therefore, what we inevitably encounter is the simultaneous growth of women's professions with women's activism and essay writing. In this sense, we may affirm our initial question that women's essays in Latin America and continental feminism have grown together and developed hand in hand.

The concept of feminism as a unifying system that would transform society and women's participation in it motivated Argentine poet and essayist Alfonsina Storni to declare feminism a process which helps "to create in the feminine soul her own life, her own being, her individual consciousness about all things and to apply this personal concept to free her from ancient chains" [*Movimiento*, 19].[24] All over the continent, we witness precisely what Storni claimed: women freeing themselves from ancient chains of prescribed femininity. In each context, the methods may vary, but the result is similar. For example, the Dominican Evangelina Rodríguez, who in 1911 was the first woman in her country to graduate from medical school, provided us with an early feminist position both on the role of the military and on U.S. intervention in Latin America. Considered one of the pioneers of Dominican feminism, she clearly demonstrated what would later be the feminist motto of the personal being the political. A strong foe of "Trujillismo" (the Trujillo dictatorship that dominated Dominican life for over thirty years), she endured the years of the U.S. intervention (1916-1924) and was inflexible in her criticism of the military occupation. Throughout these years, her essays never relented in portraying the ills of women's subservient role in Dominican society by denouncing the dehumanization of both women and men in dictatorial regimes at home and abroad.

Feminism as a distinct politics, disassociated from all other political and religious parties, and still a hotly debated issue among contemporary Latin American women in their essays and their roundtables, garnered one of its first bases in the 1930s with Zoila Aurora Cáceres's essay, "Manifiesto de feminismo peruano" [Manifesto of Peruvian feminism]. Like her contemporaries and her forebears, she published her principles and goals (including equal rights for women before the law, the right to vote, to administer her own property, to receive equal pay for equal work) as leaflets and short essays in local newspapers. She revolutionized both Latin American feminism and Latin American politics by welcoming to the ranks of her group, "Peruvian Feminism," all those who agreed with their feminist principles of organization, regardless of their political affiliations.[25]

Cáceres's perspective of feminist independence continues today, as is evidenced in Julieta Kirkwood's essay for the journal *Furia* [Anger]. Kirkwood's writings remind us of the need for Latin American women to approach political struggle from a gendered perspective. Her feminist political essays are visionary in scope for they permit women to assess where they are and where they want to go, or in Kirkwood's own words: "this is what we are, and this is what we want to be" [*Furia* n.p.].

Contemporary feminist essays in Latin America argue convincingly in favor of a coalescence of feminist activism and feminist theory, as in the case of Kirkwood's "Denial of Authoritarianism," an analysis that carries deep implications for the feminists of the continent.[26] By declaring that "there is no democracy without feminism," a slogan that has been chanted in many of the feminist marches throughout Latin America, Kirkwood effectively equates the military regimes of the seventies and eighties with their patriarchal rule while placing a feminist agenda alongside any democratic platform. Kirkwood's feminism, one of the most polemical, is also one of the most popular when she argues for a reevaluation of human production and reproduction as a way to rewrite Chile's social and political history. Her revolutionary position suggests that "women should end their exclusion from the discourses of power, and [should] work to invalidate the existing system of power and privilege, which is at the very root of that exclusion" [*Ser política en Chile*, 228].

In contrast to Kirkwood's feminist political essays, other essayists advocate women's activism and women's rights without ever articulating, in fact eschewing altogether, the word feminist. Nonetheless, feminist strategies are evident both on a rhetorical level in the essays themselves, and on a practical one in their activism. The best example of a woman's group consistently avoiding the word feminist while empowering itself through feminist tactics is Argentina's Madres de Plaza de Mayo. Even women who were (are) considered conservative, such as the nineteenth-century Colombian novelist and essayist Soledad Acosta de Samper, always exhibited a preoccupation with and an awareness of women's problems, women's position in society and the possibilities and desire for change, a politics which we call feminist.

Feminist essays were also a useful tool in the debates around the issue of national sovereignty and independence. Inasmuch as foreign military intervention had an impact on women's lives, it had a place in the feminist journal, *Femina*, that appeared in 1922 in the Dominican Republic.[27] The editorial "Educación o muerte" [Education or Death] makes explicit that connection:

> Without any doubt, the lack of a social education in our homes has brought about the destruction of our national edifice. Only a patient and intelligent task of reconstruction would be able to piece together our nation. It is up to the women to carry out such an important and delicate mission. . . . It is time that we acknowledge the importance of teaching and nurturing a socially conscious behavior in our children, right in our own homes. [Gómez, *Contribución*, 12].[28]

The idea that the home was instrumental in developing a social consciousness in children is one of the predominant and constant preoccupations in *Femina*'s editorials, as it was for its continental sisters during the nineteenth century. By claiming that the future of the country rested in women's hands, that is, the molding of young minds, these essayists not only reinterpreted women's "traditional" function in the home from a caretaker to the designers of a better society but also suggested that their task was reconstructive while they insinuated that men's task was destructive. Further, they argued that an educated mother was actually the cause for a more civilized society, as essays in *La Camelia, La Educación,* and *Album de Señoritas* continually explain in Buenos Aires. Thus, the link between family unity and the state paralleled the interconnection between the home as a private space and the nation as a public one. For all of these writers, their philosophy is summed up in the claim: "Feminism is an educational system and a social theory" [Hernández, 91, 92].[29] Repeatedly women have developed their essays around the metaphor of the family as a smaller version of the nation.

CONCLUSION

Despite their divergent political affiliations, marked differences in class status, and diversity of ethnic and racial origins, women in Latin American share a commonality of marginalization, exemplified in the construction of gender in each country. Latin American women writers, principally concerned about and preoccupied with the situation of women, have seen the essay as their genre of choice, for it alone allows them to develop a critical and cultural gendered voice. Women's essays, in turn, have subverted and redefined the nature of literature of protest in Latin America.[30] Since essay writing in the Latin American countries has traditionally been defined and formulated as a male exercise for the denunciation and criticism of social injustice, women writers in these countries have been de facto barred from joining the most coveted arena for the sociopolitical and cultural discussions of their times.

What is interesting, then, is not the observation of how women have interrupted the canon by injecting their essays into it, but rather their strategies for appropriating and redefining the genre by lending their gendered optic to the examination of all social issues.[31] Analyses of women in Latin American society have been based on different approaches in these essays, and although the writers themselves have come from very privileged backgrounds, descendants of Spanish and other European lineages, they have focused on women's concerns in ways that transcend class and ethnic barriers.

Writing has become an important act of survival and empowerment for women in Latin America: by consistently appropriating the public arena for women's concerns, women essayists have seen to it that those very issues began to gain some currency in the national discourses. Gender differences have gained validity as a necessary component for understanding the social fabric of Latin American nations. Women's education, for example, a marginalized topic reserved for women's journals in mid-nineteenth century, became *the* issue to debate all over the continent by the century's end.

For this reason, we are able to assert that women's essays became one of the most important avenues for women's politicization in Latin America. Free from the constraints of party politics, most women essayists discussed women's issues as social concerns, and thus placed themselves at the forefront of the sociopolitical debates of their times. Since essayists were educated women, they have been well equipped to enter the intellectual and political discussions of their times. In so doing, they have upheld the still operative Latin American tradition of writers as both intellectuals and activists.

The essays themselves contained both a sociological and literary value, as well as a historic and political one. In developing a voice for themselves as writers, Latin American women have also developed a consciousness as women. With their voice of the "counter discourse" or "the discourse of transgression," these essayists helped to create a space for the woman writer who practiced any other genre, as many of the essayists themselves did. By transgressing the norm requiring woman to remain silent, they simultaneously established a polyvocal voice and by their example showed how each piece of the quilt can be individually stitched in order to create a whole. The transgression consisted not only in breaking silences, but also in dismantling the injunction against women speaking. While the woman novelist was also concerned with speaking out, the woman essayist took her rebellion one step further by first issuing the complaint, and then creatively designing a social path that would better her society. It is precisely this feminist strategy that permits us to speak of a solidarity between women and the initiation of a feminist discourse of continental proportions, the underpinnings of a feminist movement.

Yet the history of Latin American feminism is the history of Latin American women's essays *only* to the extent that we consider those writings as the main, but never the only, forum for feminist thought. In the light of specific Latin American cultural indicators, important social, economic, geographic, political, and ethnic variables must always be interpreted as necessary components of the entire spectrum. At the same time, no history of Latin American intellectual thought would be complete without the inclusion of women's perspectives on self, society, and women's role in it that Latin American women's essays suggest. By intruding on and usurping a male tradition, women not only appropriate the genre, but they also require us to establish new parameters for the discussion of Latin American history.

NOTES

The authors gratefully acknowledge two individual Picker grants from our respective institutions in 1987-1988 which enabled us to travel to Latin America to consult primary sources. We are also grateful to Elena Tchalidy of Buenos Aires who permitted us access to the papers of Alicia Moreau de Justo. Thanks also to Brenda Rowe McGovern, our research assistant, who spent countless hours doing bibliographic work early on in the project. Additionally, we wish to thank the staffs of the National Libraries in Argentina, Uruguay, Peru, and Colombia who helped us find these essays.

1. Throughout this article we refer to this body of work as Latin American women's essays. In fact, the more technical term would be Spanish-American women's essays, for

we only treat those written in Spanish-speaking countries. Both Brazil and the English- and French-speaking Caribbean are outside the scope of this study. However, because of the possible confusion that would result from the term "Spanish-American," we are referring to our research as Latin American. Likewise, the term Latin American emphasizes the continental dimension of the essays, a point we wish to stress.

2. We are defining feminist thought as a way of thinking that advocates equal rights for women. Feminism, as it is understood in Latin America, is an activist position. Therefore, it is possible to be a proponent of feminist thought without actually being a feminist in Latin America.

3. Miller, 1983; Meyer and Zamora, 1983a; González and Ortega, 1984; Virgillo and Lindstrom, 1985; Magnarelli, 1985; Merrim, 1987; Arenal and Schlau, 1989; Franco, 1989; Lindstrom, 1989; Pratt and Morello-Frosch, 1989; Vidal, 1989; Bassnet, 1990; Guerra Cunningham, 1990; Marting, 1990.

For anthologies, see Meyer and Fernández-Olmos (1983b); Agosín (1989); Manguel (1986); Garfield (1985; 1988); Correas de Zapata (1990); Erro Peralta and Silva Núñez (1990); and Solá (1990). For translations of testimonial literature see Barrios de Chungara (1978); Burgos-Debray (1984); Partnoy (1986; 1988); and Alegría (1987). We have not included here the new and vast body of work by U.S. Latinas and the literary criticism surrounding it.

4. Before Latin America received its European-imposed name and colonial system of government, women poets were writing in both the Aztec and Incan empires.

5. "el campo literario y artístico . . . le ha sido disputado palmo a palmo por el exclusivismo varonil, y aún hoy día se la mira en él como intrusa y usurpadora, tratándosela en consecuencia con cierta ojeriza y desconfianza, que se echa de ver en el alejamiento en que se la mantiene de las academias *barbudas*. Pasadnos este adjetivo, queridas lectoras, porque se nos ha venido naturalmente a la pluma al mencionar esas ilustres corporaciones de gentes de letras, cuyo primero y más importante título es el de *tener barbas*." Throughout the text, the translations of the essays and essay titles are our own, except where otherwise noted.

6. For an interesting discussion of what it means to be a woman poet in Latin America, see Myriam Díaz-Diocaretz.

7. The Latin American Boom, an explosion of publications onto the international literary scene, took place during the 1960s and early 1970s. Such names as Gabriel García Márquez, Mario Vargas Llosa, Julio Cortázar, and Carlos Fuentes are some of the principal male authors.

8. See Garro; Poniatowska; Angel; Valenzuela; Lynch; Castellanos, "Oficio de tinieblas."

9. We are using "popularized" in the Spanish sense of the word, to mean used by the people.

10. Though Ripoll's work is not the first, it is considered to be the most definitive early panoramic view of the Latin American essay. Before him, José Gaos (México, 1944) published *El pensamiento hispanoamericano* [Spanish-American thought]. Aside from a few other anthologies, it is worth noting that the first collection to appear under the Latin American Thought series, published by the Mexican Ministry of Education (1942-1944), was *El pensamiento de América*. Its fourteen volumes focused on representative Latin American essayists such as Simón Bolívar, Andrés Bello, Lastarria, Eugenio María de Hostos, Enrique Rodó, José Vasconcelos, José Martí, and others. All were male. Medgardo Vitier's (1945) *Del ensayo americano* [About the American essay] examined the essay as a genre; it was a type of prose in which writers could present and discuss the most vital issues in Latin America. José Luis Martínez (1958) also published an anthology in which he studied antecedents, themes, and definitions of the genre with special attention given to the Mexican essay. Neither of these included any women. In Kurt L. Levy and Keith Ellis (1970), of the thirty-five articles, two deal with women essayists, one on Sor Juana Inés de la Cruz and another one on Puerto Rican essayists.

11. " . . . el ensayista hispanoamericano se convierte en un Diógenes angustiado que escruta al indio, interroga al conquistador, ensaya la historia, hace autopsia el tirano, convierte en oráculos a sus héroes, o se ilumina la cara del espíritu para encontrar los rasgos de su cultura. Sabe nueva su posición, se independiza del mundo y emprende su insólito camino."

12. *Caudillismo* is a political system characterized by one-man rule. The *caudillo* is usually a charismatic leader whose personality becomes identified with his power. Latin American countries endured the iron-clad rule of many *caudillos* during the nineteenth century; Juan Manuel Rosas in Argentina and Porfirio Díaz in Mexico are among the best known.

13. Rosa Guerra's newspaper *La Educación*, published in 1852, is an example of the publications which flourished after Rosas fell. *Album de Señoritas: Periódico de Literatura, Modas, Bellas Artes y Teatros*, edited in Buenos Aires by the educator Juana Manso, is another example. In the first issue, Manso [1854, 1] claims that "woman's intelligence, far from being an absurdity, a defect, a crime, or a fate, is her best adornment, the true source of her virtue" ["la inteligencia de la mujer, lejos de ser un absurdo, o un defecto, un crimen, o un destino, es su mejor adorno, es la verdadera fuente de su virtud"]. But the journal *La Camelia* [1852, 1], the longest running of the three, made the clearest references to the recent dictatorship of the "Tyrant" ["El Tirano"] or "the dark cloud which covered the horizon" ["la negra nube que cubria el orizonte"].

14. In our own experience, we have been frustrated at the unavailability of essays because the insects had arrived first, or when asked to return at later dates to find particular essays, only to be told then that (1) the collection was not available for public use; (2) the library was closed; (3) the material was misplaced; or (4) photocopying facilities did not exist or were not allowed for nineteenth-century texts. Such conditions that may be commonplace with any aspect of Latin American research appear to be all the more prevalent when the subject is women, especially women's essays.

15. In the first issue of *Album de Señoritas*, Juana Manso [1854, 1] apologizes to her readers for taking so long to get back to them. This issue, she explains, "costs me five times as much," but is preferable to a prospectus because it gives "a clearer idea of my thought and a more efficient proof of my good will" ["una idea más clara de mi pensamiento, y una prueba más eficaz de mi buena voluntad"].

16. Fragmentation was for many Latin Americans a way of life, as their history, geography, and politics could all attest.

17. "En las naciones que es honrada la mujer . . . hallaréis civilización, progreso, vida pública. En los países en que la mujer está envilecida, no vive nada que sea grande, la servidumbre, la barbarie, la ruina moral es el destino inevitable a que se hallan condenados."

18. Although we did not invent the term, we find it useful here. Among others, Eliana Rivero [218] uses it in her article on testimonial literature.

19. It is also a world apart from some women who emulate men by using the "nosotros" also, even when they are also speaking in the singular.

20. "El nuevo mundo, en el que hemos de habitar y que legaremos a las generaciones que nos sucedan, exigirá el esfuerzo y la colaboración de todos. Y entre esos todos, está la mujer, que posee una potencialidad de energía para el trabajo con la que ya cuentan los sociólogos que saben lo que traen entre manos y que planifican nuestro desarrollo. Y a quienes, naturalmente, no vamos a hacer quedar mal."

21. As Ivette Malverde Disselkoen has written in reference to Chilean women's fiction, "the subversion is found in the interstices" [72].

22. *La Camelia*, for example, devoted a section of most issues to "La Moda" (fashion) but made clear from the start that their program had a social function: "Readers should not infer that we intend to give details to such ridiculous topics as fashion, no way." ["No vaya á creerse que . . . pensamos en detallar todas las puerilidades que se llaman *Modas*, de ningún modo."] Rather, their intention was to promote decency in

dress and hair style in order to show what they considered to be their superior morality. [*La Camelia*, 1, Núm. 1 11 abril 1852:1].

Recent issues of *Furia* (Chile, 1983) and *Brujas* (Argentina, 1983–present) show that in both cases, the writers of the articles (though fearful of signing their true names because of the repressive governments of their countries) include drawings, captions, and other ways to facilitate the reading for women who might be encountering a woman's journal for the first time. Typically, these journals circulate at the continental feminist *Encuentros* (feminist meetings) as well as in their countries of origin.

23. See Mistral's anthology of readings for women at the school of her own name established in Mexico at the request of José Vasconcelos. In her introduction, Mistral, also a teacher and writer, notes "It's time we started the formation of our own feminine literature, and it should be serious." ["Ya es tiempo de iniciar entre nosotros la formación de una literatura femenina, seria."] Jean Franco offers another opinion of this volume [103]. Contemporary Mexican feminists consider Castellanos's master's thesis, "Is There a Feminine Culture?" a key text from which their political and theoretical positions derive and a landmark in Mexican feminist thought.

24. "crear en el alma femenina su propia vida, su verdadero ser, su conciencia individual de las cosas todas y aplicar este concepto personal a libertarla de trabas ancestrales."

25. "Manifesto of Peruvian Feminism" is in *folleto* form (loose leaf) and is part of Cáceres's personal correspondence. Her papers are not yet classified but are available at the Biblioteca Nacional in Lima.

26. This essay, first presented as a lecture at the XI Latin American Studies Association Congress in Mexico City in September 1983, later appeared as a pamphlet under *Documentos de Discusión*, No. 52, December 1983, published by FLASCO and was recently included in her book, *Tejiendo Rebeldías*. This essay, though contemporary, has followed the course of many earlier essays: lecture, pamphlet, book chapter.

27. Among the editors of *Femina* are Ercilia Pepín, Evangelina Rodríguez, Amanda Nivar de Paitaluga, Delia Weber Coiscou, Petronila Gómez, and Rosa Smester. Although male colleagues sometimes collaborated, they were never responsible for the publication of the journal.

28. "Incuestionablemente, la carencia de una educación civica eficiente en nuestros hogares ha producido el derrumbamiento del edificio de nuestra nacionalidad. Sólo una paciente inteligente labor de reconstrucción podrá levantar el edificio inconscientemente arruinado. Toca a la mujer el desempeño de tan delicada e importante misión y es hora ya, de que se labore con perseverancia por el establecimiento de nociones prácticas de civismo desde el santuario puro del hogar."

29. "Feminismo es un sistema educativo y una teoría social."

30. This seems to be true even of the essayists, whom we do not treat in this essay, who wrote from a conservative perspective about the impending threat of the new woman or feminism. These women believed that they were acting on women's behalf.

31. In 1895 Matto de Turner assesses this phenomenon in her "Las obreras del pensamiento" [Women workers of the mind]. Like many women's essays, these thoughts were first publicized as a lecture given at the Ateneo of Buenos Aires, 14 December 1895.

WORKS CITED

(For the benefit of our readers, we are including sources we uncovered in our archival research, not mentioned in the text.)

Acosta de Samper, Soledad. *La Mujer* 25 (1 October, 1879): 1.

Agosín, Marjorie, ed. *Landscapes of a New Land: Short Stories by Latin American Women*. Toronto: White Pine Press, 1989.

Alegría, Claribel. *They Won't Take Me Alive*. Trans. Amanda Hopkinson. London: Women's Press, 1987.

Alvarado Rivera, María. *El Comercio* (7 October 1914): 2.

Anderson Imbert, Enrique. "El ensayo por los ensayistas." *Dominical* in *La República* (2 March 1986): 5.

Angel, Albalucía. *Estaba la pájara pinta, sentada en el verde limón*. Barcelona: Ediciones Vergara, 1984.

_____. *Misiá Señora*. Barcelona: Ediciones Argos Vergara, 1982.

Arenal, Electa, and Stacy Schlau. *Untold Sisters: Hispanic Nuns in their Own Works*. Albuquerque: University of New Mexico Press, 1989.

Barrios de Chungara, Domitila, with Moema Viezzer. *Let Me Speak!* Trans. Victoria Oritz. New York: Monthly Review Press, 1978.

Bassnet, Susan, ed. *Knives and Angels: Women Writers in Latin America*. London: Zed Books, 1990.

Belsey, Catherine. "Constructing the subject: deconstructing the text." In *Feminist Criticism and Social Change: Sex, Class and Race in Literature and Culture*. Ed. Judith Newton and Deborah Rosenfelt. New York: Methuen, 1985. 45-64.

Berg, Mary. "Clorinda Matto de Turner." *Spanish American Women Writers: A Bio-Biographical Source Book*. Ed. Diane Marting. Westport, Conn.: Greenwood Press, 1990. 303–15.

Burgos-Debray, Elisabeth. *I . . . Rigoberta Menchú: An Indian Woman in Guatemala*. Trans. Ann Wright. London: Verso, 1984.

Cáceres, Zoila Aurora. "Manifiesto de feminismo peruano." Lima: Imprenta Lux de E. L. Castro (15 January 1931).

La Camelia. "Modas" 1, num. 1 (11 abril 1852): 1.

_____. "Las redactoras" 1, num. 3 (15 April 1852): 1.

Castellanos, Rosario. *Mujer que sabe latín*. México: ERA, 1973.

_____. *Oficio de tinieblas*. México: Joaquín Mortiz, 1962.

_____. *Sobre cultura femenina*. Mexico: Ediciones de América, Revista Antológica, 1950.

Correas de Zapata, Celia, ed. *Short Stories by Latin American Women: The Magic and the Real*. Houston: Arte Público Press, 1990.

Cypess, Sandra Messinger, David R. Kohut, and Rachel Moore, eds. *Women Authors of Modern Hispanic South America: A Bibliography of Criticism and Interpretation*. Metuchen, N.J.: Scarecrow Press, 1989.

Demorizi Rodríguez, Emilio. *Salomé Ureña y el Instituto de Señoritas*. Palabras de Camila Henríquez Ureña. Ciudad Trujillo: Academia Dominicana de la Historia, 1960.

Díaz-Diocaretz, Myriam. " 'I will be a scandal in your boat': Women poets and the tradition." In *Knives and Angels: Women Writers in Latin America*. Ed. Susan Bassnet. London: Zed Books, 1990. 86-109.

Earle, Peter G. "El ensayo definido por los ensayistas." *Dominical* in *La República* (2 March 1986): 7.

_____. "The Female Persona in the Spanish-American Essay." In *Women as Myth and Metaphor in Latin American Literature*. Ed. Carmello Virgillo and Naomi Lindstom. Columbia: University of Missouri Press, 1985.

Erro Peralta, Nora and Caridad Silva Núñez, eds. *Beyond the Border: A New Age in Latin American Women's Fiction*. San Francisco: Cleis Press, 1990.

Fernández Retamar, Roberto. *Calibán*. Montevideo: Aquí Testimonio, 1973.

Foster, David. *Hacia una lectura semiótica del ensayo*. Madrid: Studia Humanitatis, 1983.

Franco, Jean. *Plotting Women: Gender and Representation in Mexico*. New York: Columbia University Press, 1989.

Garfield, Evelyn Picon, ed. *Women's Fiction from Latin America: Selections from Twelve Contemporary Authors.* Detroit: Wayne State University Press, 1988.

_____, ed. *Women's Voices from Latin America: Conversations with Six Contemporary Authors.* Detroit: Wayne State University Press, 1985.

Garro, Elena. *Recollection of Things to Come.* Trans. Ruth L. C. Simms. Austin: University of Texas Press, 1969. [*Los recuerdos del porvenir.* México: Joaquín Mortiz, 1963].

Gómez, Petronila. *Contribución a la historia del feminismo dominicano.* Cuidad Trujillo, Dominican Republic: Editorial Librería Dominicana, 1952.

Gómez de Avellaneda, Gertrudis. "*La mujer*" (1860). In *Antología del feminismo.* Ed. Amalia Martín-Gamero. Madrid: Editorial Alianza, S.A., 1975. 121-24.

González, Patricia Elena and Eliana Ortega, eds. *La sartén por el mango: Encuentro de escritoras latinoamericanas.* Río Piedras: Editorial Huracán, 1984.

Guerra, Rosa. "Correspondencia." *La Educación* (Buenos Aires) 1, núm. 2 (July 31, 1852): n.p.

Guerra Cunningham, Lucía, ed. *Splintering Darkness: Latin American Women Writers in Search of Themselves.* Pittsburgh: Latin American Literary Review Press, 1990.

Hernández, Angela. *Emergencia del silencio.* Santo Domingo: Editor Universitaria, UASD, 1986.

Hostos, Eugenio María de. "La educación científica de la mujer." In *Obras completas.* Vol. 12, *Forjando el porvenir americano.* Havana: Edición Conmemorativa del Gobierno de Puerto Rico, Cultural, S.A., 1939.

Kirkwood, Julieta. "Editorial," *Furia* (Santiago) August 1981.

_____. *Ser política en Chile.* Santiago: Editorial Cuarto Propio, 1990.

_____. "Tejiendo rebeldías." In *Escritos feministas de Julieta Kirkwood hilvanados por Patricia Crispi.* Santiago: Círculo de Estudios de la Mujer y FLASCO, 1983.

Levy, Kurt L. and Keith Ellis, eds. *El ensayo y la crítica literaria en IberoAmérica.* Proceedings of the XIV International Congress on Latin American Literature, University of Toronto: Instituto Internacional de Literatura Latinoamericana, 1970.

Lindstrom, Naomi. *Women's Voice in Latin American Literature.* Washington, D.C.: Three Continents Press, 1989.

Loveluck, Juan. "El ensayo definido por los enasayistas." *Dominical* in *La República* (2 March 1986): 7.

Lynch, Marta. *La Señora Ordóñez.* Buenos Aires: Jorge Alvarez, 1967.

Magnarelli, Sharon. *The Lost Rib.* Cranbury, New Jersey: Fairleigh Dickinson University Press, 1985.

Malverde Disselkoen, Ivette. "De *La última niebla* y *La amortajada* a *La brecha.*" *Nuevo Texto Crítico: América Latina: Mujer, Escritura, Praxis.* Ed. Mary Louise Pratt and Marta Morello Frosch. 2, no. 4 (Second Semester 1989): 69-78.

Manguel, Alberto, ed. *Other Fires: Short Fiction by Latin American Women Writers.* New York: Crown Publishers, 1986.

Manso, Juana. "La redacción." *Album de Señoritas* 1, núm. 1 (1 January 1854).

Manzor-Coats, Lillian. "The Reconstructed Subject: Women's Testimonials as Voices of Resistance." In *Splintering Darkness: Latin American Women Writers in Search of Themselves.* Ed. Lucía Guerra Cunningham. Pittsburgh: Latin American Literary Review Press, 1990. 157-71.

Martínez, José Luis. *El ensayo mexicano moderno.* Mexico City: 1958.

Marting, Diane, ed. *Spanish American Women Writers: A Bio-Biographical Source Book.* Westport: Greenwood Press, 1990.

Masiello, Francine. "Between Civilization and Barbarism: Women, Family and Literary Culture in Mid-19th Century Argentina." In *Cultural and Historical Grounding for Hispanic and Luso-Brazilian Feminist Literary Criticism.* Ed. Hernán Vidal. Minneapolis: Institute for the Study of Ideologies and Literature, 1989. 517–66.

Matto de Turner, Clorinda. *Aves sin nido.* Oaxaca: Editorial Oasis, 1981.

_____. *Cuatro conferencias sobre América del Sur*. Buenos Aires: Imprenta de Juan A. Alsina, 1909.

_____. "Las obreras del pensamiento en la América del Sud." *Boreales, miniaturas y porcelanas*. Buenos Aires: Imprenta de Juan A. Alsina, 1902. 245-66.

Merrim, Stephanie, ed. *"Y yo despierta": Towards a Feminist Understanding of Sor Juana Inés de la Cruz*. Ann Arbor: Oxford Books, 1987.

Meyer, Doris, and Margarite Fernández-Olmos, eds. *Contemporary Women Authors of Latin America: Introductory Essays*. New York: Brooklyn College Press, 1983.

_____. *Contemporary Women Authors of Latin America: New Translations*. New York: Brooklyn College Press, 1983.

Miller, Beth. "A Random Survey of the Ration of Female Poets to Males in Anthologies: Less-than-Tokenism as a Mexican Tradition." In *Latin American Women Writers Yesterday and Today*. Ed. Yvette E. Miller and Charles M. Tatum. Pittsburgh: Latin American Literary Review Press, 1977. 11-17.

Miller, Beth, ed. *Women in Hispanic Literature: Icons and Fallen Idols*. Berkeley: University of California Press, 1983.

Mistral, Gabriela. *Lecturas para mujeres*. México: Porrúa, 1976. *El Mosquito*. 19 August 1877.

Ordóñez, Montserrat, ed. *Soledad Acosta de Samper: Una nueva lectura*. Bogotá: Ediciones Fondo Cultural Cafetero, 1988.

Partnoy, Alicia. *The Little School: Tales of Disappearance and Survival in Argentina*. San Francisco: Cleis Press, 1986.

_____, ed. *You Can't Drown the Fire: Latin American Women Writing in Exile*. San Francisco: Cleis Press, 1988.

Peden, Margaret Sayers, ed. and trans. *The Intellectual Autobiography of Sor Juana Inés de la Cruz*. Lime Rock, Conn.: Lime Rock Press, 1982.

Pepín, Ercilia. *Diversas consideraciones relativas a la evolución intelectual y jurídica de la mujer dominicana de los últimos cinco lustros*. Santiago: 1936.

Picón Salas, Mariano. "Y va de ensayo." In *Crisis, cambio, tradición: Ensayos sobre la forma de nuestra cultura*. Madrid, Caracas: Ediciones Edime, 1955.

Pineda, Magaly. "Feminismo y la participación política en la República Dominicana." Unpublished. 1986.

_____. "Mujeres de los sectores populares involucradas en actividades económicas en el Canbe." Centro de Investigación para la Acción Femenina. Unpublished. Presented at the Workshop on Feminismo Popular, Barranquilla, Colombia. 14-19 November 1983.

Pinto Villarroel, Patricia. "Mirada y voz femeninas en la ensayística de Amanda Labarca Hubertson: Historia de la anticipación chilena." In *Nuevo Texto Crítico: América Latina: Mujer, Escritura, Praxis*. Ed. Mary Louise Pratt and Marta Morello Frosch. 2 (Second Semester 1989): 57-67.

Poniatowska, Elena. *Hasta no verte, Jesús mío*. México: Ediciones Era, 1969.

Pratt, Mary Louise and Marta Morello Frosch, eds. *Nuevo Texto Crítico. América Latina: Mujer, Escritura, Praxis* 2 (Second Semester 1989).

Ripoll, Carlos. *Conciencia intelectual de América: Antología del Ensayo Hispanoamericano (1836-1959)*. New York: Las Américas, 1966.

Rivero, Eliana. "Testimonios y conversaciones como discurso literario: Cuba y Nicaragua." *Literature and Contemporary Revolutionary Culture* 1 (1985): 218-28.

Rojas, Lourdes. "Recent Trends in Women's Sexuality in Latin America." *Trends in History* 4, no. 4 (1990): 187-209.

Sánchez, Luz Elena. "We Are Making Inroads." *Escritos en Movimiento*. Special Issue of *¿Qué pasa mujer?* (Winter 1983): 81-90.

Smith, Sidonie. *A Poetics of Women's Autobiography: Marginality and the Fictions of Self-Representation*. Bloomington: Indiana University Press, 1987.

Solá, María, ed. *Aquí cuentan las mujeres: Muestra y estudio de cinco narradoras puertorriqueñas*. Río Piedras: Huracán, 1990.

Sommer, Doris. "*Sab* C'est Moi." *Genders* 2 (July 1988): 111-26.

_____. *Foundational Fictions*. Berkeley: University of California Press, 1991.

Sosa de Newton, Lily. *Diccionario biográfico de mujeres argentinas*, 3rd edición. Buenos Aires: Editorial Plus Ultra, 1986.

Sternbach, Nancy Saporta, Marysa Navarro, Patricia Chuchryk and Sonia Alvarez. "Feminisms in Latin America: From Bogotá to San Bernardo." *Signs* 17 (Winter 1992): 393-434.

Storni, Alfonsina. "El movimiento hacia la emancipación de la mujer en la República Argentina: Las dirigentes feministas." *La Revista del Mundo* 5 (August 1919): 12-19.

Vidal, Hernán, ed. *Cultural and Historical Grounding for Hispanic and Luso-Brazilian Feminist Literary Criticism*. Minneapolis: Institute for the Study of Ideologies and Literature, 1989.

Virgillo, Carmello, and Naomi Lindstrom, eds. *Woman as Myth and Metaphor*. Columbia: University of Missouri Press, 1985.

Vitier, Medgardo. *Del ensayo americano*. Mexico City: 1945.

CHAPTER ELEVEN

"A Weaponry of Choice"

Black American Women Writers and the Essay

PAMELA KLASS MITTLEFEHLDT

> Early on . . . this possibility of language, of writing, seemed to me magical and basic and irresistible. . . . I loved words and I hated to fight. But if, as a Black girl-child in America, I could not evade the necessity to fight, then, maybe, I could choose my weaponry at least.
>
> June Jordan, *Civil Wars*

Essay. Weapon. The juxtaposition creates an uneasy tension, a dialectic resonant with possibility, yet landmined with resistance. The essay literally is a trial, an attempt, an exploration. A cool tracking of one's thought: rumination, reflection. Nothing that sends us into the blood and smoke of battle. Yet June Jordan, Audre Lorde, and Alice Walker, three Black American writers, have appropriated the essay and fired it with the passion and particularity of their voices and experiences. A political charge sustains their writing: the conviction that words can be a weapon of choice in the struggle against racism, sexism, heterosexism, homophobia, ageism, poverty, and injustice. They have disrupted and transformed the genre as their words disrupt and challenge the world. They refuse to let us forget there is a battle raging.

In addition to their writing in other genres, Jordan, Lorde, and Walker have each published two volumes of prose in the past ten years. The essays collected in these volumes range historically from Jordan's 1964 "Testimony" to Lorde's "A Burst of Light," published in 1988. They range topically from coming alive in the Civil Rights movement to confronting death while living with cancer. And they move from Harlem to Arlesheim, from Moscow to Mississippi, from East Lansing to Juigalpa. They are peopled with family and strangers, ancestors and friends. They are about riots, Brer Rabbit, a daughter who smokes Camels, a horse named Blue, the murder of Black children. Beyond the immediacy of topic and detail, these collections are about being Black and female in twentieth-century America. They are explosions of anger and statements of power. They are a refusal to remain silent or invisible. They leave me—a white woman sharing on many levels the anger and the demand for change—charged and responsible.

Reading these essays—some of them familiar as memorized poems, others starkly new—collectively raises questions about the juxtaposition of form and impact. Why did Jordan, Lorde, and Walker turn to the essay? As a genre, it has emerged in white, Western privilege. It is presumed male: studied, authoritative. In form, it tends to be rambling, contemplative, remote, lacking urgency and fire. If the essay had a color, it would be pewter. Yet these essays by Jordan, Lorde, and Walker are obsidian and crimson, heat and lightning. They strike to the bone. They spark and flame.

What of the voices resounding through these essays? To write an essay is to assume the validity and authority of one's voice, the significance of one's experience, and the implicit value of one's insight and perspective. To write an essay is to break silence and claim authority. It is to assume the right of speech and Being. For a Black woman in America to write an essay is an act of bodacious rebellion.

The essay traditionally has assumed a measured relationship with its audience. That audience has been presumed to be a like company of good men: contemplative, erudite, immersed in the quiet pleasures of the moment. What do we make of essays that challenge and demand response?

In other words, what of essays that are intentionally political—not only in terms of content, but also in terms of form and voice? What of essays that lead not to contemplation but to action? Essays where the front lies just beyond the last sentence? What of essays that claim to be weapons? For these are reports from the front lines of America. And the Black woman is at the center of the battle. "What other creature in the world besides the Black woman has had to build the knowledge of so much hatred into her survival and keep going?" Lorde asks. "What other human being absorbs so much virulent hostility and still functions?" [*Sister Outsider*, 150, 151].

Why did these three writers turn to the essay? The most obvious response, of course, is why not? Resistance often involves the appropriation of established forms. If language is employed as a tool of rebellion, any literary genre may be of use, no matter how relentlessly white, Anglo-European, heterosexual, male it traditionally may have been. However, the essay in particular has qualities that make its appropriation intriguing. As a form, the essay has its own internal tensions which may make it both resistant and useful to Black feminist writers who select it as a weapon of choice.

The essay has been compared to a journey, to a stroll, to a portrait, to after-dinner ruminations around a fire. Traditionally, it has an aura of containment, detachment. The essay ponders, reflects, questions, probes. Yet it does so from a distance. Virginia Woolf, one of the few women writers included in the tradition of the essay, describes this quality: "It should lay us under a spell with its first word, and we should only wake, refreshed, with its last. In the interval we may pass through the most various experiences of amusement, surprise, interest, indignation; we may soar to the heights of fantasy with Lamb or plunge to the depths of wisdom with Bacon, but we must never be roused. The essay must lap us about and draw its curtain across the world" [Woolf, 294]. The essays in these collections by Jordan, Lorde, and Walker defy this quality of removed contemplation. Rather than laying the reader under a spell and drawing a curtain across the world, they tear down the blinds and challenge the reader to gaze eye to eye with the world.

On the other hand, some qualities of the essay make it a particularly appropriate tool for these Black feminist writers. The essay is personal. The author matters intensely. When that author is a Black woman, the voice which comes through is one of radical import, for it is a voice which has been traditionally obliterated in Western thought and literature. The essay makes visible the patterns of an individual's thoughts. It allows us to see the process of contemplation that results in understanding that in turn leads to action.

The essay is grounded in the particular. By their nature, essays are specific and detailed. They emerge from a specific mind, responding in a specific time and place. There is an immediacy to the genre. When Jordan, Lorde, and Walker write, they speak from their specific social contexts. They write with the immediacy of their lives as Black American women. Whether reflecting on anger or the politics of oppression or the connectedness of all living things, these essays are nevertheless firmly rooted in the specific details of their lives. Because these details reveal lives that until very recently had been excluded from the traditional record, the immediate is political.

Finally, the essay cuts against the grain. Essays can be crosscurrents. They reflect and question. They can be, as Theodor Adorno notes, heretical: "the law of the innermost form of the essay is heresy. By transgressing the orthodoxy of thought, something becomes visible in the object which is orthodoxy's secret purpose to keep invisible" [171]. Much of the energy of the essay comes not from observation and confirmation of what is, but from reconsideration and resistance.

It is these qualities of the essay—the focus on the personal, the affirmation of process, the groundedness in particular experience, the challenge—that make it a useful genre for Black feminists who are writing to change their worlds. Its versatility and flexibility allow it to be honed to a fine point and flung with precision into the struggle for survival.

Each of these writers indicates various reasons for turning to the essay. All share the imperative of refusing to be silenced, of being excluded from the public discourse. June Jordan refers to this as the "politics of exclusion"—the whitelisting and censorship—which she as a Black woman writer experienced. Black women's perspectives rarely appear in print on a national level on a regular basis in any newspaper or journal. In general, Black women's voices rarely appear in the public record. Publishing her essays is a way of redressing that omission.

While the importance of being heard underlies the creation of these essays, there is also an indication of resistance to the form. Alice Walker approached her second collection of essays after finishing her novel, *The Color Purple*, thinking she was done with words altogether. Audre Lorde turned to prose after years of expressing herself in poetry, resisting the communication of "deep feeling in linear, solid blocks of print," a process she had come to suspect because she "had seen so many errors committed in its name" [SO, 87]. However, she discovered that prose provided a context within which to work through her perceptions, to clarify her ideas, and to transform feeling into language [SO, 88]. The essay provided a place where "knowing and understanding mesh," where "knowledge [is made] available for use" [SO, 109].

In these essays, there is a pattern, a sense of movement. They begin with contemplation, with the effort to map a journey, understand a world. They end with a challenge, an imperative to action. Jordan states that "these writings document my political efforts to coherently fathom all of my universe, and to arrive at a moral judgement that will determine my further political conduct" [OC, 2]. They document the authors' awareness of the tension between contemplation and action. As Walker comments near the end of *Living By the Word*: "What of this book? I realize that, as it stands, it has the rounded neatness of contemplation, and I would like to leave the reader with the uneven (I almost said ragged) edge of activity" [LBW, 176].

Between the simultaneous intentions of preserving perceptions and providing an impetus to action, these essays function in three distinctive ways. They provide grounding. They rupture/resist. They demand transformation. The simultaneous interaction of these three qualities sparks a charge which makes these essays weapons of choice.

These essays provide grounding: an affirmation of the immediacy and power of one's reality on both a personal and a political level. They are a context within which each writer constructs a sense of her presence in this universe. They allow the evolution of an authorial self. This self is not isolate; she is shaped within a context of ancestors, family, friends, community. In these essays, a distinctive voice is heard—one that is particular, female, and Black. This voice emerges in dialogue—with itself and with others.

However, while these essays allow for the possibility of coherence and community, they also rupture. They are resistance: a refusal to be silenced, a refusal to be *said*. By telling the stories of their own and other Black women's lives, Jordan, Lorde, and Walker counter the attempts to erase and deny the experiences of Black women in American culture. At the same time, they also challenge the seductive ease of connection by engaging the dialectic tensions of difference.

The tension between grounding and rupture seeks resolution in transformation, in change: the transformation of a self from silence to voice; the tranformation of a sexist, racist, and otherwise distorted culture. That transformation begins in the text. Its challenge is passed along to the reader. One quality which permeates all of these collected essays is a sense not of complacency, but of urgency, the imperative to acknowledge and to enter the struggle.

"How can I be who I am?" June Jordan identifies this as the basic question of contemporary life. The process of grounding is the process of coming to terms with that question. On many levels, the essay provides an ideal context in which to explore that question, for at the heart of the essay is the self—the subjective *I* who observes, experiences, questions, and interprets. The voice of the essay is the voice of the self, observer and agent, who is both created in and creator of the essay. In these essays, that self is Black and female, two realities which create a complex weave of relationships and resistances. The space of the essay provides a context within which to explore these tensions and to move towards a definition of one's self. That movement towards definition is an act of self-preservation. As Lorde notes, "If we do not define ourselves for ourselves, we will be defined by others—for their use and to our detriment" [SO, 45]. It is also an act of resistance.

The self encountered in these essays is clearly defined, deliberately located in time and place:

"As a forty-nine-year-old Black lesbian-feminist socialist mother of two, including one boy, and a member of an inter-racial couple . . . " [Lorde, SO, 114].

"As a Black woman, and as a human being within the First World movement, and as a woman who loves women as well as she loves men" [Jordan, CW, 115].

"I am . . . Norte Americana, an African-American, even an African-Indian-Gringo American . . . " [Walker, LBW, 176].

Each of these statements places the individual within a specific, politically charged social context. The Self emerges on a finely webbed matrix of roles and identities.

In addition to these social descriptions, each writer also claims identities which are symbolic and which move away from the literal matrices of sociological/economic/cultural definition. "I am Nicaraguan; I am Salvadoran; I am Grenadian; I am Caribbean; and I am Central American," writes Alice Walker [LBW, 176]. "I am a scar, a report from the headlines, a talisman, a resurrection," states Audre Lorde [BL, 59]. These symbolic identities are metaphors for connection as well as another refusal to remain enmeshed on anyone's grid.

One aspect of telling one's own story—part of that process of grounding the self—includes recording and reflecting on one's experiences. Because these essays emerge from the details of the writers' experiences, they frequently provide a rich autobiographical record of self-development. Walker's earliest writings record the passion and exhaustion of a twenty-three-year-old woman "knee-deep in stories" in Mississippi, the defiant pride of a single mother encountering a white New England winter with a sick child. Jordan begins her first volume by placing herself literally in the universe: "First there was Harlem and the people of Harlem, my own birthplace." Her second volume ends with the demanding question: "Where are we and whose country is this anyway?" Jordan's essays track the territory between the conditions of her birth and the imperative of her politics. As she reflects on her father, her marriage, her mother's death, the Harlem riot of 1964, her experiences in Nicaragua, the murder of a young Black man, Jordan's commitment to the front line of social change is grounded in the details of her experience.

The self that is constructed in these essays emerges from the complexity of each writer's personal experiences as a Black woman. It is strikingly apparent that for these women, that self is multi-voiced and in constant dialogue with others. These writers speak in many tongues.

Alice Walker writes of the internal tension created by this multiplicity of voices as she embraces the slave-owning great-great grandfather as part of her circle of ancestors. "We are the African and the trader. We are the Indian and the settler. We are the slaver and the enslaved. We are the oppressor and the oppressed" [LBW, 89]. When this multiplicity of voices is acknowledged as part of the construction of one's identity, a unique self emerges, one that is complex and paradoxical. This dynamic internal pluralism is both empowering and silencing. June Jordan explores this double bind as she describes the irony of simultaneity: "As a Black woman, as a Black feminist, I exist, simultaneously, as part of the powerless and as part of the majority peoples of the world in two ways: I am powerless as compared to any man because women, per se, are kept powerless by men/by the powerful. I am the majority because women constitute the majority gender. I am the majority because Black and Third World peoples constitute the majority of life on this planet" [CW, 143].

This internal vocality is intricate and ironic. As that multi-layered voice speaks in these essays, it offers new angles of vision, unique juxtapositions of understanding and accountability. Another aspect of the voice in these essays, though, is the fact that it so often is engaged in external dialogue with others. These are not essays written in isolation. There is a passionate sense of connection in these writings, a clear impression that these words are directed towards others, and that they invite response. The self which emerges here is one which is grounded in community.

June Jordan sketches the pattern of this interactive struggle for self-definition: "My life seems to be an increasing revelation of the intimate face of universal struggle. You begin with your family and the kids on the block, and next you open your eyes to what you call your people and that leads you back to your own bed where you lie by yourself, wondering if you deserve to be peaceful, or trusted or desired or left to the freedom of your own unfaltering heart. And the scale shrinks to the size of a skull: Your own interior cage" [CW, xi].

That trajectory, from self to family to neighborhood to one's people back to one's own bed, one's own interior cage, traces a pattern of self-construction which is repeated throughout the work of these three writers. They suggest that it is through accepting the centrality of others in the formation of the self that one's identity is known. "I am who I am, doing what I came to do, acting upon you like a drug or a chisel to remind you of your me-ness, as I discover you in myself," writes Audre Lorde [SO, 146-47]. The isolate Emersonian individual traditionally speaking in the essay is supplanted by a self which resonates in dialogue with others, creating what Mae Henderson has called a "simultaneity of discourse," an exchange which is particularly revealing in the writing of Black women because of the way race and gender are refracted in the formation of the self [Henderson, 17]. Like the internal construction of the Self, the Other in these works is also multifaceted. It includes a spectrum of relationships, including ancestors, family, Black women, Black people, women, all living beings.

For each of these writers, the other on a most primary level is the mother. The connection between mother and daughter is honored, as these essays celebrate the mothers who kept alive the notion of song, who strode with "fists as well as/hands" across landmined battlefields to provide the very basics for their daughter's survival: "books/desks/a place for us" [Walker, SMG, 242]. These essays acknowledge the connection between mothers' sacrifices and a new generation of Black daughters; they also describe the distances and tensions between generations. As Jordan says, while her mother's work never "enlarged the universe of her imagination or her power to influence what happened beyond the front door of our house, [it] invented the potential for a completely different kind of work for us, the next generation of Black women: huge, rewarding work demanded by the huge, new ambitions that her perfect confidence in us engendered" [OC, 105]. Yet that confidence also included a legacy of pain. While daughters learned survival from their mothers, they also learned "isolation, fury, mistrust, self-rejection, and sadness." Audre Lorde writes that her own survival "lay in learning how to use the weapons she gave me, also, to fight against those things within myself, unnamed" [SO, 149-50].

One response to this dual legacy of survival and pain is a rigorous sense of responsibility. When Jordan's mother committed suicide, her death became an imperative for Jordan's living: "I wanted to live my life so that people would know unmistakably that I am alive, so that when I finally die people will know the difference for sure between my living and my death. . . . I came too late to help my mother to her feet. By way of everlasting thanks to all of the women who have helped me to stay alive I am working never to be late again" [OC, 26]. Mothering itself becomes a metaphor for this responsibility—to oneself and to other Black women. It means, as Lorde writes, "that I affirm my own worth by committing myself to my own survival, in my own self and in the self of other Black women" [SO, 173].

Each of these women has chosen the role of writer as a response to that commitment, and each reflects on the responsibilities of that role. A variety of images of the artist appear: voice of the people, warrior, dragonslayer, witness. The responsibility of the artist, like that of the mother, is survival. *"We are a people. A people do not throw their geniuses away.* And if they are thrown away, it is our duty *as artists and as witnesses for the future* to collect them again for the sake of our children, and, if necessary, bone by bone" [SMG, 92].

That survival is both personal and collective. The voice of the writer in these essays is one that resonates with her community. Yet the role of the writer is double-edged. If, on one hand, the artist provides illumination and collects community, on the other hand, the artist also acts in resistance, placing herself necessarily in opposition to the expectations of the other. A Black woman writer stands in the crossfire of expectations placed on her by Black and white men, as well as by Black and white women. The pressure of these expectations is intense. Walker describes this uneasy status with insight when she states that the artist often finds herself "considered 'unacceptable' by masses of people who think that the writer's obligation is not to explore or to challenge, but to second the masses' motions, whatever they are. Yet the gift of loneliness is sometimes a radical vision of society or one's people that has not previously been taken into account" [SMG, 264]. This gift of radical vision is compounded when the artist/outsider is also Black woman/outsider, a tension Lorde acknowledges in her title, *Sister Outsider*.

If, however, like a lightning rod, these essays provide grounding, that grounded charge emerges from them as rupture, resistance. One of the functions of the artist is to disrupt, to question, to resist. "I have moved from an infantile reception of the universe, as given, into a progressively political self-assertion that is now reaching beyond the limitations of a victim mentality," writes Jordan. "I choose to exist unafraid of my enemies; instead, I choose to become an enemy to my enemies" [CW, 129].

The image of writer as a warrior, of the writer's work as a battle, runs throughout these collections of essays. The sense of being on the front line creates much of the energy in these writings. This metaphor is not one of militaristic violence, for each of the writers clearly speaks with a deep affirmation of life. It is one of determined resistance and a demand for transformation. These essays acknowledge the fact that in order for change to occur, there will be struggle. Jordan comes to the understanding that "I am not against war; I am against losing the war" [OC, 17], as she reflects on the politics of racism. Lorde realizes that "I am not only a casualty, I am also a warrior" [SO, 41], as she confronts the reality of cancer. These essays repeatedly remind us that not losing means you have to fight.

There is no safety in silence: "My silences had not protected me. Your silence will not protect you" [SO, 41]. Breaking silence means moving from being victim to being warrior. The weapons have been chosen with care. Choosing words as a form of resistance necessitates acknowledging the politics of language. "For those of us who write, it is necessary to scrutinize not only the truth of what we speak, but the truth of that language by which we speak it," notes Audre Lorde [SO, 43]. The language of the essay has traditionally been that of white male privilege. It is essential to have a language of one's own to sustain own's own being, for, as Alice Walker writes, "it is language more than anything else that reveals and validates one's existence, and if the language we actually speak is denied us, then it is inevitable that the form we are permitted to assume historically will be one of caricature, reflecting someone else's literary or social fantasy" [LBW, 58]. That language, when preserved, is life-giving.

Jordan worked with children and young adults as a teacher and a poet. As a result she is particularly tuned to the politics of English. English, she claims, is not a matter of specific geography — it is a matter of privilege and oppression, a matter of survival. She explores what she calls the "politics of translation" between Black English and white English. For Black children, white English literally is a second language, and, she argues, should be approached as such. Instead, children quickly learn that they must "literally, accept the terms of the oppressor, or perish: that is the irreducible, horrifying truth of the politics of language" [CW, 66]. She ruptures the standards of mainstream publishing by writing an essay in Black English: "White Tuesday. November, 1984," which begins: "Whole campaign an' dint neither one of them joker talk about right or wrong. We knowed it was trouble" [CW, 141].

The politics of language extend beyond decisions over whether or not to use Black English. For the most part, these essays are crafted in standard/white English. Yet language is used in ways which create a strong sense of Black women's voices and presence. Jordan demands that those who choose the word as weapon must use it as agents, not victims. "By itself, our language cannot refuse to reflect the agonizing process of alienation from ourselves. If we collaborate with the powerful then our language will lose its currency as a means to tell the truth in order to change the truth" [OC, 33]. She argues that we cannot afford the luxury or the powerlessness of the passive, of the vague, of the general. Accordingly, these essays are written in an active voice, with ears attuned to the rhythms of one's people, with eyes alert to the details of the immediate lives of Black women. All three women are also poets, a fact which also shapes their use of language.

These essays disrupt. They are concrete evidence of Black women refusing silence. They resist the traditional voice of the essay by insisting on the signature of their own respective voices. They also disrupt in terms of content, for these are essays centered on the experiences and opinions of Black women. That, even in late twentieth-century America, is still a matter of opposition.

Jordan, Lorde, and Walker create a new geography of the essay marked by race and gender. The self in these essays is full bodied: Black and female. This is perhaps the most blatant rupture in the form and voice of the essay. The pain, the joy, the rage, the love, the terror, the hope are all grounded in specific bodies. The bodies of these writers become part of the text. Racism scrubbed into the grain of a young girl's skin can no longer remain an abstraction. "Did *bad* mean *Black*?" Lorde questions. "The endless scrubbing with lemon juice in the cracks and crevices of my ripening, darkening, body. And oh, the sins of my dark elbows and knees, my gums and nipples, the folds of my neck and the cave of my armpits!" [SO, 149]. Alice Walker reflects on the devastating impact that a scarred eye had on her sense of herself. It wasn't until her daughter pointed out that she had a world in her eye — that the eye looked like the "Big Blue Marble" image of the earth seen from the moon — that Walker was able to embrace herself fully as "beautiful, whole and free" [SMG, 393].

June Jordan writes of literally putting her body where her words were; "I wanted to get real; to put my life, as well as my words, on the line. I had to go to Nicaragua" [OC, 67]. She took her body to the battle.

For Audre Lorde, her body becomes the battle as she writes from the front-line of living with cancer. She writes of the immediacy of her pain and fear, and then expands the parameters of the struggle as she explores cancer as a meta-phor for racism, sexism, homophobia—disease on a cultural level. "The strug-gle with cancer now informs all my days, but it is only another face of that continuing battle for self-determination and survival that Black women fight daily, often in triumph" [BL, 49].

These essays also create rupture in terms of their focus, particularly their repeated insistence on addressing the issue of difference. While there is a strong sense of connection, while there is space for grounding, ultimately these essays refuse the seduction of easy agreement and identification. As a white woman reading these words, I found myself coming abruptly against points of differ-ence, places I could not enter, experiences I could not claim. It did not always make for comfortable reading. It did provide much of the charge in these works.

Dealing with the dynamics of difference has been one of the crucial issues of contemporary feminism. In "Age, Race, Class, and Sex: Women Redefining Difference," which was originally delivered as a speech in 1980, Lorde identi-fies the most devastating danger of difference: "our refusal to recognize those differences, and to examine the distortions which result from our misnaming them and their effects upon human behavior and expectations" [SO, 115]. That danger still threatens over ten years later.

These collections of essays provide a particularly complex and challenging perspective on difference because of the nature of the writer/self and her rela-tion to her audience. Difference resonates both internally and externally. The multiple definitions of self, each with their own dialectic of erasure/empowerment, remind us that difference occurs among and between, as well as within. Difference is simultaneously vital and lethal. These essays address both the pain and the imperative of difference. "Difference must be not merely tol-erated, but seen as a fund of necessary polarities between which our creativity can spark like a dialectic" [SO, 111].

These essays draw on a range of polarities. Over and over, they document the erasing/silencing effects of difference. The most painful silences are those which demand that one aspect of the self deny another: to be Black, but not female; to be woman, but not Black, resulting in a double erasure of self. These essays document the tensions and differences within the contemporary feminist movement. "Black feminism is not white feminism in Blackface" [SO, 60], writes Lorde. They document the repeated pattern of male privilege present within the Black community.

They also explore in more detail the differences between and among Black women. If the self is in part constructed from difference, it also longs for its own reflection. Yet that reflection in the Black female other is painfully refracted precisely because she is Black and female. Audre Lorde confronts the dynamics of the hatred of other/self which create pain and judgment between Black women in "Eye to Eye: Black Women, Hatred, and Anger." This essay traces the effects of absorbing the anger directed at Black women, and then firing it back at another Black woman in what becomes a double form of self-hatred. She calls for a reclamation of the love and tenderness possible between Black women, seeing it as an imperative first step toward change. "It would be ridiculous to believe that this process is not lengthy and difficult. It is suicidal to believe it is not possible" [SO, 175].

The Black lesbian has come to embody the most primal fear of difference as she incorporates all aspects of otherness. The "terror of Black Lesbians is buried in that deep inner place where we have been taught to fear all difference—to kill it or ignore it." [BL, 21]. This terror is the ultimate weapon for keeping Black women apart. The Black lesbian stands outside all social norms and speaks with unique insight. She is another challenge to the Cartesian dualism of constructed reality. Not married to man. Not single. Partnered/lover of women. Choosing to love another woman incurs the wrath and fear of those who struggle to keep women contained. These three writers, whether lesbian, bi-sexual, or "homospiritual" [LBW, 163], address the mindless drain of energy wasted on what Lorde calls "antilesbian hysteria" [SO, 49]. As the epitome of the fear of difference, it "ascribes false power to difference" [SO, 51], and perpetuates the isolation and loneliness of Black women.

The insistence on confronting issues of difference arises from the shared conviction that these issues are at the heart of the battle. Racism, sexism, and homophobia are all seen as forms of human blindness, a blindness which stems from the "inability to recognize the notion of difference as a dynamic human force, one which is enriching rather than threatening to the defined self . . . " [Lorde, SO, 45]. These essays address these forms of blindness. They illuminate the pain and fury of trying to assemble a self in their crossfire. They embody the politics of resistance as independent selves emerge from the smoke, striding across the minefields into each other's arms.

In these essays, Black women have refused silence, and have shattered the calm with their words. An array of selves speaks through these works; grounded, disrupting, their words demand response. They put us all "On Call." Throughout these essays, I as a reader am called beyond contemplation to action. These are not platonic abstractions pondering metaphors of truth; these are passionate injunctions declaring the immediacy of battle. The essay has become a form that melds the eloquence and urgency of poetry with the precision and potency of fine rhetoric. A weaponry of choice, which demands transformation.

This tranformation is called for on both personal and cultural levels. It begins with the need to transform the hatred—the direct by-product of racism and sexism—accumulated by Black women living in America into a force that can work constructively towards the future—that can be, as Lorde puts it, a lifewish rather than a deathwish [SO, 152]. That force is fired by anger—the result of "metabolizing hatred like a daily bread. Because I am Black, because I am woman, because I am not Black enough, because I am not some particular fantasy of a woman, because I AM" [SO, 152]. And these essays are fired by anger—anger at the murder of Reggie Jordan, anger at the imprisonment of Dessie Woods, anger at the discrimination and injustice permeating American culture. Anger is a tool of survival. It brings clarity. It is, as Lorde notes, "a powerful fuel." Yet anger alone is a less than satisfactory weapon. Like guilt, it is "an incomplete form of human knowledge" [SO, 152]. The urgency of anger drives these essays. Yet it is anger which has been translated into word and action. The raw emotion has been transformed into commitment and connection.

Anger is also a by-product of confronting difference. These essays urge the transformation of our responses to difference. Rather than fearing it, we must learn to use it. Difference is not only an issue between Black and white women. Several of these essays explore the dynamics of difference between Black women. Sharing oppression does not automatically lead to sisterhood. June Jordan reflects on this fact as she writes about Olive, the Bahamian woman who was the maid at the Sheraton British Colonial, where Jordan went for a vacation. She comes to the realization that " . . . even though both 'Olive' and 'I' live inside a conflict neither one of us created . . . I may be one of the monsters she needs to eliminate from her universe and, in a sense, she may be one of the monsters in mine" [OC, 47]. The ultimate connection between Black women cannot be the enemy. Rather it must be "the need that we find between us. It is not only who you are . . . but what we can do for each other that will determine the connection" [OC, 47].

Between Black and white women, the issue of difference has led to anger which often results in guilt, particularly on the part of white women. That guilt is a form of both silence and privilege. It allows a refusal to take responsibility. These essays confront this tension and highlight the imperative of moving beyond it. Agreement is not necessarily the point. What is essential is a shared commitment to justice, to change. "You do not have to be me in order for us to fight alongside each other. I do not have to be you to recognize that our wars are the same . . . we must allow each other our differences at the same time as we recognize our sameness" [SO, 142].

These collected essays help affirm the collective wideness of our vision as women. At the same time, they refuse an easy assumption of sisterhood. They affirm difference, and hold us all accountable for acknowledging, honoring, and using it. As the ambiguity of Lorde's title, Sister Outsider, suggests, an unresolved tension resonates throughout these works. That ambiguity, unrelieved by the clarification of punctuation, leaves open-ended the question of how we all connect, and where our differences ultimately will leave us.

That open-endedness is another quality of these essays. They are not neatly packaged. They refuse to remain tidily between the pages. They lack the crystallization of poetry and resist the sense of narrative completion which marks novels and stories. They create momentum rather than reach resolution. "Pass it on," says Alice Walker in the final line of *Living by the Word*. Pass it on.

It is that imperative which leaves me charged, responsible. The struggle that these essays call for is not over as the last line is written. On the contrary, it has just begun. June Jordan, Audre Lorde, and Alice Walker have written essays that serve as weapons in the civil wars of twentieth-century America. These essays both affirm and protest. They create grounding and rupture. They call for transformation. They are simultaneously celebration and ammunition.

> I make, demand, translate satisfactions out of every ray of sunlight, scrap of bright cloth, beautiful sound, delicious smell that comes my way, out of every sincere smile and good wish. They are discreet bits of ammunition in my arsenal against despair.
>
> Audre Lorde, "A Burst of Light"

WORKS CITED

Adorno, Theodor W. "The Essay as Form." *New German Critique* 32 (Spring-Summer 1984): 151-71.

Henderson, Mae Gwendolyn. "Speaking in Tongues: Dialogics, Dialectics, and the Black Woman Writer's Literary Tradition." In *Changing Our Own Words: Essays on Criticism, Theory, and Writing by Black Women*. Ed. Cheryl A. Wall. New Brunswick: Rutgers University Press, 1989. 16-37.

Jordan, June. *Civil Wars*. Boston: Beacon Press, 1981. [CW]

_____. *On Call: Political Essays*. Boston: South End Press, 1985. [OC]

Lorde, Audre. *A Burst of Light*. Ithaca, N.Y.: Firebrand Books, 1988. [BL]

_____. *Sister Outsider*. Trumansburg, N.Y.: Crossing Press, 1984. [SO]

Walker, Alice. *In Search of Our Mothers' Gardens*. San Diego: Harcourt Brace Jovanovich, 1983. [SMG]

_____. *Living By the Word: Selected Writings 1973-1987*. San Diego: Harvest/HBJ Book, 1988. [LBW]

Woolf, Virginia. "The Modern Essay." In *The Common Reader*. New York: Harcourt, Brace, and Co., 1948. 293-307.

CHAPTER TWELVE

Terrorism and the Essay

The Case of Ulrike Meinhof

ARLENE A. TERAOKA

[The essay] does not capitulate before the
burden of what exists.
Adorno, "The Essay as Form"

In the second scene of Heiner Müller's *Hamletmachine*, a dramatic autopsy of
the European male intellectual who acts in collusion with the patriarchal state,
the figure of Ophelia appears on stage to put an end to her suicidal past as a
prisoner in a world defined by men. In startling contrast to the aristocratic
Hamlet who engages in his famous monologic "BLABLA" [Müller, *Hamletmachine*, 53], Ophelia takes action: destroying the home in which she was oppressed and reclaiming her body as her own, she enters the street covered in
blood. In her unorthodox escape from the Hamlet story that would immortal-
ize her victimization, Ophelia defies an oppressive male, bourgeois order;
abandoning her hidden position as domestic victim, she leaves the scene with
an unspoken promise of retaliatory urban violence:

> I smash the tools of my captivity, the chair the table the bed. I destroy the battlefield
> that was my home. . . . With my bleeding hands I tear the photos of the men I loved
> and who used me on the bed on the table on the chair on the ground. I set fire to my
> prison. . . . I walk into the street clothed in my blood. [Müller, *Hamletmachine*, 54-55][1]

Müller's striking figure draws her inspiration from the life of the late West
German terrorist Ulrike Meinhof [Müller, "Viv(r)e la contradiction!" 50]. Considered next to Patty Hearst the most famous woman terrorist of the 1970s and
eulogized as the most significant woman in German politics since Rosa Lux-
emburg [Kramer, 213], Meinhof abandoned her bourgeois home for the urban
guerrilla underground in a dramatic sequence of events between 1968 and
1970. Divorcing her husband and curtailing her successful career as a political
journalist, she renounced categorically her domestic, social, and professional

life in favor of a politics of violence and the uncertainties of a terrorist exist-ence.

Born in 1934, Meinhof was the second daughter of respectable, middle-class, Protestant parents. Her father, from a family of theologians, was an art historian and director of the municipal museum in Jena, and an active member of a church that opposed the Nazi state. After her father's death, when Mein-hof was six years old, her mother began her university studies in art history. A student friend, Renate Riemeck, joined the household as a boarder; when Meinhof's mother died of cancer in 1949, the talented Riemeck, fourteen years older than Meinhof and soon to become one of the first women professors in the Federal Republic of Germany, took on the role of foster mother.

Supported by a competitive scholarship, Meinhof studied education and psychology at Marburg, moving later to Münster. Highly active in the opposi-tion movement against West German nuclear rearmament, she gained the at-tention of Klaus Rainer Röhl, editor of konkret, a student newspaper that would become the focal cultural organ of the radicalized West German stu-dents and intellectuals in the 1960s. The editor saw Meinhof as a valuable prize to be won over both politically and personally and made his conquest in a ro-mantic setting with a popular love song playing in the background [Röhl, 129, 131-32]. In general Röhl was proud of Meinhof's good looks and intellectual charisma, and gloated over the attention paid her in public by men who could not possess her [Röhl, 235-36]. Although it is difficult to assess the specific dy-namics of their relationship, their strong mixed feelings of attraction and re-pulsion formed the foundation for a productive working relationship on the journal and, simultaneously, a marriage in which, in Röhl's account, Meinhof seemed to be happy [cf. Kramer, 199-200].

Associated with konkret from 1959 to 1969, and working as editor-in-chief from 1962 to 1964, Meinhof earned fame, wealth, and unusual social respect-ability as the author of sharply critical essays published in her husband's jour-nal. With her divorce in 1968 came not only the subsequent decision to sever all professional connections to the journal but also the final stages of a shift from earlier pacifist views to an acceptance of the necessity of revolutionary violence. The change in loyalties and lifestyle was expressed in highly symbolic fashion in 1969 when Meinhof, after a thwarted attempt to occupy the edito-rial offices of her ex-husband's journal, moved the scene of the group action to their former marital home; the acts of Ophelian vandalism performed in the fashionable house in a respectable, wealthy Hamburg suburb signified Mein-hof's final rejection of her bourgeois and domestic past. One year later she took part in the spectacular armed escape of Andreas Baader from police custody, committing herself to a life underground. Soon afterward she formed, together with Baader and Gudrun Ensslin, the terrorist Red Army Faction (Rote Armee Fraktion, or RAF) in which she played an active role until her death in prison in 1976.[2]

Numerous explanations have been offered, by biographers, sociologists, political analysts, and even by Meinhof's ex-husband, of the apparently sudden turn from bourgeois acceptability to terrorist violence. None is convincing, and most focus on psychological factors, turning what might be political into the purely personal: the loss of both parents at an early age; the strong influence of Meinhof's independent, academic, and leftist foster mother; or the intense love affair with a chauvinistic and unfaithful husband all conspired somehow to create a woman desperately in need of the strong social attachments offered by a terrorist commitment.[3] But I would like to depart here from such retrospective psychologizing and take a different approach to the case.

In the following, I seek to probe the ties between essay writing and terrorism suggested by the remarkable details of Meinhof's biography. The emancipatory Ulrike/Ophelia of Müller's play destroys bed, table, chair, and home, all instruments of her oppression, before moving into the streets. Where would one place the typewriter in this scene, if at all? It is true that Meinhof resigned publicly from her ex-husband's journal soon before taking up her underground terrorist life; it is also true that she abandoned her lucrative career as a journalist and essayist for the dangers of a criminal existence. But it would be facile to conclude that Meinhof left all words and theorizing behind to take up the gun, or that essay writing and terrorist activity are incompatible or at least separate endeavors. Instead I would propose that terrorism and the form of the essay are interconnected in subtle ways that illuminate both their natural affinity and their mutual limitations.

Language and writing play an undeniable and necessary role in terrorist activity. Political analysts have pointed to the inherently rhetorical dimension of terrorist acts, which, highly symbolic in their every detail, seek to demonstrate to a broad audience the nature of the abuses perpetrated by political systems. Terrorist violence itself is also, if not primarily, an extreme mode of communication [Leeman; Miller]. Furthermore, acts of terrorism are invariably accompanied by written communiqués that claim responsibility for, and that explain the political and moral significance of, the violence undertaken. The violent act thus becomes the extreme and unexpected rhetorical flourish that captures the audience and holds its attention for the intellectual discourse that follows. The substance of that discourse is key: Ulrike Meinhof's terrorist writings, for example, constitute a crucial part of her essayistic oeuvre and offer the most incisive, comprehensive, and mature political and ideological analyses of her career.[4]

More interesting than the linguistic component of terrorism, however, is the possibility of a terrorist component of essay writing itself. I mean here first of all the possibility that we might understand Meinhof's terrorism not as the irrational and desperate end to, but as the logical continuation of, the project of her political essays. But it is also worth pursuing the further implication that the essay genre in its West German context maintains a political stance towards the institutions of power that can be seen as implicitly terroristic. Just as acts of terrorism are highly symbolic "texts," the essay in turn contains a component of terror in its uncompromisingly critical relationship to the social and political status quo of an increasingly repressive German state.

Meinhof's columns and other essays during her ten-year career with *konkret* cover a variety of topics, from the Cold War, Kennedy's assassination, and Vietnam, to German rearmament, political arson, the debates concerning the German Emergency Laws,[5] the political uniformity of the German press, and the dilemma of women bearing the burdens of both household and job [Meinhof, *Die Würde des Menschen*].[6] Yet the impressive breadth of material is governed by a single, recognizable, and consistent political project: in the best tradition of Kantian Enlightenment, Meinhof seeks to illuminate previously (or deliberately) unexamined assumptions and to educate the public citizenry in the use of its faculty of reason as a tool for political analysis and change.

In the 1964 essay "Provinz und kleinkariert" ["Province and petty"], for example, Meinhof argues that fourteen years of Adenauer's chancellorship resulted in the creation of a populace largely ignorant of political reality, a people unable to recognize, much less to act in, its own interests. "The people of the Federal Republic live without awareness of themselves and their history," Meinhof writes, "uninformed, unenlightened, disoriented, undecided between Pril and Sunil [brand-name detergents], in the know about Alete baby food and kitchen appliances, not about nonaggression pacts and nuclear-free zones" [*Die Würde des Menschen*, 44]. Consumerism had replaced informed judgment; "well nourished and ignorant" [47], the Germans were incapable of responsible political decision-making.[7]

In the face of such large-scale political *Unmündigkeit* [immaturity], the specific task of the intellectual is to analyze and to expose the mechanisms of manipulation to public scrutiny in an effort to effect serious social change: "To overcome and surmount [the Adenauer era] means to describe it, to analyze it, to see through it, and then to do everything entirely differently than HE had thought, done, and wished" [Meinhof, *Die Würde des Menschen*, 47].[8] The intellectual nurtures the development of critical thought in a populace historically blinded and immobilized by state or state-supported institutions. The goal entails a new concept of democracy, described in the following terms in an essay on the German publishing mogul Axel Springer:[9]

> instead of using the freedoms of speech and of the press to manipulate public opinion, using them to abolish the manipulation; instead of channelling and blocking information, dispersing it; instead of pounding in a certain political view, cultivating a critical consciousness; instead of letting the people fall asleep, waking them up; instead of letting them become stupified . . . , emancipating them. [Meinhof, *Die Würde des Menschen*, 1980, 106]

Stated programmatically in these excerpts, themes of rational critique, political enlightenment, informed public debate, and the need for radical change characterize the entire project of Meinhof's essays.[10] The appeal to reason is evident from her earliest work: in the essay "Der Friede macht Geschichte" ["Peace makes history"], for example, Meinhof lauds the historic meeting of Eisenhower and Khrushchev at Camp David in 1959 as a victory of "the forces of reason and humanity" [*Die Würde des Menschen*, 12]. Eight years later she appeals to those same forces in her comments on the Israeli occupation of Sinai, the West Bank, and the Golan Heights, calling for "rational" solutions and for a "reason" [*Vernunft*] that transcends political alliances [100-103].

The essay "Hochhuth" (1965) expresses her unflagging belief in the power and revolutionary potential of intellectuals who, by analyzing the causes of social discontent, can enlighten the German working class [Meinhof, *Die Würde des Menschen*, 68-70]. The project of emancipatory enlightenment continues in the 1967 essay "Enteignet Springer!" ["Expropriate Springer!"], which calls for the "education of citizens who are capable of judgment" and an end to the exclusion of "critical, thinking, oppositional voices" from the German press [104-107]. In another essay published that year, Meinhof speaks out strongly for "free discussion" and "rational debate" and against the tactics of the government that would turn democracy into a police state and its citizens into mere "receivers of orders" [108-11].

The aim in these texts is always to expose the repressive mechanisms of a capitalistic and increasingly militaristic state and to further the political maturity and independence of its citizens. The critique of state ideology is often fearless in its claims. Meinhof's essay from 1960 on the proposed German Emergency Laws, for example, points out basic similarities between the policies of the West German government towards potentially subversive groups and those of Nazi Germany, contrasting the "terror" of the West German state with the principles of true democracy [*Die Würde des Menschen*, 14-19]. An incisive analysis from 1962 argues that, as a result of amendments to the West German constitution allowing for remilitarization and of proposed changes enabling the suspension of civil rights in cases of national emergency (including massive strikes and demonstrations), "the dignity of the human being would be violable once again." In the essay bearing that title Meinhof puts forth a spectacular argument to the effect that the development of nuclear arms is incompatible with the preservation of democracy [27-30].

An essay on the Grand Coalition of the Social Democrats and the Christian Democrats from 1966 links the erosion of parliamentary discussion and political difference to the material prosperity of the German people, a prosperity that worked to obscure the regressive direction of party politics [Meinhof, *Die Würde des Menschen*, 88-91]. Even Meinhof's last work before her turn to terrorist activity continues the project to expose state oppression in all its forms: the preface to her television play *Bambule* on state homes for juvenile delinquents makes clear the political function of such institutions in a program to discipline and to suppress spontaneous attempts by disadvantaged German youths to break out of a life of poverty and abuse.

The lawsuits in 1961 and 1964 brought against Meinhof by Franz Josef Strauss, the archconservative leader of the Christian Social Union (CSU), testify to the explosive impact of such texts.[11] If the tenets and goals of the West German state are predicated on the continued political ignorance and passivity of its people as Meinhof claims, then the attempt to correct such ignorance and overcome such consenting passivity represents a fundamental, potentially violent threat to official state politics. In their attempt to create a consensus of critical knowledge, to foster a broad climate of opposition to the policies of the state, and to inspire dramatic change in the existing political order, Meinhof's essays are, I would suggest, tendentially terroristic.

Notably, their subversive enlightenment project is furthered rather than abandoned in Meinhof's terrorist writings, where it is contrasted with the specifically anti-enlightenment project of the state to foster lies and to mobilize public fears in its own interests:

> the principle of [the state's] psychological warfare, aimed at inciting the people against the guerrilla and isolating the guerrilla from the people, is: to distort the material, real goals of the revolution . . . , to mystify, to make the comprehensible incomprehensible, to make the rational appear irrational. . . . the method is: persecution, lies, dirt, racism, manipulation, mobilization of the unconscious fears of the people, of . . . reflexes of existential fear and superstition in response to forces that are uncomprehended, because they are unrecognized structures of domination. [*Texte: der RAF,* 69]

The RAF, in opposition, serves an "enlightenment function," working above all to "make the truth visible" [*Texte: der RAF,* 547]. Meinhof's essays, no less than the actions of the RAF, manifest in this way a continued programmatic refusal to capitulate before the power of the political status quo.

It is at this point that an essential affinity between terrorism and the essay genre comes to light. Despite its well-documented origins as a literary form fathered in the sixteenth century by Montaigne and Bacon, the essay as genre has remained stubbornly, elusively undefined. Indeed, much of the scholarly discussion surrounding the essay is devoted to rectifying its lack of generic definition [McCarthy; Bensmaïa]: characteristically protean and non- or openly anticonformist, the essay is a genre whose authors have claimed the right to question anything and everything, adhering to no traditions and seeming to fear no transgressions in form or content [Hardison; Gerhardt]. One line of essayistic development—its dominant tradition—has followed a paternalistic path in which the knowledge and insights of the author are handed down with an irresistible authority based on wit, stylistic elegance, and the learning that comes from class and gender privilege.[12] But I would suggest that there is freedom in the form for another lineage, one that critically aims to expose such privileges and the illusions that they support and that support them in turn, a lineage for which the female terrorist, not the aristocratic male, might be the paradigmatic author.

The theoretical statement that provides the strongest case for this critical, "terroristic" potential of the essay genre comes from Theodor W. Adorno. His philosophical treatise on "The Essay as Form" (1958) is restricted to the critical essay on works of culture, particularly literary texts, contrasting modes of knowledge and definitions of truth in the realms of art and science. But if we are sensitive to the political overtones of his assertions, Adorno's various statements become highly charged, if not incendiary.[13]

In a passage that recalls Meinhof's own essayistic project, Adorno links the essay form to both enlightenment and resistance. Again we find the identification of a specifically German problem as one of failed political emancipation: the inability of the "spirit" [*Geist*] to develop and to function independently, and its propensity to sacrifice its freedom and to subordinate itself to established authority. And again, as for Meinhof, the specific project of the essay is to engage that dormant capacity for critical reason and thereby to inspire an emancipatory resistance; this action in turn elicits a reflex of repression against the essay and the knowledge and politics it represents:

> In Germany the essay arouses resistance because it evokes intellectual freedom. Since the failure of an Enlightenment that has been lukewarm since Leibniz, even under present-day conditions of formal freedom, that intellectual freedom has never quite developed but has always been ready to proclaim its subordination to external authorities as its real concern. The essay, however, does not let its domain be prescribed for it. [Adorno, 3-4]

In its task the essay recognizes no limitations upon its birthright to critique. Its proper domain cannot be dictated (thus restricted) by external authority; neither does it have any "qualms" [the essay is "ohne Skrupel," literally, "without scruples"] about making use of the intellectual achievements of others [Adorno, 4]. Respecting neither established boundaries nor traditional rights of property, the essay is, in Adorno's characterization, "childlike" [4]; it is this same quality that makes it politically subversive.

In Adorno's analysis, the fundamental quality of the essay is its anti-authoritarian stance. Rejecting the reigning, scientific definition of truth as universal and unchanging, the essay enacts in its form and its content a radical critique of methods, principles, and categories that claim absolute and abstract validity. Instead of demonstrating its "responsibility to the status quo," it evinces a resolute "irresponsibility" [Adorno, 6]; it "raise[s] doubts," it "does not play by the rules," it "rejects primordial givens" and "rebels against . . . doctrine" [Adorno, 9, 10, 12]. Against any methodological reduction, and thus subordination, to principle, the essay champions the ephemeral, the transient, the individual, the "irritating and dangerous aspects" [Adorno, 12] that are inevitably and deliberately excised by the demand for indubitable certainty and systematic closure. The essay thereby threatens by its very nature the continued existence of an epistemological and political status quo based upon the systematic elimination of incompatible and antagonistic elements: "If science and scholarship, falsifying as is their custom, reduce what is difficult and complex in a reality that is antagonistic and split into monads to simplified models . . . , the essay, in contrast, shakes off the illusion of a simple and fundamentally logical world, an illusion well suited to the defense of the status quo" [Adorno, 15].

Stated in explicitly political terms: the essay seeks to expose as illusions the hitherto unquestioned "truths" put forth by a dominant science (read: the state) that have worked to secure its power over an audience whose intellectual and political freedom has remained (or been kept) deliberately immature. The uncompromising essay is the product of "the subject's efforts to penetrate what hides behind the facade under the name of objectivity" [Adorno, 4]: exposing accepted norms as potential instruments of subordination, categorically reject-ing every unexamined capitulation to the status quo, finding dogmatic systems abhorrent to the claims of life, the essay embodies by definition "mobility," "confrontation," and the "critique of ideology" [Adorno, 20, 18]. "Hence the essay's innermost formal law is heresy," Adorno concludes; "through viola-tions of the orthodoxy of thought, something in the object becomes visible which it is orthodoxy's secret and objective aim to keep invisible" [Adorno, 23]. In its defiance of social, political, and epistemological norms, and in its efforts to enlighten and potentially to mobilize its audience against the status quo, the essay as genre thus betrays a startling resemblance to the phenomenon of modern political terrorism. Conversely, Meinhof's descriptions of the urban guerrilla echo Adorno's statements concerning the form of the essay: the guer-rilla has no set temporal or spatial location, no set position as a secure point of origin, but constitutes herself in the process of constant motion and critique [Brückner, 176-77]; further, in her political actions she seeks above all to de-stroy the myth of the omnipresence and invulnerability of the state system [*Texte: der RAF*, 357].

Yet while the essay and terrorism share an anti-authoritarian defiance and an ideological critique of domination, the alliance of the two serves also to un-cover their mutual limitations. To claim that the essay is potentially or implic-itly terroristic is just as much a misrepresentation as it is an insight into the nature of the genre: the comparison of the essay and terrorism inevitably un-derscores the fact that the one is, especially in the context of German intellec-tual and political history, *only* words, a subversive act in the realm of "spirit." "In Germany the essay arouses resistance because it evokes intellectual free-dom," Adorno says [3]; but the act of emancipatory resistance is tantamount to, and goes no further than, the exercise of the freedom of the intellect to pierce through repressive illusions. The project of the essay exhausts itself in intellectual critique, in a heresy of ideas only. "Recoil[ing] from the violence" perpetrated by a dogmatic system in which individuality is subordinated to atemporal abstractions [Adorno, 10], the essay does not attain a position from which it might advocate a violence of its own that would be retaliatory. Re-maining solely critical, the essay offers little in the way of an alternative: "it is radical *in its non-radicalism*, in refraining from any reduction to a principle" [Adorno, 9; emphasis mine]. While the language Adorno uses invokes at times the impulse of terrorism, his words of violence in connection with the essay are, in the final analysis, purely metaphorical. The essay preserves the freedom of reason to question the scientific and political status quo—not an insignificant claim, and certainly not without threatening implications. Nonetheless, the essay in Adorno's presentation can in no way be construed as a call to armed struggle.

In this respect the German philosopher belongs to the long, much criticized tradition in German history of an idealism that, faced with a nonrevolutionary situation, upholds the value of consciousness, "spirit," or reason above that of concrete action in the material world. Selected examples may suffice as illustration. According to Kant in his essay on the definition of Enlightenment, the citizen of the world [*Weltbürger*] is "free" to exercise his reason in the pursuit of truth in the realm of ideas, but as a citizen of the state he is granted no alternative but to obey. Likewise, Hegel's seminal master-slave dialectic ends not with the slave's armed liberation from his chains but with the philosophical realization of his freedom, that is, with the attainment of a purely philosophical freedom in the form of stoicism. Meinhof summarizes a related trend in recent German political history: "The history of the Germans, of German monopoly capital, of German social democracy, of the unions, not to have prevented two imperialistic world wars and twelve years of fascism, not even to have fought against them in meaningful ways—that is the history of the German workers' movement" [*Texte: der RAF*, 56-57]. Finally, in a context tied directly to the development of West German terrorism, the testimony offered in 1967 by a panel of experts including Peter Szondi and Peter Wapnewski, both distinguished professors of literature, categorized a student pamphlet calling for acts of department store arson as a "play with words" in the classic Surrealist tradition, thus not to be taken seriously as an inspiration for actions in the real world.[14]

Unlike the programmatic isolation from the material or practical realm, however, another aspect of this German philosophical tradition has for too long gone unacknowledged. Namely, the gendered pronouns in my synopsis of paradigmatic arguments in Kant and Hegel, more than simply a matter of outmoded stylistic convention, carry deliberate philosophical meaning. In their consistent privileging of a contemplation freed from the burdens of material or social life; of a sovereign reason over the claims of sensation, emotion, and the body; and of the sphere of public and political activity over the (rarely discussed) domestic sphere of home and family, both philosophers project a philosophic subject that has been traditionally male.[15] Even Heiner Müller calls our attention to the masculinist character of this European bourgeois tradition when he attributes the philosophical "BLABLA" of his play to Hamlet; the political history spawned by the prince's repressive idealism and his male gender are graphically demonstrated in Müller's text when Hamlet, in his father's armor, executes not his murderous uncle and stepfather (only the latest representative of the paternalistic state), but the revolutionaries Marx, Lenin, and Mao, appearing as naked women [*Hamletmachine*, 58]. The German idealistic tradition and its ideal of reason, far from being neutral with regard to gender, have functioned implicitly to secure and to strengthen the continued political and philosophic dominance of men and of a "male" reason.

In this broad cultural context, Meinhof's turn from the essay to terrorist violence takes on manifold meaning. Deliberately rejecting a tradition that would restrict the project of criticism to a purely intellectual or aesthetic realm in which the concerns of the material world remain irrelevant, Meinhof's turn to terrorism enacts also, in symbolic and paradigmatic fashion, a woman's rebellion against a male order. For Meinhof, the value of critical thought must be measured solely by its concrete political effect; thus the inability of the student protest to end Germany's support of the United States' war against Vietnam, for example, was taken as de facto complicity [Die Würde des Menschen, 110]. In contrast, the appeal of, and justification for, terrorist violence was its specific "will to efficiency" [111].[16] The "primacy of praxis" proclaimed by the RAF [Texte: der RAF, 47, 349-54; see also 70], pointing to the incomplete nature of words alone, responds heretically to the masculinist Kantian and Hegelian heritage that asserts the values of pure reflection and practical indifference. Terrorism thereby emerges in its German context as a radically extended and explicitly gendered "essay" in ideological analysis and emancipatory political change, a feminist enactment of the political project implied by the essay form.[17]

The so-called first generation of the RAF reached a controversial end with the deaths of Ulrike Meinhof, Andreas Baader, and Gudrun Ensslin in prison in 1976 and 1977.[18] RAF members of later generations, although greater in number, never attained the same level of intellectual intensity or political notoriety. If one judges the RAF by the results of its actions, and this would not be to apply criteria that it would itself find inappropriate, then the conclusion is inevitable that the terrorist organization failed in its goals to educate and mobilize its German audience. The actual deeds of the RAF in fact seem miniscule in comparison to the violent dimensions of the government's repressive response: a handful of bank robberies, a handful of bombings, and a handful of victims, on the one side, versus a massive escalation in state surveillance and counterinsurgency techniques, new legislation restricting the constitutional rights of the West German citizens, and a deformed judicial process in which defendants could be tried in absentia, on the other [Aust; Böll; Kramer, 216, n. 38; Wasmund, 192; Weiss].[19]

Ironically, the inability of the Baader-Meinhof group to mobilize the German public through its attacks against the system has something to do with, and something to say about, the kinship between terrorism and the politics of essay writing. As hard-hitting, as comprehensive, and as compelling as the analyses offered by Meinhof in her essays can be, they nonetheless present the reader at times with syntactically complex and rhetorically sophisticated arguments that presuppose an intimidating familiarity with German and American politics, history, and economics. Klaus Wagenbach thus finds it necessary to provide explanatory footnotes in his posthumous edition of Meinhof's essays [Die Würde des Menschen], and Peter Brückner devotes his volume largely to his own detailed exposition of German political conditions and events, excerpting only selectively from Meinhof's essays. Further, despite the self-proclaimed attempt to communicate political insights and goals to a broader audience, the difficulties for the reader become intensified, while the analyses grow sharper and more encompassing, in the essays written after Meinhof's turn to terror-ism. Adopting at times an almost telegraphic style, with unorthodox orthogra-phy and sentence breaks, the terrorist prose ranges boldly over historical anal-yses of German fascism, philosophical discourses on the identity of the urban guerrilla and her ties to the proletariat, political critiques of American imperi-alism in the Third World and in Western Europe, and ideological exposés of the irregular judicial process brought against the terrorists.

The textual difficulties become all the more notable in light of the fact that the RAF saw itself as writing and acting for the proletariat. Against the trans-national organization of capital, RAF members championed a "proletarian in-ternationalism" that encompassed the working class and marginalized groups in German society—the poor and the homeless, the mentally ill, inmates of homes and prisons, and others—as well as independence movements in the Third World [*Texte: der RAF*, 63, 67; also 392-94]. Their communiqués were intended as "newspapers" that would explain to the people the need for sup-porting the guerrillas [*Texte: der RAF*, 50]; above all they desired to make themselves—their actions as well as their "propaganda, [their] language, [their] words"—understood by the masses they claimed to represent [*Texte: der RAF*, 432]. While critics noted the upper- or middle-class background of many of the key terrorists, they themselves emphasized the proletarian roots of their membership: "half of us come from proletarian backgrounds—primary school, apprenticeship, factory, state home, prison" [*Texte: der RAF*, 52]. The concept of the proletariat was itself redefined, so that membership in it was a matter not of social class, but of political choice:

> the struggle itself proletarianizes the fighters. . . . this is certainly not a sociological concept of the proletariat. that doesn't interest us anyway. proletariat is not a con-cept taken from the fascists' doctrine of descent—it denotes a relationship, the re-lationship of the guerrilla to the people—denotes the *relationship* of the proletariat to the imperialistic state, defined as an enmity to the death. [*Texte: der RAF*, 52]

At least one scholar has pointed to the tension between populism and elit-ism as an inherent characteristic of terrorist discourse: the claim to be "for the people" is counterbalanced by a disparaging view of the masses as politically brainwashed [Leeman, 60-62]. But while the former predominates in the RAF's texts, and because it predominates, the contradiction deepens between the po-litical philosophy of West German terrorism and the often inaccessible manner of its writing. Indeed, this tension between the revolutionary politics and the style of the terrorist treatises is suggestive of the contradictory nature, and ge-neric limitations, of the essay in its German context.

In the final analysis, the terrorist communiqués probably remained as in-comprehensible as the terrorist acts themselves to an audience at the level of the average *Bild-Zeitung* reader [Miller, 190, 223, 280; Bachem, 63-64, 73].[20] As Peter Demetz notes, West German terrorists tended to come largely from aca-demic and professional families—this is certainly true of Ensslin, Baader, and Meinhof—and found stronger support among white-collar professionals (lawyers, journalists, and teachers) than among the working class [Demetz, 66-67]. The political analyses that provided the motivation and justification for terrorism were accessible to, and could be understood by, only the privileged few of German academics, writers, and other highly trained intellectuals. Thus the terrorism of the RAF in West Germany, which sought in radical ways to educate and to inspire political change, achieved in the end its own extreme political and intellectual isolation. A privileged discourse by and for the educated middle class, it repelled rather than attracted those who lacked at the outset the intellectual and economic qualifications for inclusion.

Heiner Müller's Ophelia, appearing one last time in the concluding scene of *Hamletmachine*, sits alone in an underwater world and recites a text that offers a clear promise of continued revolution [58]. On a deeper level, as a highly literary intertext weaving together the voices of Frantz Fanon, Jean-Paul Sartre, Joseph Conrad, and undoubtedly others, Ophelia's pronouncements remain enigmatic, elusive, and disturbingly elitist. The same structural tension characterizes the essayistic and terroristic attempts at revolutionary change enacted by Ulrike Meinhof. Despite the intensity of her efforts to reach a proletarian audience and to liberate herself from the burden of a tradition of intellectual critique and political compliance, her emancipatory project nonetheless seems tragically flawed in its form. Both terrorism and the essay, unlikely but natural siblings in their German context, engage in an explicitly subversive project to undermine the illusions that support a politics of oppression. But both are also historically and perhaps generically impaired by the privileged education and learning that they continue to presuppose.

NOTES

I wish to thank Karen Storz, who provided invaluable assistance in the collection of materials for this study.

1. Original German text, *Die Hamletmaschine*, in Heiner Müller, *Mauser* (Berlin: Rotbuch, 1978), 89-97.

2. Meinhof, Baader, and Ensslin were arrested in 1972; two years later Meinhof was sentenced to eight years in prison for her role in Baader's escape. For accounts of Meinhof's life and the development of the RAF, see Aust, Becker, Kramer [196-204], Krebs, and Röhl. Demetz [57-68] and Wasmund [193-96] offer concise summaries of the political and historical background of the West German student movement. Kramer provides a preliminary discussion of Meinhof's case within the context of the history of women and the development of radical feminism in West Germany. The special German Issue of *Semiotext(e)* contains a number of relevant texts in English translation, including interviews with former terrorists, articles on German terrorism by Félix Guattari and Jean Baudrillard, and various terrorist communiqués.

3. See in particular the interpretations offered by Becker and Röhl. Wasmund presents

the need for strong group attachments as a general characteristic of terrorist biographies.

4. The terrorist writings of the RAF are often collectively authored, generally fragmentary, and sometimes edited by third parties [Brückner, 166-67, n. 6]. In *Texte: der RAF* see "fragment über struktur" ["Fragment on structure," 23-26], "konzept a./u. zu einem anderen prozess" ["Concept A./U. of a different process," 27-32], "teile zu der erklärung der gefangenen aus der raf" ["Parts of the statement of the RAF prisoners," 40-54], "geschichte der brd, alte linke" ["History of the FRG, the old Left," 55-61], "rede von ulrike zu der befreiung von andreas" ["Speech by Ulrike on the freeing of Andreas," 62-74], "Das Konzept Stadtguerilla" ["The concept of the urban guerrilla," 337-67], "Stadtguerilla und Klassenkampf" ["The urban guerrilla and class struggle," 368-410], and "Den antiimperalistischen Kampf führen! Die Rote Armee aufbauen!" ["Lead the antiimperialist fight! Build the Red Army!" 411-47]. The letters to the defense lawyers for the RAF provide an especially devastating analysis and critique of the West German judicial system, the development of counterinsurgency as a state program, and the role of the Federal Republic in worldwide imperialism [517-73].

5. The Emergency Laws were added to the Basic Law (constitution) of the Federal Republic of Germany in June 1968. In addition to providing for greatly increased police powers, extensive command of the economy and labor force, and centralization of power in a declared state of emergency, the amendments allow for peacetime surveillance of mail and telecommunications for security purposes. A response to massive student protests of the time, the passage of the laws was seen by many as an ominous means of curtailing and suppressing legitimate dissent.

6. For Meinhof's discussion of women's issues see the essays "Jürgen Bartsch und die Gesellschaft" ["Jürgen Bartsch and society"], "Falsches Bewußtsein" ["False consciousness"], and "Die Frauen im SDS oder in eigener Sache" ["Women in the SDS or in our own cause"] in Meinhof, *Die Würde des Menschen*, [112-16, 117-33, 149-52]; also Kramer [207-10]. The SDS is the Socialist Federation of German Students.

7. All translations of Meinhof's writings are my own.

8. I use the German term to make an explicit connection to Kant's definition of Enlightenment. "Unmündigkeit" denotes immaturity in terms of both physical development and legal responsibility; the immature person has not yet "come of age" as an adult and as a citizen of the state. Kant's definition from 1784, which continues to play a powerful role in German political discourse, emphasizes the autonomy of reason and the critical examination of beliefs: "Enlightenment is man's release from his self-incurred tutelage [*Unmündigkeit*]. Tutelage is man's inability to make use of his understanding without direction from another" [Kant, 3]. Original German in Immanuel Kant, "Beantwortung der Frage: Was ist Aufklärung?" *Werke*, ed. Wilhelm Weischedel, vol. 11 (Frankfurt am Main: Insel, 1964), 53-61, here 53.

9. Springer's vast publishing empire included the national daily *Bild-Zeitung*, Europe's best-selling tabloid with a circulation estimated in 1987 at 5.4 million. Founded by Springer in 1952, the newspaper adopted a decidedly cold-warrior position under his guidance and campaigned aggressively against rapprochement with East Germany and against the student Left in West Germany in the 1960s.

10. In Wagenbach's opinion the essays were exemplary in this regard [Meinhof, *Die Würde des Menschen*, 188].

11. Strauss, then Minister of Defense, first sued in response to the publication of Meinhof's "Hitler in Euch" ["Hitler in You"] which, as its title promised, drew parallels between the West German politician and Adolf Hitler. Meinhof and *konkret* prevailed with the help of Gustav Heinemann, former Minister of the Interior under Adenauer and future President of the Federal Republic, as their defense attorney. Strauss won the second lawsuit three years later in the amount of 600 Marks. See Aust [37], Becker [139-40, 145], and Röhl [159-60]. Brückner provides a detailed presentation of Meinhof's essays in the specific context of West German politics.

12. Haefner challenges this view.

13. For other discussions of Adorno's essay see McCarthy [45-46] and Kauffmann [229-32]. Kauffmann notes the historical centrality of the German philosophical tradition in theoretical discussions of the modern essay genre [227]. While he distinguishes the German from a competing French poststructuralist "school" of the essay, he goes on to emphasize their commonalities [232-35].

14. See Taubes for the text of their testimony, given at the trial brought against the authors of the student pamphlet. Holthusen offers a politically conservative but interesting discussion of the trial and the relationship between literature and terrorism.

15. List offers a wide-ranging evaluation of androcentric notions of reason and rationality in Western philosophy and social theory.

16. See also Meinhof's vehement critique of the failed movement against the passage of the Emergency Laws—a protest that was launched "only with sentences" and "verbal acts of aggression" [Die Würde des Menschen, 142]—and her rejection of "verbal radicalism" [Texte: der RAF, 66]. This is not to say, however, that words (or essay writing) are insignificant or nonessential as a medium for political change. While the critique of ideology is not the same as the dismantling of its institutions, the one can constitute the necessary intellectual precondition of the other. See Meinhof's comments on theoretical insight and political action in "Natürlich kann geschossen werden" ["Of course shots can be fired"]. It is significant that the focus on reason in the konkret essays is replaced by an emphasis on will in the RAF writings; see, for example, Texte: der RAF [23-26].

17. Compare Bohrer's analysis, which presents terrorism not as a rejection but as a desperate outgrowth of the tradition of German idealism. Morgan argues against any feminist aspect of terrorism, characterizing the female terrorist's actions as mere " 're-bellion' for love's sake" [208]. See also the feminist critiques of women terrorists noted in Kramer [212-13] and the varied analyses in Frauen und Terror.

18. Meinhof was found hanging from the bars of the window in her cell in May 1976. Baader, Ensslin, and Jan-Carl Raspe died in October 1977, Ensslin by hanging, the two others by gunshot. A fourth RAF member, Irmgard Möller, was stabbed in the chest four times with a table knife but survived. The deaths, all ruled suicides, occurred in a maximum security prison built especially to hold the terrorist prisoners and equipped with unparalleled surveillance devices. Numerous inconsistencies in the circumstances and evidence relating to the four deaths have never been resolved. See Aust [3-6, 345-47, 535-41, 542-52] and Krebs [261-67].

19. The hope of the RAF, which remained unrealized, was that the retaliatory response of the state would awaken mass protest. See Texte: der RAF [28-29, 72] and Brückner's critique [183-92].

20. Springer claimed that the clear, uncomplicated style and orientation of Bild-Zeitung spoke to and for the real masses of ordinary Germans. Among Bild-Zeitung readers (one quarter of the German population over 14 years of age), Germans with the equivalent of a high school education or less are overrepresented in relation to their proportion of the total population. In addition to its trademark aggressive right-wing politics, the newspaper built its reputation on sensationalized stories on topics ranging from murder and rape to the intimate lives of the rich and famous. There is considerable evidence that stories are routinely distorted or even fabricated.

WORKS CITED

Adorno, Theodor W. "The Essay as Form." *Notes to Literature*. Vol. 1. Ed. Rolf Tiedemann. Trans. Shierry Weber Nicholsen. New York: Columbia University Press, 1991. 3-23.

Aust, Stefan. *The Baader-Meinhof Group: The Inside Story of a Phenomenon*. Trans. Anthea Bell. London: The Bodley Head, 1987.

Bachem, Rolf. "Sprache der Terroristen: Analyse eines offenen Briefes." *Der Deutschunterricht* 30, no. 5 (1978): 61-79.

Becker, Jillian. *Hitler's Children: The Story of the Baader-Meinhof Terrorist Gang*. Philadelphia: J. B. Lippincott, 1977.

Bensmaïa, Réda. "The Essay." *The Barthes Effect: The Essay as Reflective Text*. Trans. Pat Fedkiew. Minneapolis: University of Minnesota Press, 1987. 95-100.

Bohrer, Karl Heinz. "Authentizität und Terror." *Kursbuch* 60 (June 1980): 143-50.

Böll, Heinrich. "Will Ulrike Gnade oder freies Geleit?" *Der Spiegel* 10 January 1972: 54-57.

Brückner, Peter. *Ulrike Marie Meinhof und die deutschen Verhältnisse*. Berlin: Klaus Wagenbach, 1976.

Demetz, Peter. *After the Fires: Recent Writing in the Germanies, Austria, and Switzerland*. San Diego: Harcourt Brace Jovanovich, 1986.

Frauen und Terror: Versuche, die Beteiligung von Frauen an Gewalttaten zu erklären. Ed. Susanne v. Paczensky. Reinbek bei Hamburg: Rowohlt Taschenbuch, 1978.

Gerhardt, Marlis. "Nachwort: Über den Essay." *Essays von Frauen des 20. Jahrhunderts*. Ed. Marlis Gerhardt. Frankfurt am Main: Insel, 1988. 331-43.

Haefner, Joel. "Unfathering the Essay: Resistance and Intergenreality in the Essay Genre." *Prose Studies: History, Theory, Criticism* 12 (1989): 259-73.

Hardison, O. B., Jr. "Binding Proteus: An Essay on the Essay." *Essays on the Essay: Redefining the Genre*. Ed. Alexander J. Butrym. Athens: University of Georgia Press, 1989. 11-28.

Hegel, G. W. F. *Phenomenology of Spirit*. Trans. A. V. Miller. Oxford: Oxford University Press, 1977.

Holthusen, Hans Egon. "Sartre in Stammheim: Literatur und Terrorismus." *Sartre in Stammheim: Zwei Themen aus den Jahren der großen Turbulenz*. Stuttgart: Klett-Cotta, 1982. 99-239.

Kant, Immanuel. "What is Enlightenment?" Trans. Lewis White Beck. *On History*. Ed. Lewis White Beck. Indianapolis: Bobbs-Merrill, 1963. 3-10.

Kauffmann, R. Lane. "The Skewed Path: Essaying as Unmethodical Method." *Essays on the Essay: Redefining the Genre*. Ed. Alexander J. Butrym. Athens: University of Georgia Press, 1989. 221-40.

Kramer, David. "Ulrike Meinhof: An Emancipated Terrorist?" *European Women on the Left: Socialism, Feminism, and the Problems Faced by Political Women, 1880 to the Present*. Ed. Jane Slaughter and Robert Kern. Westport: Greenwood Press, 1981. 195-219.

Krebs, Mario. *Ulrike Meinhof: Ein Leben im Widerspruch*. Reinbek bei Hamburg: Rowohlt Taschenbuch, 1988.

Leeman, Richard W. *The Rhetoric of Terrorism and Counterterrorism*. New York: Greenwood Press, 1991.

List, Elisabeth. "Reason, Gender, and the Paradox of Rationalization: A Feminist Perspective on Theories of Modernisation and Rationality." Symposium on Women in Austria. Center for Austrian Studies, University of Minnesota, Minneapolis, Minnesota, 18-20 April 1991.

McCarthy, John A. *Crossing Boundaries: A Theory and History of Essay Writing in German, 1680-1815*. Philadelphia: University of Pennsylvania Press, 1989.

Meinhof, Ulrike Marie. *Bambule: Fürsorge—Sorge für wen?* Berlin: Klaus Wagenbach, 1987.

_____. "Natürlich kann geschossen werden." *Der Spiegel* 15 June 1970: 74-75.

_____. *Die Würde des Menschen ist antastbar: Aufsätze und Polemiken*. Berlin: Klaus Wagenbach, 1980.

Miller, Bowman Howard. "The Language Component of Terrorism Strategy: A Text-based, Linguistic Case Study of Contemporary German Terrorism." Diss. Georgetown University, 1983.

Morgan, Robin. *The Demon Lover: On the Sexuality of Terrorism*. New York: Norton, 1989.

Müller, Heiner. *Hamletmachine and Other Texts for the Stage*. Ed. and trans. Carl Weber. New York: Performing Arts Journal Publications, 1984.

_____. "Viv(r)e la contradiction!" *France nouvelle* 29 January 1979: 43-50.

Röhl, Klaus Rainer. *Fünf Finger sind keine Faust*. Köln: Kiepenheuer & Witsch, 1974.

Semiotext(e). The German Issue 11 *(1982):* 80-158.

Taubes, Jacob. "Surrealistische Provokation: Ein Gutachten zur Anklageschrift im Prozeß Langhans-Teufel über die Flugblätter der 'Kommune I.'" *Merkur* 21 (1967): 1069-79.

Texte: der RAF. Malmö, Sweden: Bo Cavefors, 1977.

Wasmund, Klaus. "The Political Socialization of West German Terrorists." *Political Violence and Terror: Motifs and Motivations*. Ed. Peter H. Merkl. Berkeley: University of California Press, 1986. 191-228.

Weiss, Peter. "Joe McCarthy is Alive and Well and Living in West Germany: Terror and Counter-Terror in the Federal Republic." *New York University Journal of International Law and Politics* 9 (Spring 1976): 61-88.

Contributors

TUZYLINE JITA ALLAN, Assistant Professor of English at Baruch College, the City University of New York, is currently at work on a critical study of African women novelists.

MARGRET BRÜGMANN is Associate Professor at the Centre of Women's Studies and in the Department of Comparative Literature at the University of Nijmegen, the Netherlands. She is the author of *Amazonen der Literatur. Studien zur deutschsprachigen Frauenliteratur der 70er Jahre* [Amazons of Literature: Studies of German Women's Literature of the 1970s] and *Verstilde verhalen—sprekende beelden. Mythen, vrouwelijkheid en het postmoderne* [Silenced Stories—Talking Images: Myths, Femininity, and Postmodernism].

SUSAN GRIFFIN, a member of the faculty at Mills College, is the author of *Woman and Nature: The Roaring Inside Her, Rape: The Politics of Consciousness, Pornography and Silence*, and *A Chorus of Stones: The Private Life of War*. Her most recent collection of poetry is *Unremembered Country*.

RUTH-ELLEN BOETCHER JOERES is Professor of German at the University of Minnesota and editor of *Signs: Journal of Women in Culture and Society*. She is the author of *Die Anfänge der deutschen Frauenbewegung: Louise Otto-Peters* and coeditor of several volumes, including *German Women in the Eighteenth and Nineteenth Centuries: A Social and Literary History, Interpreting Women's Lives: Feminist Theory and Personal Narratives*, and *Out of Line/Ausgefallen: The Paradox of Marginality in the Writings of Nineteenth-Century German Women*.

AMY KAMINSKY, Associate Professor of Women's Studies at the University of Minnesota, has published articles on Spanish and Latin American literature. She is the author of *Reading the Body Politic: Latin American Women Writers and Feminist Criticism* and the editor of the forthcoming anthology *Flores del agua/Waterlilies: Spanish Women Writers from 1400 to 1900*.

PAMELA KLASS MITTLEFEHLDT, Assistant Professor of American Studies at St. Cloud State University, was a member of the Personal Narratives Group that wrote and edited *Interpreting Women's Lives: Feminist Theory and Personal Narratives*. Her work concerns the relationship between women's stories and social change.

ELIZABETH MITTMAN, Mellon postdoctoral fellow at Emory University, recently completed a dissertation on East German literature entitled "Encounters with the Institution: Woman and *Wissenschaft* in GDR Literature." She is also the coeditor and cotranslator of a forthcoming collection of early German romantic texts.

LOURDES ROJAS, Associate Professor of Spanish and Coordinator of Latin American Studies at Colgate University, is author of the forthcoming *Mujer, Mito y Novela*. She has published numerous essays on the feminist literary criticism of contemporary Latin American fiction.

BARBARA SICHTERMANN studied sociology in Berlin and Hannover and lives today as a free-lance writer in Berlin. She has worked extensively for both newspapers and radio and is well known for her books on work, motherhood, and gender roles. Her 1983 collection of essays, *Weiblichkeit: Zur Politik des Privaten* has been translated into English as *Femininity: The Politics of the Personal*.

EILEEN BOYD SIVERT is Associate Professor of French at the University of Minnesota. She is currently at work on a study of women and narration in Barbey d'Aurevilly's *Diaboliques*, and her work on d'Aurevilly, Merimee, George Sand, and Balzac has appeared in a variety of journals.

KATHERINE V. SNYDER, Instructor of English at Wesleyan University and Yale University, has recently completed a dissertation at Yale University entitled "Bachelor Narrative: Gender and Representation in Anglo-American Fiction, 1850-1914."

NANCY SAPORTA STERNBACH is Assistant Professor of Spanish at Smith College. She is the co-editor of *Breaking Boundaries: Latina Writing and Critical Readings* and the author of articles on Latin American women and the canon.

CONSTANCE A. SULLIVAN, Associate Professor of Spanish and chair of Women's Studies at the University of Minnesota, has published articles on Spanish theater, novels, essays, and literary history. Her current research concerns Josefa Amar y Borbon, and women and traditional Spanish proverbs.

ARLENE A. TERAOKA, Associate Professor of German at the University of Minnesota, has published articles on German drama, postwar German literature, and minority literature in Germany. She is author of *The Silence of Entropy or Universal Discourse: The Postmodernist Poetics of Heiner Müller* and coeditor of a special issue of *New German Critique* on minorities in German culture.

Index